The Old West Quiz and Fact Book

Also by Rod Gragg

The Civil War Quiz and Fact Book
Pirates, Planters and Patriots
Bobby Bagley: POW

THE OLD WEST QUIZ AND FACT BOOK

Rod Gragg

PERENNIAL LIBRARY

HARPER & ROW, PUBLISHERS

New York, Cambridge, Philadelphia,
San Francisco, Washington, London, Mexico City,
São Paulo, Singapore, Sydney

For Skip—an authentic mountain man

PHOTO CREDITS

American Heritage Center, University of Wyoming: 9
Custer Battlefield National Monument: 162, 174
Given Memorial Archives: 22
Kansas State Historical Society: 15, 124, 131, 158
Library of Congress: 117, 121, 166, 195
Museum of Modern Art: 199
Paramount Pictures: 189
RKO General Pictures: 184
20th Century–Fox: 192
U.S. Military Academy: 152, 169, 179, 180
Warner Brothers: 201
All other photos courtesy National Archives.

Library of Congress Cataloging-in-Publication Data

Gragg, Rod.
    The Old West quiz and fact book.

    Bibliography: p.
    Includes index.
    1. Frontier and pioneer life—West—Miscellanea.
2. West (U.S.)—History—Miscellanea   3. Questions and answers.   I. Title.
F596.G76   1986   978'.0076   85-45574
ISBN 0-06-055002-3   86 87 88 89 90 RRD 10 9 8 7 6 5 4 3 2 1
ISBN 0-06-096077-9 (pbk.) 86 87 88 89 90 RRD 10 9 8 7 6 5 4 3 2 1

Contents

R
978
GR

Acknowledgments   vi

Introduction   ix

1: Bad Men, Lawmen and Shootists   1

2: Mountain Men, Frontiersmen
   and Trailblazers   24

3: Tribes and Warriors of the West   49

4: Indian-Fighting Army   73

5: Pioneers, Sodbusters and Town Raisers   93

6: Wranglers, Rustlers and Roundups   116

7: Words from the West   136

8: Custer and the Little Big Horn   161

9: Hollywood's Wild West   183

Bibliography   203

Index   213

Acknowledgments

Separating truth from legend is an occupational challenge for any historian, especially when dealing with the Old West. Much of the history of the American West is based on personal recollections and long-savored stories. With the passage of time and the republishing of legend as truth, it becomes almost impossible in many cases to determine what is fact and what is fiction. Eventually, the author must simply weigh the evidence and make a decision. Every author must bear ultimate responsibility for his or her work, but the hard decisions are made easier by dependable advice—and *The Old West Quiz and Fact Book* was influenced and improved by many competent advisers.

Neil Mangum, chief historian at the Custer Battlefield National Monument, offered knowledgeable advice on some of the perplexing questions surrounding the Battle of the Little Big Horn. Dr. Robert Hollow, curator of collections at the State Historical Society of North Dakota, provided valuable information on a variety of topics related to the Old West. Historian Robert M. Utley, author of several definitive works on the Western Indian Wars, provided expert counsel on a number of subjects. Custer authority Dr. Lawrence Frost responded to many inquiries and clarified confusing details related to the life of General George A. Custer. Lieutenant

Colonel James Browning of The Citadel shared his extensive knowledge on numerous subjects and supplied more than a few elusive details.

I'm indebted to the staff of the Kimbel Library at USC-Coastal Carolina College in Conway, South Carolina, and especially to public service librarian Mary Bull, who helped track down countless obscure and elusive facts and who demonstrated great courtesy and competent professionalism. Librarian Janice Schuster put the University of South Carolina's interlibrary loan system to a mighty test and uncovered important documents and rare books on the Old West from distant corners of the nation. Other members of Dr. Lynne Smith's staff who also assisted in this work are Paul Fowler, Margaret Fain, Peggy Bates, Charmaine Tomczyk, David Wilkie and Kay Alford.

My editor at Harper & Row, M. S. Wyeth, Jr., provided valuable advice throughout the research and writing of this work. Associate editor Terry Karten also provided assistance, and so did Florence Goldstein, Jim Armstrong, and Daniel Bial.

The staff members of the Still Pictures Section of the National Archives and the Prints and Photographs Division of the Library of Congress were especially helpful in locating the photographs for this book. I'm also grateful to the Academy of Motion Picture Arts and Sciences; the American Film Institute; the Film Stills Archives of the Museum of Modern Art; the Horry County Memorial Library in Conway, South Carolina; Moore County Library in Carthage, North Carolina; and Given Memorial Library in Pinehurst, North Carolina.

Michael Wayne, son of film star John Wayne, patiently and pleasantly answered all my questions about his father's film career.

Special thanks are also due Nancy Sherbert of the Kansas State Historical Society; Renee Klish, registrar of the West Point Museum; Marie Capps, the director of Special Collections at the U.S. Military Academy's West Point Library; the American Heritage Center at the University of Wyoming; the Western History Collection of the University of Oklahoma; and photographers Bill Edmonds and Lisa Graham.

Mae Reid-Bills, managing editor of *American West* magazine, shared informed advice, and so did Bob Edgar of Cody, Wyoming; Clark Hogan of Palmerdale, Alabama; Rodney A. Douglas of Porter, Texas; Jeff Cooper of Paulden, Arizona; Douglas Scott of the National Park Service's Midwest Archaeological Center; Edna

Cahoon of Almo, Idaho; and Gilbert Campbell of Palmer Lake, Colorado.

Ted Gragg offered knowledgeable advice on period firearms. George Taylor provided valuable encouragement and assistance, and so did Bill and Margaret Outlaw, Charles Lunsford, Bob Melton, Connie Gragg, Jackie Outlaw, Bud Chandler, Randy Riddle and Tommy and Kay Swaim.

Brenda Cox skillfully typed and retyped the manuscript, proofed copy and corrected errors. Her assistance was invaluable.

I'm grateful to the Lindseys, the Davies and the Boyds of the 2:7 Bible Study at Grace Presbyterian Church, P.C.A., and to my parents, L. W. and Elizabeth Gragg. But the greatest contribution to this work came from my children—Faith, Rachel, Elizabeth, Joni and Penny—who endured my long-term preoccupation with the Old West in good humor, and from my wife, Cindy, who consistently exhibits the virtues recorded in Proverbs 31:10–31.

Introduction

The Old West is uniquely American. Nothing like it exists any-where else. Other lands have wilderness marvels and rowdy histo-ries, but the Old West belongs only to America. Immersed as we are today in the mythology of the Old West, however, it's easy to wonder if it ever really did exist. Yet stand on the rim of Wyoming's Yellowstone Canyon; study the treeless horizon of Montana's east-ern grasslands; walk the shore of Bear Lake on the Utah-Idaho border; or watch the twilight shadows climb the walls of Arizona's Canyon de Chelly—then you'll know. You'll *feel* the Old West and you'll know it was real; because the history of the West—like its lure and its legend—was shaped by its awesome geography.

The colorful drama unfolded quickly and ended within a single long lifetime. From the day Lewis and Clark set out on their jour-ney to the Pacific to the time the great buffalo herds vanished, barely eighty years elapsed. Yet despite its brief life, the Old West left a permanent legacy—and for good reason. The familiar image of men and women struggling against the odds in a wilderness land of gigantic proportions has an irresistible appeal. Admittedly the image has become a cliché, but even the cliché retains a basic truth. The Old West *was* a remarkable region tamed by remarkable people—Indians, mountain men, pioneers, soldiers, settlers, cowboys, gunmen, gamblers and townspeople—whose images are rightfully chiseled into our mental mural of the Old West.

For the serious history buff and the novice student of the Old West, here are some surprises, some forgotten facts, some neglected truth and a huge splash of color from that which is uniquely American—the Old West.

1 | Bad Men, Lawmen and Shootists

Q: What famous gunfighter was indicted for horse stealing by officials in Van Buren, Arkansas, on May 8, 1871?

A: The horse-stealing indictment was handed down against future lawman Wyatt Earp, who escaped trial by jumping bail and fleeing to Kansas.

Q: On December 21, 1876, gunfighter Clay Allison shot and killed Deputy Sheriff Charles Faber at the Olympic Dance Hall in Las Animas, Colorado. What act led to the shootout?

A: The law enforcement officer was reportedly summoned to the dance hall because the mean-tempered Allison was purposely stomping on the feet of dancers.

Q: What famous aliases were used by Old West outlaws Robert LeRoy Parker and Harry Longabaugh?

A: The two were better known as Butch Cassidy and the Sundance Kid.

Q: When and where was Billy the Kid born?

A: Billy the Kid was born on September 17, 1859, in New York City.

Q: Who was Phoebe Anne Mozee, and by what name did she achieve international fame?

A: Phoebe Anne Mozee was an expert rifle and shotgun markswoman who became famous in Buffalo Bill's Wild West Show under the stage name Annie Oakley.

Q: What physical handicap plagued Texas Judge Roy Bean, who was known for his harsh and often bizarre frontier justice?

A: The self-proclaimed "law west of the Pecos," Bean was unable to turn his head due to an injury he had received in California as a young man. He had killed a Mexican official in a dispute over a girl, and the dead man's friends hanged Bean, who was cut down, injured but alive, by the contested damsel.

Q: Who was Sheriff Frank M. Canton, and what was the big secret in his past?

A: Canton was sheriff of Johnson County, Wyoming, in 1892 and helped lead the cattlemen and gunfighters who sought to destroy the small farmers in the violent Johnson County War. Unknown to his followers, Frank M. Canton's real name was Joseph Horner, and he was wanted in Texas for murder and for a string of other crimes.

Q: What notorious gunfighter used the names Henry McCarty, Henry Antrim and William Bonney at various times?

A: All were used by William ("Billy the Kid") Bonney.

Q: What was the usual price of the .45-caliber 1873 Colt Peacemaker, the weapon that became known as "the gun that won the West"?

A: The Peacemaker, which was made by Colt's Fire Arms Manufacturing Company in Hartford, Connecticut, could be purchased by mail order for $17.

Q: **What was Jesse James's full name, where was he born and who were his parents?**

A: **Jesse Woodson James was born September 5, 1847, in Clay County, Missouri, to Robert and Zerelda Cole James. When Jesse was a child, his father left the family in order to join the California Gold Rush. He died in the gold fields.**

Q: How did the infamous Cole Younger spend his last years?

A: After serving more than twenty years in prison, Cole got a job selling tombstones; worked for a while in a Wild West show with Frank James; and died quietly in 1916 in Lee's Summit, Missouri, where he was known as an elderly churchgoer.

Q: What famous Old West shootist was born in Troy Grove, Illinois, on May 27, 1837?

A: James Butler ("Wild Bill") Hickok.

Q: By what name was California resident Charles E. Boles best known from 1875 to 1882?

A: Boles was best known by the alias "Black Bart," the name under which he robbed a succession of stagecoaches and evaded lawmen and Wells Fargo detectives—until he was finally arrested.

Q: What famous Old West badman used the alias "J. D. Howard"?

A: Jesse James used this alias at different times in his career and was so known to his neighbors in St. Joseph, Missouri, at the time of his murder there.

Q: What did the following locations all have in common: Delta, Colorado; Tipton, Wyoming; Montpelier, Idaho; Belle Fourche, South Dakota; Folsom, New Mexico; Exeter, Montana; and Winnemucca, Nevada?

A: All were sites of major robberies by members of Butch Cassidy's Wild Bunch.

Q: What famous Old West lawman was named Bartholomew and was born in Quebec, Canada?

A: Bartholomew ("Bat") Masterson, who adopted the name William Barclay Masterson, was born in Henryville, Quebec, on November 26, 1853.

Q: How did fast-gun Harry Longabaugh become known as "the Sundance Kid"?

A: In 1887 Longabaugh served a jail term for horse stealing in Sundance, Wyoming—an experience that prompted Longabaugh's colleagues to refer to him thereafter as the Sundance Kid.

Q: What was the "border draw" used by some gunfighters?

A: The border draw was a method of drawing a pistol worn butt-forward, in which the gunman would reach across his body to draw the weapon. It was so named because of its popularity near the Mexican border.

Q: How long did the infamous Dalton Gang operate?
A: The Dalton Gang gained notoriety when accused of robbing a train
     at Wharton, Oklahoma, on May 9, 1891, and dissolved in a bloody
     shootout at Coffeyville, Kansas, on October 5, 1892, one year and
     five months later.

Q: At the time of the famous gunfight at the O.K. Corral, was Wyatt
     Earp the town marshal or the sheriff in Tombstone, Arizona?
A: Neither. At the time of the legendary shootout Wyatt Earp, pictured
     in this studio photograph, was a private citizen employed as a saloon
     keeper in Tombstone. His brother Virgil was town marshal in Tomb-
     stone and had temporarily deputized Wyatt, brother Morgan Earp
     and friend Doc Holliday in time for the gunfight.

Q: What did Bat Masterson do with his famous "Buntline Special"—the .45-caliber Colt Peacemaker with an extralong barrel—that was reportedly presented to him in a Dodge City ceremony by an Eastern dime novelist?

A: When the ceremonies were over and the "dignitaries" were gone, Masterson is said to have quietly sawed off the pistol's famous long barrel and reduced it to standard size.

Q: Where on the Western frontier did the famous target shooter Annie Oakley reside?

A: Despite her portrayal as a heroine of the Old West, Annie Oakley never lived farther west than Ohio.

Q: What kind of Old West character was referred to as a "leather slapper," a "gun fanner," a "gun tipper," "bad medicine," a "curly wolf" or a "shootist"?

A: A gunfighter.

Q: By what name was Butch Cassidy's outlaw gang popularly known?
A: The Wild Bunch.

Q: Under what circumstances did Judge Roy Bean of Texas impose a court fine on a dead man?

A: During the 1880s, when his combination barroom-courtroom was known as "the law west of the Pecos," Bean learned that the clothes of a deceased cowboy contained $40 and a six-gun, whereupon the judge charged the corpse with carrying a concealed weapon and fined it $40.

Q: What famous outlaw pair visited New York City in February 1901 and posed for photographs at De Young's Broadway Studio?

A: The New York tourists were Harry Longabaugh—the Sundance Kid—and his consort, Etta Place, who toured New York City en route to South America and a new career in crime with their accomplice, Butch Cassidy.

Q: What famous Western shootist operated a saloon in Nome, Alaska, at the beginning of the twentieth century?

A: Wyatt Earp operated a Nome barroom during middle-age wanderings that took him to Texas, California, Idaho, Kansas, Colorado, Arizona, Nevada and Alaska, before he retired in Los Angeles in 1906.

Q: When was Jesse James murdered, what was he doing at the time of his death and who killed him?

A: On April 3, 1882, Jesse James was killed from behind by a single shot to the head fired by gang member Bob Ford. The notorious outlaw leader was brushing the dust off a wall picture in his home at St. Joseph, Missouri, when he was killed.

Q: In 1871 Deputy Sheriff Charles H. Nichols of Dallas, Texas, was shot to death trying to arrest John Younger, a member of the Jesse James–Cole Younger gang. Why was the sheriff trying to arrest Younger?

A: Younger, who escaped after gunning down the sheriff, was wanted by Dallas authorities for taking off a cowboy's nose while trying to shoot a pipe out of his mouth.

Q: What was the weight and speed of the bullet fired from the famous Colt .45 of the Old West?

A: The metallic cartridge originally designed for the .45-caliber Colt handgun, loaded with 40 grains of black powder, normally held a lead bullet weighing 233 to 265 grains, which was fired at a speed of 700 to 900 feet per second.

Q: What infamous Old West gunman was described in a physician's report as "partly maniacal," with a personality that in "emotional or physical excitement produces paroxysmal of a mixed character"?

A: Gunfighter Clay Allison, a native of Tennessee, was so described in 1862 when medically discharged from the Confederate Army.

Q: Who killed the notorious gunfighter John Wesley Hardin?

A: On August 19, 1895, Hardin was shot and killed from behind by John Henry Selman, an outlaw-turned-constable who had a grudge against Hardin and surprised him in El Paso's Acme Saloon.

FACT: Billy the Kid was *not* left-handed. Contrary to Hollywood portrayals, like the 1958 film *The Left-Handed Gun*, Billy the Kid was right-handed. Popularizers of the Billy the Kid legend were sometimes misled by old photographs that were carelessly transposed when printed and made the young gunman appear to be wearing his weapon on his left side.

Q: What three brothers, infamous Old West outlaws, began their sensational careers as law enforcement officers?

A: Grat, Bob and Emmett Dalton—leaders of the Dalton Gang—all spent time wearing badges before going to the other side of the law. Grat was briefly a deputy U.S. marshal; Bob served as chief of police for the Osage Indians and Emmett assisted his brothers in both posts.

Q: Who was Charles B. Richards, and how did he affect the history of the Old West?

A: Charles B. Richards, an assistant superintendent of Colt's Fire Arms Manufacturing Company of Hartford, Connecticut, received a patent on July 25, 1871, for conversion of Colt's Army Model 1860 handgun to cartridge loading, a design that produced the famous Colt Peacemaker.

Q: When did Jesse James rob his first bank, and where was it?

A: On February 13, 1866, Jesse James pulled his first bank job, holding up the Clay County Savings Bank and Loan Association in Liberty, Missouri.

Q: What did shootist Clay Allison do to the Cheyenne dentist who drilled the wrong tooth while treating Allison's toothache?

A: He forcibly pulled one of the dentist's teeth.

Q: What was the real name of Belle Starr, the "bandit queen" of the Old West, and how was she introduced into the outlaw life?

A: Belle Starr's real name was Myra Belle Shirley, and as an eighteen-year-old farmer's daughter in Scyrene, Texas, she met Cole Younger and Jesse and Frank James, who were en route to Missouri after fencing stolen gold with a Mexican contact. The rendezvous led Myra Belle into a relationship with Cole Younger and a life of crime.

Q: What practices did Wild Bill Hickok employ to avoid being shot from ambush?

A: Worried that his notoriety as a shootist made him an attractive target for assassination, Hickok never used a front door; he normally walked in the center of the street so he could watch alleyways; usually avoided sitting with his back to a door; slept with wadded-up newspapers around his bed to deter crawling assassins; and was never out of arm's reach from his gun. When shot to death in 1876, he was sitting with his back to a door.

Q: How much did Wyoming's big ranchers pay the hired gunmen they recruited for use against the settlers during the 1892 Johnson County Wars?

A: The gunmen, who were sent out to shoot or hang the small-time ranchers and nesters on the Johnson County range, were paid $5 a day plus expenses, with a $50 bonus for each settler they killed.

Q: Who was Tom ("Bear River") Smith, and what happened to him?

A: He was the town marshal who briefly tamed wild and violent Abilene, Kansas, during its heyday as a cow town. He was later murdered on the job and was succeeded by Wild Bill Hickok.

Q: What was Wyatt Earp's full name?

A: Wyatt Berry Stapp Earp.

Q: Where were Butch Cassidy and the Sundance Kid born?

A: Butch Cassidy, seated far right, was born in Beaver, Utah, in 1866, and the Sundance Kid, seated far left, was born in Phoenixville, Pennsylvania, in 1870. Here they pose with other members of Cassidy's gang during a visit to Fort Worth, Texas.

Q: What was the birthplace of shootist Ben Thompson, whose twenty-year career as a gunfighter ended in a bloody shootout?

A: Thompson, who earned his deadly reputation through gunfights in Texas and Kansas, was born in Knottingly, England, on November 11, 1842.

Q: In the late 1890s U.S. Marshal Albert Lowe of Nome, Alaska, reportedly slapped an intoxicated saloon keeper and took his gun away after the barkeeper threatened to demonstrate how guns were handled "down Arizona way." Whom did Marshal Lowe disarm and manhandle?

A: The object of Lowe's discipline was Wyatt Earp, the former Tombstone, Arizona, shootist who had wandered up to Nome.

Q: How many people were sentenced to hang by Isaac C. Parker, the "Hanging Judge," who presided over the federal court of the Western District of Arkansas between 1875 and 1896?

A: In presiding over his district, which included the violence-prone Indian nation, Parker sentenced 168 persons to hang—and 88 *were* hanged.

Q: What secret occupation was pursued by Montana sheriff Henry Plummer, and how did his law enforcement career end?

A: Personable and attractive, Plummer was elected sheriff in the Montana mining community of Bannack but secretly led a band of outlaws who robbed or killed more than a hundred victims. His hidden life was eventually discovered, and in 1864 Plummer and his gang were hanged by Montana vigilantes.

Q: What was the scene of the robbery conducted in April 1872 by Robert ("Bob") Younger, who was the brother of T. Coleman ("Cole") Younger and two other outlaw brothers in the notorious Younger gang?

A: In April 1872 Bob Younger and accomplices robbed the box office of the Kansas City Fairgrounds.

Q: What two outlaw brothers engineered the first armed robbery of a train in American history?

A: America's first train holdup is believed to have occurred on October 6, 1866, in Jackson County, Indiana, when two masked men took $13,000 from an Ohio and Mississippi Railroad express car. The innovative bandits were John and Simeon Reno.

Q: Who was older, Jesse James or his brother Frank?

A: Frank James—born Alexander Franklin James on January 10, 1843 —was more than four years older than brother Jesse.

Q: What did Old West gunfighters mean when they said they only carried "five beans in the wheel"?

A: As a safety practice, many Old West gunmen loaded five cartridges —"beans"—in their six-shot revolvers so they could leave the pistol hammer resting on an empty cylinder chamber, a precaution designed to prevent the gun from discharging accidentally.

Q: In 1853 Captain Harry Love and a company of California lawmen shot it out with bandit Joaquin Murieta, for whom a $1,000 reward had been posted. What proof did Captain Love present to claim the reward for Murieta's demise?

A: Love and his posse reportedly returned from the shootout with Joaquin's head pickled in a jar.

Q: What famous law enforcement agency was created on November 24, 1835, and how much were its members originally paid?

A: On this date the Republic of Texas established a force of rugged frontiersmen called the Texas Rangers to protect the republic's residents—at a salary of $1.25 a day.

Q: Who was the first woman tried for a serious crime in the court of Judge Isaac Parker?

A: Outlaw Belle Starr was tried for horse stealing by Parker, who presided over what is now Oklahoma from a federal court in Fort Smith, Arkansas. She was convicted and sentenced to five months in prison, becoming the first woman tried for a major crime in Parker's court.

Q: Name the English rancher whose murder by a rival ranching ring on February 18, 1878, touched off New Mexico's Lincoln County War and led to Billy the Kid's notoriety as a gunman.

A: John Tunstall.

Q: What did outlaw Jules Reni bequeath to the heritage of the Old West?

A: Jules Reni was a station operator for the Overland Stage and had several towns named for him—of which only Julesburg, Colorado, survives. He later fell into bad company and was eventually shot to death.

Q: How many banks and trains were robbed by Jesse James and his gang in their sixteen-year crime spree?

A: From the date they robbed their first bank in 1866 until Jesse's death in 1882, the notorious James gang reportedly held up seven trains and robbed twelve banks.

Q: What American magazine made Wild Bill Hickok into a national hero?

A: In 1867 a story by Eastern journalist George Ward Nichols profiled Wild Bill Hickok in *Harper's Magazine*, exaggerating Hickok's exploits and making him a national symbol of the West.

Q: How did Billy the Kid escape from the Lincoln County jail while awaiting his sentence of hanging for murder?

A: On April 28, 1881, he escaped from jail after shooting his two guards. His escape was aided by someone who hid a handgun in the jail outhouse.

Q: Who was Johnny Ringo, and what happened to him?

A: John Ringo, or Ringold, was a mysterious shootist and outlaw who earned a deadly reputation from numerous gunfights in Texas, New Mexico and Arizona. He was an opponent of the Earp clique in Tombstone, Arizona, where he reportedly committed suicide in 1882—although Wyatt Earp claimed to have killed him.

Q: What Old West lawman, nicknamed "Uncle Billy," served with distinction as marshal of Dodge City, held a variety of lawman's posts in Oklahoma and single-handedly captured the leader of the notorious Dolin gang?

A: William M. ("Uncle Billy") Tilghman took his first full-time law enforcement post in 1884 and held numerous law enforcement jobs until 1924, when, serving as an elderly city marshal in Cromwell, Oklahoma, he was shot and killed by a drunk.

Q: What famous firearm popular in the Old West was developed as an improvement of the Henry repeating rifle of the Civil War?

A: The Model 1866 Winchester.

Q: How many people were executed by the Montana vigilantes in 1884?

A: Harassed by an extended period of lawlessness, citizens of Montana Territory organized a large-scale vigilante force and in that one year executed thirty-five accused horse and cattle thieves.

Q: Who was Zerelda Mimms?

A: On April 24, 1874, at a private ceremony in Kansas City, Zerelda Mimms was married to her first cousin—the notorious outlaw Jesse James.

Q: Why was Yuma, Arizona, a place to be avoided by outlaws of the Old West?

A: The Arizona territorial prison was located there.

Q: Where was Wyatt Earp's first job as a law enforcement officer, and whom did he defeat for the post?

A: In 1870 Wyatt Earp was elected constable of Lamar, Missouri, in a race against Newton J. Earp, who was his half-brother.

Q: How did Belle Starr, the "Bandit Queen," meet her end?

A: Glorified as "braver than Joan of Arc" by the dime novels, Belle Starr was a horse thief, outlaw and part-time prostitute who was shot in the back and killed in 1889 by an unknown assailant.

Q: How much reward was the state of Missouri offering for Jesse and Frank James at the time of Jesse's murder?

A: $10,000.

Q: Who was Frank P. ("Windy") Cahill, and what was his claim to Old West fame?

A: On August 17, 1877, Cahill, a blacksmith at Fort Grant, Arizona, was shot to death by a young delinquent during an argument, becoming Billy the Kid's first recorded victim.

Q: What lawman captured the infamous gunfighter John Wesley Hardin in 1877, and where did the arrest occur?

A: Texas Ranger John Armstrong trailed Hardin to Pensacola, Florida, cornered him on a train and disarmed the deadly shootist when Hardin somehow got his gun entangled in his suspenders.

FACT: Despite Hollywood's depiction to the contrary, Jesse and Frank James were never cowboys. Both were raised on a farm in Missouri, where many of their crimes occurred, and neither spent time as a cowpuncher.

Q: When, where and by whom was Wild Bill Hickok killed, and what was he holding in his hand at the time?

A: Hickok was shot in the back of the head by an alcoholic drifter named Jack McCall while playing poker in Saloon No. 66 in Deadwood, South Dakota, on August 2, 1876. When killed he was holding a poker hand of aces and eights—thereafter known as the Dead Man's Hand.

Q: For the capture of what California outlaw was a reward of $1,000 offered—only to be raised to $3,000 before his eventual capture in 1874?

A: The reward was offered for Tiburcio Vásquez, who was the leader of a bandit gang that terrorized much of southern California in the 1870s. Vásquez was finally caught and was hanged in San José in 1875.

Q: Who was governor of New Mexico Territory when Lincoln County Sheriff Pat Garrett killed Billy the Kid, and what was the governor's principal contribution to American history?

A: The territorial governor of New Mexico at the time of Billy the Kid's death was Lew Wallace, a prominent Union general in the Civil War and later the author of the literary classic *Ben Hur*.

Q: What became of Jesse James's brother Frank, who rode with his infamous relative for sixteen years of banditry?

A: After his notorious brother was murdered in 1882, Frank James surrendered to authorities and was tried and acquitted by a sympathetic Missouri jury. He later worked at a racetrack, served as a security guard, farmed in Missouri, directed a Wild West show, and lived until 1915.

Q: What did a Western gunman mean when he referred to his "ace in the hole"?

A: An ace in the hole was a hidden pistol that some gunfighters, gamblers and cowboys concealed in a shoulder holster, in a boot, in a waistband or in some other hideaway.

Q: At what age did the famous target shooter Annie Oakley begin to earn an income with her marksmanship?

A: Annie Oakley's father died when she was six, and to help support her Ohio family, she shot wild game for sale to a Cincinnati hotel, earning her first shooting money as early as age eight.

Q: How many men died in gunfights with Wyatt Earp during his service as a lawman in Dodge City, Kansas?

A: One. On July 26, 1878, a drunken cowboy named George Hoyt
was mortally wounded while trading shots with Earp and other
gunmen.

Q: Who was Nelson King and how did his invention affect the Old
West?

A: King invented a way to load the sixteen-shot Henry repeating rifle
from the side instead of from the awkward tube under the gun's
muzzle. His invention popularized the Henry repeater's improved
successor—the Model 1866 Winchester.

Q: Did Dodge City really have a Long Branch Saloon?

A: Yes. During its roaring days as a booming cattle town, Dodge City
boasted numerous saloons, and one of the most popular with lawmen
and the lawless was the Long Branch, shown here as it appeared in
the 1880s. One of the owners of the establishment, William Harris,
was a former resident of Long Branch, New Jersey, and the notorious Long Branch Saloon was named in honor of that faraway Eastern city.

FACT: What was perhaps the most heroic defense against the odds ever made by an Old West lawman did not involve Wyatt Earp, Wild Bill Hickok, Bat Masterson or any other famous Old West lawmen. Instead it involved a volunteer deputy sheriff named Elfego Baca, who set out to disperse a band of wild cowboys who were shooting up the town of Frisco, New Mexico, in 1884. In response to Baca's attempts to bring law and order to Frisco, some eighty gun-toting cowhands cornered the young lawman in an adobe-and-log hut and fired more than four thousand rounds into his hiding place over a thirty-six-hour period. Before being relieved by lawmen, Baca managed to kill four of his assailants, wounded eight more and walked away from the fight unhurt—at age nineteen.

Q: When did Wyatt Earp die, and where is he buried?

A: Earp died at his home at 4004 West Seventeenth Street in Los Angeles, California, on Sunday, January 13, 1929, at age seventy-nine. His remains were cremated, and his ashes were buried in Hills of Eternity Memorial Park at Colma, California.

Q: What was Butch Cassidy's most successful robbery?

A: Although reports of Cassidy's crimes could not always be verified, his biggest haul—if he participated—was probably the robbery of a railroad express car near Folsom, New Mexico, on July 11, 1899, which yielded approximately $70,000.

Q: Of the twenty-eight stagecoach holdups attempted by Old West robber "Black Bart," how many succeeded—and how was he finally caught?

A: Between 1875 and 1882 Black Bart successfully robbed twenty-seven stagecoaches in California, failing only on number twenty-eight—when he dropped a handkerchief bearing a laundry mark that led lawmen to his door.

Q: What kind of firearm was Wild Bill Hickok wearing when he was shot to death in 1876?

A: Although he did not have a chance to use it, on the day of his murder Hickok was wearing a .32-caliber Smith & Wesson Model No. 2 revolver.

Q: What happened to Bob Ford—the man who killed Jesse James?
A: Although he received a huge reward, Ford was reviled for shooting
     Jesse James from behind. Ten years after he shot the infamous bandit
     leader, Ford was shot and killed while running a tent saloon in
     Creede, Colorado. Here he poses with the gun he said he used to kill
     Jesse James.

Q: Who was Jesse James, Jr., and what became of him?

A: Jesse James, Jr., was the son of the famous outlaw, and after his father's death he became a respected attorney in Kansas City.

Q: What was the last law enforcement post held by frontier lawman Bat Masterson?

A: After somewhat controversial service as a lawman in Dodge City and a variety of other jobs around the West, Masterson moved to New York City and was appointed deputy U.S. marshal for southern New York by President Theodore Roosevelt—an appointment later revoked by President Taft.

Q: Who were the partners who developed the Smith & Wesson handguns so popular on the Old West frontier?

A: In 1852 Daniel Wesson and Horace Smith formed a partnership in Norwich, Connecticut, and began producing the Smith & Wesson firearms that competed with Samuel Colt's popular revolver.

Q: How long did the famous gunfight at the O.K. Corral last?

A: Approximately 30 seconds.

Q: Where are Wild Bill Hickok and Calamity Jane buried?

A: Both are interred in Mount Moriah Cemetery in Deadwood, South Dakota.

Q: Where was outlaw Sam Bass killed?

A: Bass, who was more notorious than successful as an outlaw, was mortally wounded in a gunfight with Texas Rangers during a bungled bank robbery in Round Rock, Texas, on July 21, 1878.

Q: Where was the Long and Norton Bank, which was robbed of $14,000 by Jesse James and his gang in 1868?

A: Russellville, Kentucky.

Q: How many deputy U.S. marshals were killed in the line of duty between 1875 and 1891 while enforcing the law for "Hanging Judge" Isaac C. Parker of Fort Smith, Arkansas?

A: Sixty-five.

Q: How did gunfighter Ben Thompson meet his end?

A: Thompson, who earned a fierce reputation with shooting scrapes from Texas to Kansas, was shot to death in March of 1884, when he drunkenly confronted an old adversary in San Antonio's Vaudeville Variety Theatre.

Q: What cattlemen's organization hired a mob of Texas gunmen to invade Johnson County, Wyoming, with the mission of killing settlers and nesters who threatened the future of the giant ranches?

A: The army of hired gunmen which launched the Johnson County War was recruited and bankrolled by the influential Wyoming Stock Growers Association.

Q: In what 1896 sports event did Wyatt Earp participate, and why was it controversial?

A: In 1896 Earp served as referee of the Tom Sharkey–Bob Fitzsimmons prizefight in San Francisco, which had a purse of $10,000. Earp created controversy by allegedly wearing a six-gun into the ring and by awarding the fight to Sharkey on a foul—a decision critics claimed was made so Earp could collect his bets.

Q: What happened to Mattie Earp, Wyatt Earp's second wife, who was with him in Tombstone, Arizona, at the time of the gunfight at the O.K. Corral?

A: Reportedly despondent because Earp had left her for another woman, Mattie Earp committed suicide with an overdose of laudanum on July 3, 1888, in Pinal, Arizona.

Q: On June 24, 1889, the San Miguel Valley Bank of Telluride, Colorado, was robbed by four gunmen, who escaped with approximately $20,000. What was significant about the holdup?

A: It was believed to have been the first bank robbed by Butch Cassidy.

Q: Who was Virgil Earp's famous in-law?

A: Virgil Earp's wife, Allie Sullivan Earp, was the sister of Amelia Sullivan, twenty-fifth wife of Mormon leader Brigham Young.

Q: What was the "road-agent's spin," which was employed with deadly consequences by some Western shootists?

A: The road-agent's spin referred to the practice of pretending to surrender a handgun butt first, only to spin the weapon into firing position.

Q: Who was the man who killed the man who killed gunfighter John Wesley Hardin?

A: Hardin was shot to death in 1895 by El Paso resident John Henry Selman. A year later Selman, while intoxicated, was shot and killed by Deputy U.S. Marshal George Scarborough.

Q: When, where and by whom was Billy the Kid killed?
A: He was shot to death on the night of July 14, 1881, at the home of rancher Pete Maxwell at Fort Sumner, New Mexico, by Lincoln County Sheriff Pat Garrett.

Q: How long after Billy the Kid's death did the first "biography" of the young gunman appear?
A: About three weeks.

Q: How did Pat Garrett—the celebrated killer of Billy the Kid—meet his end?
A: On February 29, 1908, while en route from his New Mexico ranch to nearby Las Cruces, Garrett was shot and killed by a business associate or a hired gunman during an argument over a land lease.

Q: What was the Hole in the Wall?
A: Located southwest of Buffalo, Wyoming—near the modern community of Kaycee—the Hole in the Wall was a region of rugged badlands that became a "robbers' roost" for outlaws on the run.

Q: What was Jesse James's favorite firearm?
A: At the time of his death in 1882, Jesse's first choice in firearms was the 1875 Smith & Wesson Schofield, a .45-caliber single-action handgun that was popular on the Western frontier.

Q: What was Butch Cassidy's last holdup in the Old West?
A: Cassidy's last holdup was probably the robbery of a Great Northern Railway express car in Exeter, Montana, on July 3, 1901—a job that netted the robbers approximately $65,000.

Q: By what nickname was Jesse James known to his friends?
A: Jesse's best buddies called him "Dingus."

FACT: The last Old West outlaw of renown to die "on the job" was Henry Starr, who began his career of Western banditry in 1893 and led a gang of mounted outlaws for more than twenty-five years. Starr's career finally ended on February 18, 1921, when he was shot to death trying to rob a bank in Harrison, Arkansas.

Q: Who gave famous markswoman Annie Oakley the heralded title of "Little Sure Shot"?

A: Annie Oakley received this much-publicized nickname from the Sioux leader Sitting Bull, who saw her perform in 1884.

Q: What was a Westerner doing when he was said to be "among the willows"?

A: The phrase described men on the run from the law and may have come from the desperado's practice of traveling across open country by night and hiding by day among the willows that shaded many Western waterways.

Q: How many men were killed in the 1871 "Newton Massacre" in Newton, Kansas, and how did it affect the town?

A: In 1871 the notorious cow town was the site of a saloon shootout that left five dead, including a town policeman. Following the gunfight, infuriated townsmen ordered every gambler, outlaw and harlot to leave Newton within twelve hours—or else—and they left.

Q: What was the "street howitzer" with which Doc Holliday was known to arm himself?

A: Holliday's so-called street howitzer was one of his favorite weapons —a 10-gauge Meteor double-barrel sawed-off shotgun.

Q: What eventually happened to Butch Cassidy and the Sundance Kid?

A: After a much publicized string of bank and train robberies in the West, Butch and Sundance reportedly moved their operations to Bolivia, where they were believed to have been killed in a shootout with Bolivian troops in 1911. Evidence exists, however, that Butch Cassidy relocated in Spokane, Washington, where he lived under the alias William T. Phillips until he died of cancer in the county poorhouse on July 20, 1937. Persistent reports claimed the Sundance Kid also returned to the United States, where he allegedly lived under an alias until his death in Wyoming in 1957.

Q: Did Old West gunman Bat Masterson, survivor of numerous frontier gunfights, die with his boots on?

A: Yes, sort of. On October 25, 1921, Masterson suddenly collapsed and died at his desk at the offices of New York's *Morning Telegraph*, where he had spent his last years as sports editor.

Q: Where did Annie Oakley conclude her career?

A: In 1915, after seventeen years of trick shooting with Buffalo Bill's
Wild West Show, on a grand European tour and in other appearances
across the United States, Annie Oakley and husband Frank Butler,
another shooting exhibitionist, joined the staff of the Carolina Hotel
in Pinehurst, North Carolina, as the resident attractions. With time
out for a visit to U.S. troops during World War I, she remained in
Pinehurst until forced to retire by an automobile accident in 1921.
Here, Annie Oakley, far right, gives shooting instructions at Pinehurst shortly before her retirement. In the insert she is pictured as
she appeared in her prime.

> **FACT:** The famous gunfight at the O.K. Corral did not occur in the O.K. Corral. When the Earps and the Clantons shot it out in Tombstone, Arizona, in 1881, their famous battle took place in a vacant lot between Fly's Photograph Gallery and the Harwood house on Tombstone's Fremont Street. The O.K. Corral was located nearby, however, and somehow its name became attached to the Old West's most famous shootout.

Q: What famous Old West gunman was dispatched with a .44 Colt Single Action Revolver bearing serial number 55093?

A: Colt # 55093 was the gun with which Pat Garrett killed Billy the Kid.

Q: How did death come to Clay Allison, the infamous gunfighter who shot an uncounted number of victims over a period of approximately twenty years?

A: On July 1, 1887, Allison was mortally injured near Pecos, Texas, when run over by a wagon. Reportedly drunk at the time, he was trying to retrieve a fallen sack of grain when one of the vehicle's wheels rolled over his neck.

2 | Mountain Men, Frontiersmen and Trailblazers

Q: How much was a beaver pelt worth at the height of the fur trade era?

A: The average price for a beaver pelt was four dollars a pound, and a typical beaver pelt weighed almost two pounds, so an average pelt was worth approximately eight dollars.

Q: From what Green River did the famous Green River knife take its name?

A: One of the most popular tools in the Old West and a standard weapon for mountain men, the Green River knife was manufactured by John Russell at a site on New England's Green River near Greenfield, Massachusetts.

Q: When and where was mountain man Jim Bridger born?

A: Bridger was born in Richmond, Virginia, in 1804. His parents moved the family to St. Louis when Bridger was a child, and he was orphaned at age fourteen.

Q: What famous symbol of the Western frontier was established by a Catholic priest named Antonio de San Buenaventura Olivares in 1718?

A: The Alamo.

Q: Who was the famous son of Sir Jennings Beckwith and Miss Kill?

A: Beckwith, a Virginia planter, and Miss Kill, a mulatto slave woman, were the parents of James Pierson ("Jim") Beckwourth, a prominent trapper and scout who lived for several years with the Crow Indians. Beckwourth, pictured here, became famous in 1856 when his exploits were embellished in a sensational biography that made him the best-known black man in the history of the Old West.

Q: How many miles were covered in the famous Lewis and Clark expedition of 1804–06, and how many lives were lost during the twenty-eight-month wilderness trek?

A: From St. Louis to the Pacific coast and back, Lewis and Clark covered 7,689 miles. The expedition suffered one fatality, when Sergeant Charles Floyd died from what was probably a ruptured appendix.

Q: What famous Western scout won the Congressional Medal of Honor—only to lose it more than forty years later?

A: For acts of bravery during service with the U.S. Army in the Indian Wars, William F. ("Buffalo Bill") Cody was awarded the Medal of Honor in 1872, but in 1917—the year of his death—it was withdrawn because of his status as a civilian scout.

Q: At the 1829 trappers' Rendezvous on the Popo Agie River in what is now Wyoming, greenhorn mountain man Joe Meek was reportedly shocked to see four trappers playing cards on a peculiar makeshift table. Why did the "table" shock Meek?

A: According to Meek, the table on which the mountain men played was the still-warm body of a dead friend who had been killed in a Rendezvous fracas.

Q: What favorite delicacy did mountain men refer to as "trapper's butter?"

A: Buffalo marrow.

Q: What caliber was the famous Hawken rifle used by many mountain men, and who manufactured it?

A: The favored weapon for much of the fur era was the .50-caliber percussion muzzle-loading Hawken rifle, made in St. Louis by Samuel and Jacob Hawken.

Q: Early in the nineteenth century American wildlife painter and naturalist John J. Audubon made several expeditions into the Western wilderness to paint its wildlife. With what did he "harvest" the birds he used as models for his famous paintings?

A: A shotgun.

Q: What body of water located on what is now the border of Idaho and Utah was a favorite Rendezvous site for mountain men?

A: Bear Lake.

FACT: The steel trap so familiar to the beaver men who operated trap lines in the Rocky Mountains was invented in 1823 by Sewall Newhouse, who was the son of a New York blacksmith. At the height of the beaver trade, according to some estimates, as many as a half-million beaver were trapped in a single year, most of them in some variation of Sewall Newhouse's invention.

Q: What was the average speed of the keelboat, the river vessel that moved trappers and their furs up and down the large Western rivers in the early nineteenth century?

A: The typical keelboat was sixty to seventy feet long, with a keel running bow to stern. In good weather a keelboat could make an average of fifteen miles a day on large rivers like the Missouri.

Q: What famous Westerner was described as being unafraid of "hell or high water," as reliable as "the sun comin' up" and with morals as "clean as a hound's tooth"?

A: Mountain man and scout Christopher ("Kit") Carson was so depicted by a frontier relative who knew him well.

Q: What explorer incorrectly labeled the Great Plains as the "Great American Desert"?

A: Army officer Stephen H. Long, who explored the Western wilderness for the U.S. Army's Topographical Engineer Corps in the early nineteenth century, so labeled the Great Plains in his official reports, causing a generation of Americans to ignore the region that would one day become one of the world's greatest food producers.

Q: What was the procedure used by mountain men to trap beaver?

A: Wading to a trap site on the edge of a stream, the trapper would place a small steel trap in shallow water near the bank and anchor it with a light five-foot chain fastened to a stick. He would then suspend a twig dipped in castorum from the bank over the trap. To reach the bait, the beaver would have to move under the twig, where he would be caught by the trap. He would usually drag the trap into deeper water, where he would drown—and later would be retrieved by the trapper.

Q: How did buffalo hunters butcher their game, and what parts of the buffalo did they consider to be choice cuts?

A: Instead of dressing the slain bison from the front, as was customary with most domestic or game animals, the buffalo hunters propped the huge animals on their stomachs and skinned along the backbone. The select cuts of buffalo meat were the tongue, hump ribs, fleece fat, marrow bones, gall and liver.

Q: Where was famous mountain man Joseph R. Walker born, and where did he die?

A: Walker was born in Roan County, Tennessee, on December 13, 1798, and died peacefully at age seventy-seven at Martinez, California, on October 27, 1876.

Q: What was a "free trapper"?

A: Free trappers were trappers who worked as free-lance agents, supplying furs to various buyers without serving as employees of any particular fur company.

Q: What mountain man was known to friends as "Old Gabe," and what was his pet hate?

A: The nickname belonged to Jim Bridger, who hated cities.

Q: How much profit did pioneer fur merchant William H. Ashley record on his first fur trapping expedition?

A: None. In 1822 Ashley's first trapping expedition ended with the loss of the expedition's keelboat and a cargo estimated at $10,000. Undaunted, Ashley, founder of the Rocky Mountain Fur Company, persevered and built a fortune from furs.

Q: What Old West commodity was produced by this recipe: one gallon of alcohol, one pound of black twist tobacco, one pound of molasses, one handful of Spanish red peppers, ten gallons of river water and two rattlesnake heads?

A: These were the ingredients of the infamous "frontier whiskey," which was sometimes traded to Indians for beaver pelts and was frequently consumed by iron-bellied mountain men.

Q: When the Grand Duke Alexis of Russia came to the United States for a buffalo hunt in the Old West, what prominent frontiersmen served as his guides?

A: The duke was escorted by Buffalo Bill Cody and General George Armstrong Custer.

FACT: Western explorer John Charles Fremont, known as "the Path-finder" for his treks through the Old West wilderness, received his first independent commission to explore the West because of romance. In 1841 Fremont was commissioned to explore and map the wilds of Iowa by Secretary of War Joel R. Poinsett upon the urging of Senator Thomas Hart Benton, who was hoping to end a romance between his teenage daughter Jessie and young Fremont. The two later eloped.

Q: When chasing buffalo on horseback, where did early buffalo hunters keep their rifle balls?

A: In their mouths.

Q: Who gave California's Eel River its name and why?

A: The river was named by pioneer trader and traveler Josiah Gregg, who was inspired when he saw a large catch of eels hauled from the stream by local Indians.

Q: What did fur trappers François Duchouquette, Edward Rose, Jean Baptiste Point-au-Sable and James Beckwourth have in common?

A: All were black men who earned prominent positions in the American fur trade.

Q: How much did a mountain man usually pay for the common steel beaver trap used in the fur industry?

A: A five-pound steel beaver trap with accompanying chain sold for twelve to sixteen dollars at the height of the fur trade.

Q: Who was the first American citizen on record to enter California by an overland route from the east?

A: In 1826 mountain man Jedediah Smith discovered a central route from the Rockies to the Pacific, and, in doing so, became the first American citizen known to have reached California by an overland route.

Q: What important landmark of the Old West was established on the Arkansas River in present-day Colorado by Ceran St. Vrain and two other fur trappers in 1833?

A: That year St. Vrain and two well-known trapper brothers, William and Charles Bent, chose a site on the Arkansas River and built Bent's Fort, which became a primary stop on the Santa Fe Trail.

Q: What famous frontiersman and long hunter died near St. Louis in 1820 at age eighty-five, and what did he keep under his bed?

A: Explorer and frontiersman Daniel Boone died peacefully in a relative's home on the Missouri frontier in 1820, years after he had helped open the West through his explorations of Kentucky. In his seventies and eighties he was said to have explored as far west as the Platte River, and in his later years he kept a custom-designed cherrywood coffin under his bed for his eventual use.

Q: What giant British fur company dominated the fur industry in the northern Rockies during the trappers' era?

A: The Hudson's Bay Company.

Q: By what name was Edward Z. C. Judson best known, and what Western hero and frontier legend did he create from the exploits of an unknown army scout in the West?

A: Judson, whose famous pen name was Ned Buntline, an author of countless sensationalistic dime novels, exaggerated and glorified the unknown scout William F. Cody so successfully that Cody became internationally famous as the legendary Buffalo Bill.

Q: What explorer gave the mighty Columbia River of the Northwest its name, and for what was the waterway named?

A: Spanish explorers named the river the San Rogue in 1775, but an American sea captain, Robert Gray of Boston, "discovered" the waterway on a voyage to the Pacific coast in 1792 and renamed the river in honor of his vessel, the *Columbia Rediviva*.

Q: Who was the first American explorer on record to see Pike's Peak?

A: The first recorded sighting of Pike's Peak by an American citizen occurred in 1806, when an expedition led by U.S. Army Lieutenant Zebulon M. Pike sighted the huge mountain.

Q: What Western mountain range was known to early-nineteenth-century trappers, explorers and geographers as the Shining Mountains, the Snowy Mountains, the Stony Mountains, the Missouri Mountains, the Mexican Mountains and, more formally, the Chippewyan System?

A: All were names applied to the Rocky Mountains. Not until the second half of the nineteenth century were the Rockies commonly called by their popular name, which was adapted from *Montagnes Roucheuses,* as the rugged range was known to French fur trappers.

Q: What city was the jumping-off point for explorers and the center of the Rocky Mountain fur trade?

A: St. Louis, Missouri.

Q: When and how did the great buffalo herds disappear from the Old West?

A: By 1883 the great herds of bison that had once sprawled across the Western plains from Mexico to Canada had disappeared. For the previous ten years, from 1872 through 1882, professional hunters had slaughtered millions of buffalo for their hides and tongues, yet the shaggy beasts seemed inexhaustible in numbers. However, buffalo hunters who set out in search of their quarry in the fall of 1883 were surprised to find the great herds gone, eliminated by overhunting and by a sudden epidemic of some disease such as tick fever. During the height of the buffalo-hunting era, thousands of buffalo hides were collected at railhead hide yards like this one in Dodge City, for shipment to Eastern buyers; but by 1889 less than a hundred wild buffalo were believed to exist on the Western plains.

Q: What famous Western frontiersman was born on Tennessee's Nolichuky River in 1786 and at various times in his career was a cattle
drover, a farmer, a justice of the peace, a militia colonel, a state
legislator, a three-term U.S. congressman—and the victim of violent death on the Western frontier?

A: All these occupations were pursued at times by Davy Crockett,
who was killed in battle at the Alamo in 1836.

Q: Where was Kit Carson born, and what was his first occupation?

A: Carson was born near Richmond, Kentucky, in 1809, was raised
on the Missouri frontier and began his professional life as an ap-
prentice to a Missouri saddler—a job he ended after a few months
by running away to New Mexico.

Q: In 1832 mountain man James Clyman, who had temporarily left
the Rocky Mountain fur trade, campaigned against the Sauk and
Fox Indians in a militia unit that included a young volunteer des-
tined for international fame. Which of the mountain man's fellow
soldiers was bound for glory?

A: Clyman, who soon returned to his mountain traps, served in the
1832 Black Hawk War, where he marched alongside a young volunteer named Abraham Lincoln.

Q: What were the primary commercial uses for buffalo robes?

A: In the nineteenth century millions of buffalo were slaughtered by
hunters to meet a demand by the garment industry in the northeastern United States and Europe, which sold the woolly robes as
overcoats and lap robes.

Q: What important event in the history of the Rocky Mountain fur
trade occurred on April 11, 1822?

A: On this date fur merchant William H. Ashley was licensed to
operate a fur company along the upper Missouri River—an event
that created the famous Rocky Mountain Fur Company.

Q: Who discovered the Great Salt Lake and why?

A: Although known to Indians for centuries and seen by white men
probably as early as 1790, the huge lake was "discovered" during
the winter of 1824–25 when mountain man Jim Bridger found it
while on an expedition directed by William H. Ashley. Bridger had
accepted a bet that he could not find the source of Bear River, and
in his search he stumbled onto the Great Salt Lake.

Q: Who built a fortified trading post on the Oregon Trail at the Black Fork of the Green River in 1843, and what was its name?

A: Fort Bridger was built on this site in this year by mountain men Jim Bridger and Louis Vásquez, who together operated it for ten years as a primary stop on the Oregon Trail.

Q: What weapon accessory vital to the early mountain men was produced at sites in England near Brandon, Suffolk, Norwich, Salisbury, Tuddenham and Cavenham?

A: Before percussion rifles were available, the early mountain men depended on flintlock weapons that used gun flints quarried at these sites in Great Britain as well as sites in America.

Q: What was "jerky"—the food regularly consumed by mountain men —and where did it originate?

A: Jerky was a form of dried meat used by the Indians of Mexico, who called it *charqui*. They dried thin strips of buffalo meat in the sun, ground it into a mealy substance, then carried it in leather pouches when traveling. When cooked in a soup, the *charqui* would swell, creating a filling and nourishing meal. Mountain men found it convenient and so did the later cowboys, who substituted beef for buffalo and called it jerky.

Q: Who was the first man on record to discover the Bighorn River Valley, the headwaters of the Colorado and Snake rivers, the Grand Teton Mountains and Yellowstone Lake?

A: Although familiar to Indians for untold generations, all these sites were officially discovered by trapper and trailblazer John Colter, a former member of the Lewis and Clark Expedition, who made a solitary journey to these and other Western wonders in 1807.

FACT: The Alamo was named for a town in Mexico. Originally named San Antonio de Valero, the former Catholic mission was occupied in 1801 by a company of Spanish colonial troops who renamed the facility in honor of their home town, San José y Santiago del Alamo de Parras. It was the shortened form of this name by which the Alamo was known to the frontiersmen who were martyred there in 1836, making the old mission building famous.

Q: How did the notorious boatman Mike Fink meet his end?

A: In 1822 Fink "accidentally" shot and killed a former friend named Carpenter while attempting to shoot a cup of whiskey off the man's head. A year later, in a fit of drunken boasting, Fink bragged of the killing, and the dead man's best friend—a boatman named Talbot —drew his pistol and killed Fink.

Q: Who were the principals in the early-nineteenth-century trapping firm of Smith, Jackson and Sublette?

A: Active in the Rocky Mountain fur trade in the 1820s, the firm was composed of mountain men Jedediah S. Smith, David E. Jackson and William L. Sublette, and was sold to the Rocky Mountain Fur Company in 1830.

Q: What was mountain man David E. Jackson's primary contribution to the history and geography of the American West?

A: Jackson left his name on two prominent Wyoming landmarks: Jackson Hole and Jackson Lake. He died of typhoid fever in Paris, Tennessee, in 1837.

Q: What milestone in the fur trade occurred at 3:30 A.M., June 2, 1823, at the Arikara Indian village near the Missouri River in what is now South Dakota?

A: On this date William H. Ashley and a large party of trappers aboard two keelboats suffered a surprise attack by Arikara Indians, with whom they had been trading. After serious loss of life and property the trappers retreated downriver, leaving behind the first serious disaster of the Rocky Mountain fur trade.

Q: What mountain man was known as the "Thunderbolt of the Rocky Mountains"?

A: Trapper Milton G. Sublette, a principal of the Rocky Mountain Fur Company, was so named by his fellow trappers because of his reckless deeds.

Q: When did the Alamo fall to the Mexican army; how many Mexican troops opposed the Alamo's 188 frontiersmen; and how many troops did it cost to take the stronghold?

A: On March 6, 1836, after a thirteen-day siege, Mexican General Antonio López de Santa Anna's 5,000-man army finally captured the Alamo and reportedly killed all its defenders—at a cost of some 600 to 1,500 casualties.

Q: What was the birthplace of John Jacob Astor, founder of the American Fur Company and known in his day as "the greatest of fur merchants," and what product launched his fabulously rich business empire?

A: Astor, who eventually made a gigantic fortune in the fur trade, was born in Germany in 1763, immigrated to the United States in 1784 and began his business career by selling a load of musical instruments in New York City.

Q: What was the Northwest Gun, which was so popular in the Old West during the trappers' era?

A: Also called the Mackinaw Gun, the Northwest Gun was a lightweight smoothbore flintlock musket designed by the Hudson's Bay Company for trade with the Indians in the early nineteenth century. Made in England, the gun was worth up to twenty beaver pelts and remained popular with the Indians of the West for decades.

Q: What was the first wheeled vehicle to cross the Continental Divide on the Oregon Trail?

A: In 1827 fur entrepreneur William H. Ashley led a party of trappers over the Rockies through South Pass on part of the route later known as the Oregon Trail. With Ashley's party was the first wheeled vehicle to cross the Rockies on the trail—a four-pounder cannon drawn by mules.

Q: What killed 2,500 buffalo, 1,600 deer and elk, 105 grizzly bears and countless smaller game animals in the Old West between 1854 and 1856?

A: All were slain during a two-year hunting trip organized by mountain man Jim Bridger for visiting English hunters.

Q: What did these forts have in common: Fort Bonneville, Fort Hall, Fort Lisa, Fort Mandan, Fort Benton, Fort Bridger, Fort Walla Walla, Grant's Fort and Fort Davy Crockett?

A: All were trading posts established during the era of the Rocky Mountain fur trade.

Q: What were the two favorite forms of recreation for Andrew Henry, who was one of the early leaders in the Western fur trade?

A: Henry spent his spare time playing his violin or reading any book he could find.

Q: What famous Western frontiersman died of a hemorrhage at Fort
     Lyon, Colorado, on May 23, 1868?
A: Kit Carson.

Q: Who was the first person on record to scale Pike's Peak?
A: On an 1806 expedition explorer Zebulon M. Pike failed to scale the
     Colorado peak that bears his name. Fourteen years later the 14,110-
     foot mountain was conquered by Dr. Edwin James, a physician on
     Major Stephen H. Long's 1820 expedition to the Rocky Mountains.
     Long named the peak in honor of James, but Zebulon Pike's earlier
     sighting of the mountain had made it famous and it was his name,
     not the obscure Dr. James's, that remained popularly attached to the
     peak. In this photograph, two later adventurers work their way up
     Pike's Peak.

Q: What were the primary firearms used by the buffalo hunters?

A: Although early hunters used flintlock rifles, the numerous buffalo hunters who swarmed to the plains after the Civil War conducted their slaughter with large-caliber Sharps, Remington, Winchester and Ballard rifles.

Q: What happened to mountain man John Colter at Three Forks of the Missouri?

A: In 1807, following service with the Lewis and Clark Expedition, John Colter returned to the northern Rockies. There he and another trapper were ambushed by Blackfoot warriors near present-day Three Forks, Montana, where the Madison and the Jefferson rivers form the Missouri. His companion was killed, and Colter, stripped by the Indians, was ordered to run for his life. He outran the warriors, hid under a river log jam and eventually walked naked back to civilization—some two hundred miles away.

Q: How long was the Battle of San Jacinto, in which Sam Houston's army of Texas frontiersmen won independence from Mexico for the fledgling Republic of Texas?

A: Although the victorious Texans continued mopping-up operations against Mexican forces for two days, the actual Battle of San Jacinto lasted but eighteen minutes. Mexican casualties included 630 dead, while the Texans recorded two killed in action.

Q: What prominent trapper with the Hudson's Bay Company is remembered today by a city in Utah?

A: Peter Skene Ogden, a native of Quebec and the son of an American Loyalist refugee from the Revolution, was a leader in the Hudson's Bay Company and trapped throughout the northern Rockies. Ogden, Utah, bears his name.

Q: What famous Western landmark was discovered by prospector John Wesley Hillman in 1853?

A: Hillman discovered Crater Lake, which became the highlight of Crater Lake National Park in Oregon.

Q: In 1827 famed mountain man Joseph Walker interrupted his trapping career to hold a new job in Missouri. What was it?

A: Walker was elected sheriff of Jackson County, Missouri—which included the bustling town of Independence—but returned to the mountains after two terms of office.

Q: In 1824 a band of Shoshone Indians tricked veteran mountain man Etienne Provost and fourteen trappers into putting down their weapons, then killed most of the trappers. How did the Indians trick their victims?

A: The Shoshones invited the trappers to smoke a peace pipe, told them it was "bad medicine" to have metal present, then attacked when the mountain men carelessly put aside their weapons—killing all but Provost and four others.

Q: What unusual weapon was sometimes carried by mountain man Jim Bridger?

A: Sometimes Bridger equipped himself with an over-under swivel-barrel rifle made by Pennsylvania gunsmith John Schuler.

Q: Where did the American Fur Company and the Rocky Mountain Fur Company stage the Rendezvous of 1832?

A: The 1832 Rendezvous was held at Pierre's Hole, west of the Grand Teton Mountains, in what is now Idaho.

Q: How long did it take to load and fire a Hawken rifle?

A: An inexperienced man usually needed a full minute to load and fire the muzzle-loading Hawken—a process that required measuring and pouring powder down the gun barrel, wrapping a rifle ball in a cloth patch, ramming the ball down the barrel with a ramrod, replacing the ramrod, fitting a percussion cap to the rifle's nipple, cocking the hammer and pulling the trigger. Veteran mountain men, however, could load and fire a Hawken three or four times a minute.

Q: In the time normally required to reload and fire a Hawken rifle, how many arrows could be fired by an expert Indian bowman?

A: A skilled bowman could fire ten or more arrows in a minute.

Q: Why was mountain man John Johnson known as "Crow Killer Johnson," and what was his bizarre trademark?

A: Johnson conducted a personal war with the Crow Indians and killed so many of the tribe's warriors that he became known as "the Crow Killer." After slaying an opponent, Johnson allegedly dined on his victim's liver.

Q: For whom were the Provo River and the city of Provo, Utah, named?

A: Both were named for trapper Etienne Provost.

Q: How did Frenchman Eleuthère Irénée du Pont de Nemours help "tame" the Old West?

A: Du Pont, a former gunpowder chemist for the French government, immigrated to the United States in 1800 and eventually developed the high grade of gunpowder used by the mountain men, explorers and frontiersmen who opened the West.

Q: How did frontiersmen protect themselves when they found themselves caught on the open plains in the path of a rapidly moving prairie fire?

A: The safest defense, if time allowed, was to start a small break fire to burn off a section of the prairie that was in the path of the larger blaze, then remain in the burned-out area as the prairie fire swept past.

Q: Who were the famous Sublette brothers active in the Rocky Mountain fur trade, and why did they come West?

A: Sons of a Missouri tavern keeper, Andrew, Solomon, Pinckney, Milton and William Sublette all went into the mountains seeking relief from tuberculosis.

Q: What prominent official of the American Fur Company was killed by Blackfoot Indians near Montana's Jefferson River on October 14, 1832?

A: On this date William Henry Vanderburg, a principal with the American Fur Company, was killed in a skirmish with the Blackfeet while competing with the rival Rocky Mountain Fur Company.

FACT: After being savagely mauled by a sow grizzly in what is now South Dakota in 1823, trapper Hugh Glass was left in the care of two volunteers while the rest of his trapping party retreated. Afraid of hostile Arikara Indians and certain Glass would die, the two trappers took the injured man's weapons and deserted him. Glass did not die, however, and slowly regained his strength. Surviving on wild berries and raw meat taken from a buffalo killed by wolves, he crawled and walked across much of South Dakota to civilization. Ironically, one of the frightened trappers who abandoned Glass was a greenhorn who later became famous as mountain man Jim Bridger.

Q: Who was the first explorer on record to navigate the Colorado River through the Grand Canyon, and what was his physical handicap?

A: In 1869 explorer John Wesley Powell took a handful of men down the Colorado River in four small boats, conquering the treacherous waters of the Grand Canyon and becoming an American hero. The first man on record to navigate the Colorado through the Grand Canyon, Powell accomplished the feat despite the loss of his right arm during the Civil War. Here, Powell and fellow explorers camp on the Green River in Wyoming Territory during an 1871 expedition.

Q: Who was first to travel overland from Oregon south to Mexico's Gulf of California?

A: Fur trapper and explorer Peter Skene Ogden was first to blaze this trail.

Q: How did buffalo hunters find the great herds?

A: The hunters would trail a herd into a general area, then arise at dawn and search the treeless horizon for a huge, low-hanging frost cloud—the vapor created by the warm breath of thousands of buffalo.

Q: In the parlance of the mountain man, what was a *bourgeois*?

A: A *bourgeois* was the leader in charge of a party of trappers.

Q: What wilderness fort was known as "Fort Nonsense" to the mountain men?

A: The name was applied to Fort Bonneville, which was built by explorer and fur trader Benjamin Louis Eulalie de Bonneville near the Green River, where Bonneville unsuccessfully tried to establish a major trapping operation in the 1830s. Although he was a failure as a trapper, Bonneville's expedition made important geographical discoveries.

Q: How were keelboats usually propelled upstream on Western waters?

A: To go upstream the keelboat crew would either pole the craft forward or use the cordelle, a long line running from a high mast to the shore, which was used by twenty to forty men to tow the keelboat toward its destination. Other means of propulsion included oars and sails.

Q: What did mountain men William Sublette and Robert Campbell do to each other moments before engaging in combat with Blackfoot warriors at the Battle of Pierre's Hole?

A: The Battle of Pierre's Hole, fought near the Grand Tetons during the 1832 Rendezvous, ended inconclusively but included fierce fighting. During the fighting, Sublette and Campbell made an oral will with each other—but both survived the battle.

Q: What famous mountain man was known to Indians as "Bad Hand"?

A: Mountain man Thomas Fitzpatrick was so known to Indians because of a crippled left hand that had been injured when a rifle exploded in his hands as a young man. The Indians also called him "Broken Hand" and "Withered Hand."

Q: What did the early Western frontiersmen use to make powder horns, and how much did store-bought horns cost?

A: Most powder horns were made from oxen horns, although buffalo horns were used frequently. Powder horns sold on the frontier for prices ranging from forty-five cents to more than two dollars.

Q: What did Henry's Fork, Pierre's Hole and the Cache Valley have in common with the Popo Agie, the Green River and Bear Lake?

A: All were Rendezvous sites for the mountain men between 1825 and 1840.

Q: How did trapper Andrew Sublette die?

A: After years of following trap lines, Andrew Sublette became a businessman in California, where he practiced a favorite pastime— bear hunting. In 1853 he was mortally injured by two giant grizzlies.

Q: What was the difference between a mackinaw, a bullboat and a dugout—all means of water transportation used by fur trappers?

A: The mackinaw was a flat-bottom boat pointed at both ends and usually manned by a crew of four oarsmen. The bullboat was a round craft made of buffalo skins stretched over a willow or cottonwood frame. A dugout was a single- or double-man canoe usually cut from a large cottonwood tree.

Q: Why was mountain man Jean Baptiste ("Pompey") Charbonneau's birth unusual, and who was his famous mother?

A: Charbonneau was born on the historic Lewis and Clark Expedition in 1805, and his famous mother was Sacagawea, the Shoshone Indian who served as interpreter and guide for Lewis and Clark.

Q: What important Old West waterway was known in the early nineteenth century as the *Seeds-Kee-Dee,* or Prairie Hen River?

A: The fur trappers so named the mighty Green River, which courses through Wyoming and Utah. The river's later name came from the color of its water, the foliage on its banks, or a man named Green who trapped on it in the 1820s.

Q: When employees of the American Fur Company established a settlement on the Columbia River in what is now the state of Washington, what did they call their post and for whom was it named?

A: Named for fur merchant John Jacob Astor, the settlement of Astoria was established on the Columbia River in 1811 to expand the American fur industry into the Pacific Northwest.

Q: How did mountain man Jedediah Smith meet his end?

A: After exploring thousands of miles of wilderness and surviving numerous narrow escapes, Smith was killed by a war party of Comanche Indians on May 27, 1831, while searching for water near the Cimarron River in what is now southwest Kansas. The Indians frightened his horse, then attacked him with lances; but before he went down, Smith picked off their chief with his last shot.

Q: In 1850 trapper Edwin T. Denig, then commander of the Missouri River fur post of Fort Union, trapped a large number of fur-bearing animals and sent them—carcasses and all—back east to Washington, D.C. Why?

A: Denig, who died of appendicitis on the frontier eight years later, trapped the animals for the fledgling Smithsonian Institution, sending the nation's new museum its first acquisition of mammals from the upper Missouri River region.

Q: What part of the beaver was considered a diner's delicacy among the mountain men?

A: The tail.

Q: During the Lewis and Clark Expedition the explorers encountered such severe winter weather that the liquid in one of their containers reportedly froze solid within fifteen minutes of being exposed to the outside. What was the quick-freezing beverage?

A: Whiskey.

Q: About what particular aspect of Western cuisine did Lewis and Clark express a definite difference of opinion during the Lewis and Clark Expedition?

A: Lewis liked the traditional Indian dish of dog stew, but Clark found the recipe repugnant.

FACT: Walker Pass in California, Walker River in Nevada and Walker Lake in Nevada are all named for mountain man and trailblazer Joseph Reddeford Walker, who served as a guide for Benjamin Bonneville's 1832 exploratory expedition and also for John C. Fremont's second and third expeditions in the West. In his sixties, after retiring from the wilderness, he discovered gold in Arizona.

Q: How much did the Lewis and Clark Expedition cost the U.S. government?

A: Although the expedition's chief promoter, President Thomas Jefferson, estimated the trek's cost at $2,500, the venture actually cost $38,722.25.

Q: When recalling all his exploits, what did frontiersman Kit Carson consider to have been his worst moment?

A: Although he survived repeated Indian fights and other grueling episodes, Carson said his most harrowing experience came in 1834, when he was treed by two furious grizzlies and was forced to remain on his perch for hours.

Q: How did a hurricane lead noted trapper Lucien Fontenelle into the Rocky Mountain fur trade?

A: Raised on a Louisiana plantation, Fontenelle was orphaned when a hurricane killed his parents. Placed in the care of a stern aunt, he ran away to St. Louis, where he eventually joined the fur trade and rose to a key post in the American Fur Company.

Q: Where was mountain man Thomas Fitzpatrick born, and where was he buried?

A: Born in County Craven, Ireland, in 1799, Fitzpatrick became a leader in the fur industry, served later as a prominent Indian agent, died in Washington, D.C., on February 7, 1854, and was buried in the Congressional Cemetery.

Q: What was unusual about mountain man Robert Campbell's career after the decline of the fur trade?

A: Unlike other ex-mountain men, who became guides, traders or farmers, Campbell became a St. Louis businessman and eventually rose to be president of the Merchants National Bank of St. Louis —after spending twenty years setting traps in the wilderness.

Q: What unusual gift was bestowed on mountain man Jim Bridger during the 1837 Rendezvous?

A: In appreciation for Bridger's services as a wilderness guide, Scottish nobleman Sir William Drummond Stewart—who had paid Bridger thirty dollars a day to lead him on a hunting trip—presented Bridger with a European-style suit of armor. Bridger reportedly donned the outfit and paraded around the Rendezvous, to the delight of his fellow trappers.

Q: Where, when and how did mountain man Jim Bridger meet his end?

A: After almost half a century in the Western wilds, Jim Bridger retired to a farm near Westport, Missouri, in 1868. There, nearly blind and in poor health, he died in bed on July 17, 1881, at age seventy-seven. Bridger went to the Rocky Mountains in 1822; spent more than twenty years in the fur trade; discovered Bridger Pass through the Rockies; was believed to have been the first white man to have seen the Great Salt Lake; established Fort Bridger on the Oregon Trail; and measured the entire length of the Bozeman Trail. At the time of his death no one knew more about the Rocky Mountains than Jim Bridger.

> **FACT:** The first American trappers to establish a post on the western slope of the Continental Divide were the members of a party led by Andrew Henry, who erected a temporary trapping post on Henry's Fork of the Snake River in what is now Idaho during the winter of 1810–11. Henry and his trappers, all members of the Missouri Fur Company, thereby became the first American trapping party to operate west of the Rockies.

Q: What did these mountain men have in common: Martin McCoy, John Gaither, Thomas Daw, Charles Swift, Thomas Virgin, Joseph Palmer, Emanuel Lazarus and Joseph Lapoint?

A: They were among a party of nineteen trappers led by mountain man Jedediah Smith who were massacred in 1828 by Kelawatset Indians on the Umpqua River in what is now Oregon.

Q: Trapper Charles Bent left the mountains in the late 1820s, became a partner in the largest mercantile business in Santa Fe and, at the outbreak of the Mexican War, was made the first American governor of New Mexico Territory. How long did his political career last?

A: Less than a year after assuming the governorship, Bent was killed and scalped by Taos Indians during an uprising in 1847.

Q: How long did the era of the mountain man last, and what ended it?

A: The Rocky Mountain fur trade began after the Lewis and Clark Expedition in 1807 and peaked with the first wave of immigrants in the 1840s. The demand for beaver furs decreased dramatically in the 1840s, when silk replaced beaver as the garment of choice for men's hats in Europe and urban America—a fashion trend that, combined with increased immigration and a decrease in the beaver population, brought an end to the era of the mountain man.

Q: Who was first to climb Grand Teton, the highest peak of Wyoming's Grand Teton Mountains?

A: Grand Teton, which is almost fourteen thousand feet high, was not scaled by any recorded mountain climbing attempt until 1872, when climbers N. P. Langford and James Stevenson reached its summit.

Q: In 1849 mountain man William Bent offered to sell Bent's Old Fort —his trading post on Colorado's Arkansas River—to the federal government as a military post. How did Bent react when the government made him an offer he considered absurdly low?

A: He reportedly blew up his fort and rebuilt downriver.

Q: What eventually happened to Zebulon M. Pike, for whom Colorado's Pike's Peak is named?

A: Famous for his exploration of the Far West in 1806–07, in which he and his troops unsuccessfully tried to scale the peak that bears his name, Pike was later killed leading an assault on British fortifications in Toronto during the War of 1812.

Q: What was the cause of death for mountain man John Colter?

A: Colter, who survived months of solitary travel through the deepest Western wilds and who once outran a host of Blackfoot warriors, died quietly at home in Charette, Missouri, in 1813, as a victim of jaundice.

Q: What was the mountain man's advised method of killing a charging grizzly bear?

A: No beast of the Old West was more dangerous than an enraged nine-hundred-pound grizzly. Most mountain men avoided the animal when possible and would unashamedly climb the nearest tree to escape. When escape was impossible, the mountain man's advice was to remain calm, stand still, and wait for the huge beast to stand up—which the bear invariably would do in the final seconds of its attack. At that moment a steady frontiersman could bring down a grizzly with a shot between the eyes.

Q: What gruesome chore did trapper Jedediah Smith assign mountain man James Clyman on a trapping trek through the Rocky Mountain wilderness in 1824?

A: After he was seriously mauled by a grizzly, Smith asked Clyman to sew on a damaged ear, which the bear had almost torn from Smith's head. The surgery was successful.

Q: How was Captain Meriwether Lewis wounded during the Lewis and Clark Expedition?

A: In the wilds of what is now Montana, Lewis was accidentally shot in the buttocks by an expedition member who mistook the great explorer for an elk.

Q: What famous mountain man was involved in the three worst disasters of the Rocky Mountain fur trade?

A: In 1832 fifteen trappers in a large party led by fur merchant William H. Ashley were killed by Arikara Indians on the Missouri River; in 1827 Mojave Indians surprised and killed ten trappers in the Mojave Desert; and in 1828 fifteen trappers were massacred by Kelawatset Indians in what is now Oregon. The only mountain man present at all three disasters was Jedediah Smith, who survived them all.

Q: What was the rarest and most valuable pelt sought by trappers?

A: Many trappers considered the most valuable fur to be that of the albino beaver, whose all-white pelt was viewed as an extraordinary prize by Indians, trappers and fur merchants.

Q: Who was T. D. Bonner, and what did he do for mountain man James Beckwourth?

A: After retiring from his trap lines, Beckwourth operated a tavern in California, and T. D. Bonner, an imaginative writer, was a drinking partner there. The two collaborated on an "autobiography" of Beckwourth—*The Life and Adventures of James P. Beckwourth, Mountaineer, Scout, Pioneer, and Chief of the Crow Nation*—which appeared in 1856 and made Beckwourth an Old West celebrity.

Q: Where and how did noted mountain man Hugh Glass meet his end?

A: Famous for his 1823 trek through the wilderness after his colleagues abandoned him, Hugh Glass spent another decade trapping in the Rockies from Santa Fe to Montana. During the winter of 1832–33 he and two other trappers were caught unprotected on the frozen Yellowstone River by Arikara warriors, who killed them all.

3 | Tribes and Warriors of the West

Q: What was the dreaded Comanche Moon, and why was it so feared in the Old West?

A: For much of the nineteenth century, the warlike Comanches conducted deadly raids against settlers during the full moon of late summer, which became known as the fearsome Comanche Moon.

Q: Who killed Crazy Horse?

A: In reaction to a rumor that Crazy Horse was plotting an escape from his reservation, the Red Cloud Agency, Army troops and Indian police seized the famous chief. When he discovered he was being taken to the post jail, Crazy Horse began pulling away from his guards and was either accidentally stabbed with a knife or was bayoneted by an army sentry, Private William Gentles. Mortally wounded, Crazy Horse died that night, September 5, 1877.

Q: What did the Plains Indians produce from a mixture of bullberries, clay, moss, roots and buffalo gallstones?

A: Yellow body paint.

Q: How did the Comanches and Apaches punish women who committed adultery?

A: They clipped off the tips of the offenders' noses.

Q: In 1874 an estimated seven hundred Comanche and Kiowa warriors attacked a group of twenty-nine buffalo hunters and merchants who had established a base at Adobe Walls near an abandoned adobe trading post in the Texas Panhandle. Who led the Indian attack?

A: Encouraged by a medicine man named Coyote Droppings, Comanche Chief Quannah Parker led the assault on the hunters, which became famous as the Battle of Adobe Walls. Despite their numerical superiority, the Indians were repulsed by the well-armed frontiersmen.

Q: When an Indian warrior "counted coup" on an enemy, what was he doing?

A: Among Plains tribes, warfare was primarily a means of displaying courage. Counting coup was a traditional practice in which a warrior touched an enemy with his hand or with some object like a coupstick or a lance. Afterward, if possible, the enemy would be slain.

Q: In the summer of 1832 four Nez Percé Indians from the distant Northwest arrived in St. Louis after a grueling trek through enemy territory and some of the roughest terrain in the West. What was the motivation for their arduous journey?

A: The four Nez Percé said they were delegates from their tribe sent to get a copy of the "White Man's Book of Heaven"—the Bible—which they had heard of from Canadian trappers. Their request launched a great missionary campaign to the Northwest during the 1830s.

Q: How many Minnesota settlers were killed by Chief Little Crow and the Santee Sioux during the 1862 Minnesota Sioux Uprising?

A: At least 400 settlers died in the uprising, which began on August 17, 1862. Hundreds more were captured by the Sioux and an unknown number disappeared.

Q: **What notorious Indian warrior was named One-Who-Yawns?**

A: **One-Who-Yawns—or Goyakla in his language—was an Apache leader better known by his Spanish name, Geronimo. Here, Geronimo strikes a fierce pose in a studio photograph made in 1886, shortly before he was sent to prison in Florida.**

Q: What kind of tree did Plains Indians and mountain tribes prefer for tepee poles and why?

A: Because of its consistent girth, unusual length and light branches, the lodge pole pine was preferred for tepee poles and thus acquired its common name.

Q: What Apache leader was named Red Sleeves, and how did he die?

A: Mangas Coloradas ("Red Sleeves") was an Apache chief known for his height and his skill as a warrior. After sustained fighting with soldiers and settlers in Arizona, New Mexico and Mexico, he was captured and killed by U.S. troops in 1863.

Q: Why were California's Digger Indians so named, and what happened to them?

A: Numbering almost 100,000 in 1846, the Diggers were named for their practice of living on roots and berries. Their culture was destroyed by the California Gold Rush.

Q: What Sioux leader directed the only war against the United States ever won by Indians?

A: In 1866–68, the Oglala Sioux leader Red Cloud directed Red Cloud's War to keep Army posts off Sioux property. Under the terms of the 1868 Fort Laramie Treaty, which ended the war, the Army abandoned the forts and withdrew from Oglala lands, meeting Red Cloud's demands.

Q: What act did the Dog Men of the Arapaho routinely perform in battle?

A: Members of this warrior society would drive a stake or a lance through the sashes they wore and into the earth, staking themselves to the ground to demonstrate their refusal to retreat from the enemy.

Q: In 1867 the Kiowa chief Satanta chased away most of the Army livestock at Fort Dodge in western Kansas. What was Satanta wearing at the time of his daring raid?

A: He was attired in a U.S. major general's uniform, which had been given to him as a peace token a few weeks earlier by General Winfield S. Hancock.

Q: By what name did the Indian leader Kintpuash become famous for a time?

A: Kintpuash acquired national fame as Captain Jack, the leader of the Modoc Indians in the brief, bitter Modoc War of 1872–73.

Q: In 1821 more than three thousand American settlers lived in Texas. How many Indians lived there?

A: Approximately twenty thousand.

Q: What dramatic feat caused a Pawnee warrior named Man Chief to be lauded in Washington, D.C., as "the bravest of the brave," and what eventually became of him?

A: In 1817 Man Chief courageously rescued a captive Comanche girl who was about to be killed in a Pawnee ritual, and brought an end to human sacrifice among the Pawnees. Man Chief was honored for his heroism in Washington, but died a few years later in a smallpox epidemic.

Q: What prominent Oglala Sioux leader, given the childhood name of Curly, was born in 1842 on Rapid Creek in the Black Hills of what is now South Dakota?

A: Crazy Horse.

Q: In the 1880s, the U.S. Army employed forty-two companies of cavalry and infantry and the Mexican Army fielded approximately four thousand troops in a campaign against Geronimo and his Apaches. How large was Geronimo's force?

A: Geronimo led approximately fifty warriors.

Q: What were the Crazy Dogs, the Crooked Lances, the Bow Strings, the Red Shields, the Kit Foxes and the Dog Soldiers?

A: All were Cheyenne soldier societies, of which the Dog Soldiers was the most prestigious.

Q: What famous Indian leader was known to his people by the name Thunder-Rolling-Down-from-the-Mountains?

A: Chief Joseph of the Nez Percé, who became famous in the 1877 Nez Percé War, was so named at birth.

FACT: Apache warriors were known for their great endurance and their ability to cover long distances quickly on foot. At an early age Apache boys were taught how to survive in rugged terrain, learning, for instance, how to run for miles while holding a mouthful of water. Some Apache warriors were known to have run more than seventy miles in a single day.

Q: What was pemmican, which was consumed in great quantity by the Indians of the Old West?

A: Pemmican was a form of buffalo meat prepared for use over long periods of time. Strips of buffalo meat would be smoked or cured by hanging in the open air, as in the Arapaho camp pictured above, which was photographed near Fort Dodge, Kansas, in 1870. After curing, the meat would be pounded with stones to a powder and mixed with buffalo fat or marrow. The mixture—pemmican—would then be poured into skin pouches, where it would harden and be available for consumption for an indefinite period.

Q: What happened to the Kiowa leaders who surrendered to the Army near Fort Sill, Oklahoma, in 1875?

A: Seventy-two of them were shipped by rail to Florida, where they were imprisoned for three years in St. Augustine's aging Fort Marion.

Q: What Apache chief, called Angry-Men-Stand-in-Line-for-Him by his people, survived the infamous Camp Grant Massacre of 1871; performed in a St. Louis theater in 1876; appeared before Washington, D.C., dignitaries—then was imprisoned for years in Florida and Alabama as an Apache renegade?

A: Five years after his family was murdered at Camp Grant, Arizona, in 1871, the Apache chief Eskiminzin was taken on a tour of St. Louis and Washington by Indian agent John Clum, who later arranged Eskiminzin's release from prison.

Q: What ceremonial act was the climax of the Plains Indians' Sun Dance?

A: Practiced regularly among the Sioux, Cheyennes, Arapahoes, Kiowas and other tribes, the Sun Dance usually lasted for days, ending when the last dancer pulled free from a rawhide line skewered through the skin of his chest.

Q: How did Geronimo die, and where is he buried?

A: On February 17, 1909, the old war leader of the Chiricahua Apaches died quietly of pneumonia in the post hospital at Fort Sill, Oklahoma, a few months before his eightieth birthday. He was buried in the fort's Apache cemetery, but tribal legend says his remains were secretly removed to the Arizona mountains of his childhood.

Q: What famous Sioux leader, the son of Lone Man and Walks-as-She-Thinks, was born on Blue Creek near what is now North Platte, Nebraska, sometime in 1822?

A: Red Cloud.

Q: What was unusual about the Sioux heyokas?

A: A heyoka, or "clown," was a member of a tribal society that did everything backward. In 1804, according to Sioux tradition, a heyoka went into battle against the enemy riding backward on his horse and shooting his arrows at his own people—until he was killed.

Q: The red claystone used by some Western tribes for making pipe bowls was called catlinite by whites. What was the origin of the name?

A: Catlinite was named for artist George Catlin, whose travels and paintings of Western Indians made the stone familiar to Easterners.

Q: What tribe of Western Indians was described by an observer in 1832 as "the most powerful tribe of Indians on the continent"?

A: Frontier artist George Catlin so described the Blackfeet, who dominated much of the upper Missouri region.

Q: What famous breed of horse is said to have been developed by the Nez Percé Indians?

A: The Appaloosa.

Q: What was the "Long Walk" of 1864, and who made it?

A: The Long Walk was made by eight thousand Navahos, who were forced from their fortresslike home in Arizona's Canyon de Chelly by U.S. troops and driven more than three hundred to a reservation.

Q: Why did the Sioux refer to a small child as "he who wears his navel"?

A: The description was based on the Sioux practice of storing a newborn child's severed umbilical cord in a small, carefully decorated hide pouch, which the child wore for good fortune through the toddler stage.

Q: What eventually became of Chief Black Kettle, whose Cheyenne followers were brutally decimated in the 1864 Sand Creek Massacre?

A: Black Kettle continued to counsel peace with his tribesmen after narrowly escaping death at Sand Creek. On November 27, 1868, Black Kettle and his wife were killed when the Seventh Cavalry attacked their village at the Battle of the Washita.

FACT: The famous Oglala Sioux war leader Crazy Horse routinely prepared for battle by painting a lightning streak on his face and hailstones on his chest. He also tied a small stone behind one ear and pinned a stuffed red-backed hawk to his hair.

Q: What big game animal did many Plains Indians consider superior in taste even to buffalo?

A: Pronghorn antelope.

Q: What message did an Indian send his enemies when he decorated his horse with human handprints?

A: Each handprint stood for an enemy killed in battle by the horse's owner.

Q: What was the role of the Omaha Thunder Society?

A: Members of the Thunder Society protected the Omahas' sacred pipes—ceremonial tools that were smoked reverently on special occasions.

Q: What eventually became of the Mandan Indians, who were once among the most numerous and powerful tribes of the upper Missouri River region?

A: The Mandans were decimated by a series of smallpox epidemics caused by white carriers, and by 1838 only 130 Mandans remained. In the mid-nineteenth century, to escape raids by Sioux enemies, the survivors joined Hidatsa and Arikara remnants on what became North Dakota's Fort Berthold reservation, where the Mandans soon became culturally extinct.

Q: By what common name were the Absarokas, or "bird people," known?

A: The Crows.

Q: Who was the most feared Indian in America in 1862, and what became of him?

A: In 1862 no Indian in America instilled more fear than the Santee Sioux chief Little Crow, the reluctant leader of that year's bloody Minnesota Uprising. After his followers were defeated by an army of troops, Little Crow went into hiding, but was discovered, shot and scalped by Minnesota frontiersmen who threw his body into a slaughterhouse offal pit.

Q: Where is Crazy Horse buried?

A: No one knows. After his death in 1877, Crazy Horse's body was given to his elderly parents, who secretly buried the renowned Sioux leader somewhere in the wilds near Nebraska's Red Cloud Agency.

Q: When did scalping become a common practice among the Indians of the Old West?

A: No one knows. Although a popular myth claims scalping was introduced by the English during the American colonial period, the custom was actually a long-standing practice among many North American Indian tribes and was probably derived from an ancient custom of taking heads as war trophies.

Q: What camouflage was commonly used by Plains Indians when stalking buffalo on foot?

A: By cloaking themselves in wolf hides, Indian hunters could crawl close enough to a buffalo herd for a sure shot with bow and arrow.

Q: Why was Comanche Chief Quannah Parker removed as a judge of the Comanche reservation's Court of Indian Offenses?

A: Reservation officials disapproved of Parker's polygamy: he had eight wives.

Q: In the spring of 1877, after a year-long military campaign against them, more than three thousand Sioux and Cheyennes surrendered and settled on reservations in South Dakota and Nebraska. Who arranged the mass surrender?

A: The mediator between the U.S. Army and the hostile Sioux and Cheyennes was the Sioux chief Spotted Tail, who improved the Army's terms and persuaded the war-weary Indians to surrender.

Q: Whom did Shoshone Chief Washakie entertain in his lodge on August 8, 1883?

A: Long known as allies of the U.S. government, Washakie and his Shoshone tribesmen successfully negotiated a large reservation along Wyoming's Wind River. It was here on this date in 1883 that Chief Washakie entertained President Chester A. Arthur, who was en route to a fishing holiday in the newly created Yellowstone National Park. It was the first official visit to Western Indians by an American president.

Q: How did the famous and feared Kiowa leader Satanta meet his end?

A: A leader in the warfare between the Kiowas and the white residents of the Texas Panhandle, Satanta finally surrendered in 1874 and was imprisoned in the Texas state prison, where he committed suicide by jumping from an upper-story window in 1878.

Q: How did Chief Gall of the Hunkpapa Sioux receive his name, and how did he die?

A: One of the principal strategists of the Custer massacre, Gall reportedly received his unusual name as a child when he was found hungrily trying to eat the gallbladder of butchered game, although another story claims he was given the name to reflect a belligerent personality. Gall surrendered to U.S. officials in 1881 and settled on the Standing Rock reservation, where he became an Indian judge. He died in 1894, allegedly from an overdose of medicine, and is buried at St. Elizabeth's Episcopal Church in Wakpala, South Dakota.

Q: Why were the Flathead Indians of the Northwest so named?

A: Some Indian tribes of the Pacific Northwest purposely deformed the heads of infants with tightly bound straps to give them a flattened forehead—a practice the Flatheads did *not* follow. Early white visitors to the Flatheads, who were also called the Salish, saw captured flatheaded slaves among the tribe, thought they were tribe members and incorrectly gave the Salish the name Flatheads, with which they entered American history.

Q: What prominent Cheyenne chief was killed by U.S. troops in Georgia, and why was he there?

A: In 1875 Chief Grey Beard, a Cheyenne leader who had eluded U.S. troops for months during the Red River campaign, was sentenced to imprisonment with other Plains Indians at Fort Marion in Florida. En route, he was killed in Georgia while trying to escape.

Q: Consumption of what organ of the grizzly bear was believed by some Indian tribes to give the hunter the strength and powers of the bear?

A: The heart—eaten raw.

Q: In the early nineteenth century what post was the Nez Percé equivalent of a newspaper?

A: The Nez Percé appointed tribal criers, who yelled the news throughout Nez Percé villages.

Q: Where did Crazy Horse receive his name?

A: Although the naming of the famous chief may have been inspired by a wild pony his parents saw gallop through their village one day, Crazy Horse was not the first to bear the name: the great Sioux leader was named for his father.

Q: What tribe of Western Indians had such a fierce reputation that other Indians referred to them as "the people who fight us all the time"?

A: Their relentlessly warlike nature earned the Comanches this name.

Q: What Cheyenne chief, also called Morning Star, was a principal leader in the Cheyennes' 1878 breakout from their reservation in Oklahoma?

A: Dull Knife, a leading chief of the Northern Cheyennes, joined by Cheyenne leader Little Wolf, led the attempted escape from Oklahoma in 1878, which became known as the Dull Knife Outbreak.

Q: On April 19, 1867, a large force of U.S. troops under General Winfield S. Hancock burned a combined Sioux-Cheyenne village on Pawnee Fork of the Arkansas River in southwest Kansas. How many lodges did Hancock destroy?

A: To punish warriors he believed had slain civilians in western Kansas, Hancock destroyed the abandoned Pawnee Fork village, which contained 241 Sioux and Cheyenne lodges.

Q: From what stock did the Indian pony originate?

A: The hardy Indian pony of the Great Plains was a descendant of the Arabian and Andalusian horses brought to the Americas by the Spanish in the sixteenth century.

Q: What Cheyenne leader was killed at the Battle of Summit Springs?

A: On July 11, 1869, while encamped on Colorado's South Platte River following a raid on white settlements, Chief Tall Bull's Cheyennes were surprised and defeated by the U.S. Fifth Cavalry. Chief Tall Bull was killed in action while defending his village.

Q: What animal was known to the Plains Indians as "Holy Dog," "Medicine Dog" or "Spirit Dog"?

A: The horse was so named because of its immense value to the Plains Indians.

Q: Why did Cheyenne warriors normally leave their dead enemies lying facedown?

A: The Cheyennes considered it bad luck to leave a slain enemy's face to the sky, so they usually tried to leave their enemies lying on their stomachs.

FACT: Sitting Bull, the famous Hunkpapa Sioux medicine man and chief, was named for his father, Returns-Again, who had renamed himself Sitting Bull after a buffalo bull mysteriously wandered into his camp one night. The name was meant to symbolize the power and regal bearing of the male bison, which was revered by the Sioux and other Plains Indians. When his son killed his first enemy at age fourteen, the senior Sitting Bull recognized the act by bestowing his name on his son, whose later exploits made the name famous.

Q: What was the largest tribe among the Plains Indians?

A: The Sioux were the most numerous of the Plains tribes, with approx-
      imately twenty-five thousand members at the beginning of the nine-
      teenth century. By 1891, when this photograph of a Brule Sioux
      village was made at Pine Ridge, South Dakota, the Sioux had been
      greatly reduced in numbers but were still the dominant tribe of the
      northern plains.

Q: What peculiar monument was constructed by Indians at the junction of the Missouri and Yellowstone rivers in the early nineteenth century?

A: In the first years of the nineteenth century, passing Indian hunters began discarding elk antlers in a pile at the junction of the Missouri and the Yellowstone. The antlers were casually amassed until by 1833 they formed a monument fifteen feet wide and eighteen feet high.

Q: Who was Jack Wilson, and what celestial event in 1889 made him into a famous Indian leader—and also led to one of the worst massacres in American history?

A: Jack Wilson was the name by which whites called Wovoka, a Paiute Indian from Nevada who claimed to have had a vision during a solar eclipse in 1889. His celebrated vision launched a revival of the Ghost Dance Movement, designed to restore Indian power and culture, which reached a climax with the 1890 massacre of Sioux Indians by U.S. troops at Wounded Knee.

Q: What Western Indian leader became an American army general?

A: Stand Watie, a Cherokee leader in Oklahoma, organized a regiment of Cherokee cavalry for Confederate service in the Civil War, led several actions against Union forces and by war's end was a Confederate general.

Q: How did the Cheyenne Indians get their name?

A: They were named by the Sioux. The word *Cheyenne* is derived from the Sioux term *Shā hī' ē la,* which means "people speaking language not understood." The Cheyennes called themselves *Tsĭs tsĭs' tăs,* which means "the people," "our folks" or "us."

Q: What unusual graveside ceremony was conducted upon the death of the Ute chief Walkara?

A: Famous for the devastating raids that captured thousands of horses from his enemies, Walkara died in 1855, and as a memorial relatives killed fifteen Indian ponies at his graveside.

Q: Why would Mandan, Sioux and other tribal warriors sometimes sever their fingers in the Sun Dance ritual?

A: The severed fingers, along with flesh ripped from chests or backs, would be offered as sacrifices to tribal spirits in an attempt to increase personal power and stature.

Q: How did the Mojave Indians poison their arrows?

A: The Mojaves dipped their arrowheads in a mixture of antelope liver and rattlesnake venom.

Q: When one of their tribesmen died, how did the Apaches respond to his death?

A: Apache tradition called for the burning of the deceased's possessions and lodge, an act meant to prevent ghosts from harassing the tribe.

Q: Who led the Nez Percé Indians in battle and directed their combat strategy during the 1877 Nez Percé War?

A: The Nez Percé war leader Olikut made most combat decisions with approval of a war council, although his older brother, Chief Joseph, received most of the credit. Olikut was killed in the war's last fighting, and Joseph, the official tribal guardian, was left to surrender the Nez Percé survivors to the Army.

Q: What disaster was brought to the Indians of the northern plains by the steamboat St. Peters in 1837?

A: On June 24, 1837, the St. Peters arrived at Fort Union in what is now North Dakota with a cargo of trade goods for the Indians— and several contagious cases of smallpox. Although white authorities tried to prevent an epidemic, a devastating smallpox plague swept through the Indian tribes of the region, virtually destroying the Mandans and seriously affecting the Arikaras, the Crows, the Minnetarees, the Assiniboines and the Blackfeet.

Q: How did the Gros Ventre tribe receive its name?

A: The Gros Ventres reportedly called themselves the "Always Hungry" people, a name expressed in sign language by rubbing hands across the stomach. French trappers mistranslated the sign as "Big Bellies," or Gros Ventres.

FACT: The Hopi town of Old Oraibi, the center of Hopi culture in the nineteenth century, is believed to be the oldest continuously occupied settlement in the United States. Located in an isolated region of northeastern Arizona, Old Oraibi was inhabited as long as eight hundred years ago and has been an active community since.

Q: What job was Chief Sitting Bull given in 1885, and how much was he paid?

A: Scout-turned-showman Buffalo Bill Cody persuaded Sitting Bull to tour with Buffalo Bill's Wild West Show and paid the former warrior $50 a week. After a tour of cities around the country, Sitting Bull quit.

Q: Who killed Sitting Bull?

A: On July 19, 1881, after four years of self-exile in Canada, Sitting Bull and his followers surrendered to U.S. officials at Fort Buford in what is now North Dakota and were placed on the nearby Standing Rock Indian reservation. Nine years later, during the Ghost Dance Movement, Indian police were sent to arrest Sitting Bull, who was accused of encouraging Indian rebellion. At dawn on December 15, 1890, Sitting Bull was pulled from his cabin bed by Indian police, and when he resisted, the famous chief was shot and killed by an Indian police officer named Red Tomahawk.

Q: In what engagement, fought on September 29, 1879, did Ute warriors led by Chief Jack repulse and besiege a force of cavalry and infantry led by Major Thomas T. Thornburgh?

A: At the Battle of Milk Creek in Colorado, Thornburgh's troops were forced to withdraw to a fortified position. Thornburgh was killed, and his troops remained under siege until they were rescued by reinforcements.

Q: What peculiar development preceded the death of the prominent Cheyenne war leader Roman Nose, who was killed at the Battle of Beecher's Island on September 17, 1868?

A: On the day of the battle Roman Nose learned he had eaten food served with a metal utensil, which he believed broke his "medicine" and made him vulnerable in combat. He publicly announced his impending death, led a brazen charge against the Army force entrenched on Beecher's Island—and was mortally wounded.

Q: What incident ignited the Ute War of 1879?

A: In a well-meaning attempt to persuade the Utes to become farmers, Indian agent Nathan C. Meeker erected agency buildings on Ute hunting land and plowed up the Indian range for farming. The incensed Utes retaliated by killing Meeker and waging a brief but fierce war with the U.S. Army.

Q:　What Sioux leader surrendered to U.S. officials at Nebraska's Red
Cloud Agency on May 6, 1877?

A:　After more than a decade of resistance against U.S. forces, the
Oglala chief Crazy Horse surrendered on this date.

Q:　How did the Sioux leader Red Cloud receive his name?

A:　Although explanations for the origins of Red Cloud's name are
numerous, the likeliest story is related to his birth in 1822. That
year a large meteor passed over Oglala Sioux country and its red
glow inspired the names of a host of newborn Red Clouds, including the famous one.

Q:　What tribe of Southwestern Indians was regarded as the best horse-
men in the West?

A:　The Comanches deservedly claimed this reputation: short in stature
and noted for their stubby legs, they were remarkably skilled in
horsemanship and had no equestrian equals, white or red, in the
West.

Q:　What became of Captain Jack, the Indian leader of the Modoc
War?

A:　After months of battle with U.S. troops and the assassination of
two U.S. peace commissioners under a flag of truce, Captain Jack
was finally captured. He was tried and hanged at Fort Klamath,
Oregon, on October 3, 1873.

Q:　When Kiowa warriors set out on a buffalo hunt, they agreed that
no one would ride ahead of the hunting party and risk frightening
the buffalo herd. What happened to a warrior who violated the
agreement?

A:　He would be beaten by his companions, and his dogs and horses
would be killed.

Q:　How many miles did Chief Joseph and the Nez Percé travel in the
1877 Nez Percé Retreat?

A:　For 108 days approximately three hundred Nez Percé warriors, accompanied by five hundred women and children, covered more
than seventeen hundred miles through some of the roughest country in the West. En route they evaded more than five thousand
soldiers, inflicted almost three hundred casualties and were barely
thirty miles from the Canadian border when they were forced to
surrender on October 5, 1877.

Q: Where is Sitting Bull buried?

A: Debate surrounds the chief's burial site. After Sitting Bull was shot
to death by Indian police on South Dakota's Grand River in 1890,
he was buried in the post cemetery at Fort Yates in what is now
North Dakota. In 1953 what many believed were the remains of
Sitting Bull were moved from Fort Yates to a memorial overlooking
the Missouri River near Mobridge, South Dakota. However, many
North Dakotans believe the wrong remains were moved and today
both states staunchly claim to have Sitting Bull's burial site.

Q: What was the Tucson Committee of Public Safety, and what atrocity did it commit on April 30, 1871?

A: Composed of American and Mexican residents of Arizona and aided by a large force of Papago Indian warriors, the Tucson Committee of Public Safety launched a surprise attack on a sleeping village of peaceful Apaches near Camp Grant, Arizona, on this date, killing approximately a hundred women and children in what became known as the infamous Camp Grant Massacre.

Q: Why did Blackfoot hunters normally examine buffalo embryos in wintertime?

A: When butchering slain buffalo cows, the Blackfeet routinely examined unborn calves for signs of hair—an indication of approaching spring.

Q: With what symbolic practice did the Comanches demonstrate their dominance over newly broken horses?

A: Roped and pulled to the ground, wild horses being broken by the Comanches were haltered and tied to docile old mares—after the Comanche horse trainer symbolically depicted his power over each horse by blowing his breath into the animal's nostrils.

Q: Why would a mounted Indian lancer strike a running buffalo from a different side than a mounted bowman?

A: Each weapon required a different approach in buffalo hunting. A right-handed bowman would ride along the buffalo's right side for the best shot, while a right-handed lancer could strike an easier, more powerful blow from the animal's left side.

Q: What did Sioux medicine men fashion from a buffalo bladder and the leg bone of a turkey?

A: By fastening a turkey's hollow leg bone to a buffalo bladder filled with pulverized bark and water, the Sioux created an enema.

FACT: Although the history and culture of the Oumessourits Indians have disappeared, their name—at least a form of it—is known to every educated American. The Oumessourits, whose name meant "Living at the Mouth of the Waters," lived along the great river of the West that bears their name—the Missouri.

Q: In fighting enemy tribes in the early nineteenth century, what trophies would Sioux warriors claim from slain adversaries?

A: According to trappers who knew the Sioux, the first Sioux warrior to reach a dead enemy would take his scalp; the second, the right hand; the third, the left hand; and the fourth and fifth, the right and left feet. The grisly trophies were reportedly worn on necklaces by the victorious Sioux.

Q: What well-known Sioux leader was mortally wounded at the Battle of Slim Buttes?

A: On September 9, 1876, U.S. troops under General George Crook engaged a band of Sioux led by American Horse, a tribal elder and prominent chief. In the fighting American Horse received a severe stomach wound. He surrendered to Crook and died several hours later despite attempts by Army surgeons to save him.

Q: Who were Cynthia Ann Parker and her famous son?

A: Cynthia Ann Parker was a white woman captured by the Comanches and claimed by Comanche Chief Peta Nacona. Their son was Quannah Parker, a fierce Comanche war leader never defeated by U.S. troops. He voluntarily brought his followers to an Oklahoma reservation in 1875.

Q: When and to whom did the Apache warrior Geronimo finally surrender?

A: Geronimo gave himself up to General George Crook twice—in 1883 and 1886—but his final surrender occurred after Crook had resigned his command and was made to General Nelson A. Miles on September 4, 1886, at Fort Bowie in Arizona.

Q: In the fall of 1876 a contingent of Sioux chiefs on the Great Sioux reservation signed a treaty providing regular government food rations in exchange for a concession. What did the Sioux give up for government food?

A: The Black Hills of South Dakota.

Q: What battle resulted in the death of the Apache war leader Victorio, who fiercely contested U.S. troops for more than a year in the vain hope of regaining his tribal land in Arizona?

A: Victorio's War ended on October 16, 1880, when Mexican troops led by Colonel Joaquín Terrazas defeated Victorio's warriors and killed Victorio in the Battle of Tres Castillos in northern Mexico.

Q: On May 18, 1871, a large Kiowa war party led by Chief Owl Prophet decided *not* to attack a lightly defended Army ambulance as it crossed Salt Creek Prairie in Texas, choosing instead to wait for a wagon train. Who was aboard the vehicle the Kiowas chose to ignore?

A: Inside the ambulance on an inspection tour was General William T. Sherman, the commanding general of the U.S. Army.

Q: What nationally known Indian warrior eventually converted to Christianity, joined the Dutch Reformed Church, dictated an autobiography and was a guest of honor at the inauguration of President Theodore Roosevelt?

A: Geronimo.

Q: How did Blackfoot mothers diaper their newborn children?

A: Blackfoot infants were customarily wrapped in soft animal skins and diapered with moss.

Q: What ingredients did the Indians of the West mix to produce blue paint?

A: Blue mud, boiled rotted wood and duck droppings were used to create a blue pigment.

Q: When and where did Chief Joseph of the Nez Percé die?

A: On September 21, 1904, Chief Joseph collapsed in his lodge on Washington's Colville reservation. For more than twenty-five years he had unsuccessfully petitioned the government for permission to return to his home in the Wallowa Valley. The reservation doctor described Joseph's cause of death as "a broken heart."

Q: What were buffalo chips and how were they used by the Indians of the Old West?

A: Buffalo chips were the dried buffalo manure found in great quantity on the plains. Indians valued buffalo chips because they provided an easy and hot fire and were especially useful in regions where wood was scarce.

Q: What substances did some Western tribes administer to pregnant women to induce delivery?

A: A favorite Indian remedy for extended labor was a potion of rattlesnake rattles—which, physicians later declared, was void of medical value.

Q: How did the Snohomish Indian chief Patkanim of Oregon use his slaves to make a profit in 1856?

A: During a period of hostilities between Oregon Indians and white settlers, a bounty of $20 was offered for the head of any hostile Indian. Chief Patkanim, who was friendly to the whites, killed several enemy Indians for the bounty but then decided such acts were too dangerous. So he killed all his Indian slaves and produced their heads for the bounty.

Q: How many engagements between Western Indians and the U.S. Army occurred between 1866 and 1891, and when did peace finally come to the West?

A: According to U.S. Army records, there were 1,065 combat actions between Western Indians and U.S. forces between 1866 and 1891. The fighting between the Sioux and U.S. troops at the Wounded Knee Massacre on December 29, 1890, and the sporadic skirmishing that followed for several days brought an end to the Western Indian wars—which had lasted more than a half century. With the major tribes voluntarily or forcibly located on reservations, peace came to the West and scenes like this turn-of-the-century image, recorded near Fort Stanton, New Mexico, became common.

Q: What was the Society of the Ten Bravest?
A: It was an elite, demanding and highly regarded warrior society of the Kiowas.

Q: What prominent Indian leader was born on the Grand River in what is now South Dakota in 1831 and was named Slow by his father, a Hunkpapa Sioux warrior called Returns-Again?
A: Sitting Bull.

Q: What unique act in the history of the Plains Indians was accomplished by a party of Cheyenne warriors led by Spotted Wolf in the summer of 1867?
A: Spotted Wolf and his followers managed to derail and wreck a freight train on the Union Pacific Railroad in Nebraska that year —the only time a train was wrecked and plundered by Western Indians.

Q: What was the practice of "blanket courting" common among many Plains tribes?
A: It was the primary method by which a young man romanced a young woman in some tribes. The suitor, if accepted by the young woman, would be allowed to stand in front of her lodge wrapped with her in a blanket while the two conversed.

Q: The Apache leader Chato, who attacked Arizona settlers in a series of raids in 1882, later served as a scout for the U.S. Army and eventually helped arrange the surrender of Geronimo, yet, despite his assistance, was imprisoned for a time in Florida and Oklahoma. How did Chato meet his end?
A: He died in an automobile wreck in 1913.

4 | Indian-Fighting Army

Q: What was the average age of an Army recruit in the 1870s and 1880s?

A: Twenty-five.

Q: What famous military organization was created by an Act of Congress on July 28, 1866?

A: The U.S. Seventh Cavalry.

Q: How often were soldiers required to bathe by official regulations?

A: Whether or not they needed it, soldiers of the Old West were required to bathe at least once a week—a regulation many had difficulty following.

Q: What were the most common diseases on Army posts in the West?

A: The leading illnesses among troops in the Old West were venereal disease, malaria, respiratory illnesses and dysentery—in that order.

Q: What headgear—immensely unpopular with the troops—was issued by the Army Quartermaster Department to some troops in the West in 1880?

A: That year the Quartermaster Department authorized the issue of British-style white cork helmets for summer wear—a temporary headgear avoided by most Western troops whenever possible.

Q: How many black soldiers received the Congressional Medal of
    Honor during the Western Indian Wars of 1870–1890?
A: Fourteen.

Q: Where were the soldiers of the West trained before being assigned
    to duty on the frontier?
A: Recruits in the post–Civil War Army received only basic instruc-
    tion. Infantry troops were trained at David's Island, New York;
    cavalry were trained at Jefferson Barracks in Missouri and artillery
    recruits were trained at Columbus Barracks in Ohio.

Q: What was the standard diet for soldiers in the West?
A: Army rations in isolated Western outposts consisted primarily of
    low-grade beef, salt pork, rice, beans and a limited supply of canned
    vegetables, consumed with bread or hardtack and large quantities of
    black coffee. Officers, like these lieutenants from the First and
    Eighth Cavalry, could afford to supplement meals with food bought
    from post traders and thus fared somewhat better than enlisted men
    in the West.

Q: What was the standard firearm used by the Army in the West following the Civil War?

A: For the first seven years after the Civil War, cavalry troops used a variety of carbines and infantry used Springfield rifles converted from muzzleloaders to breechloaders. However, beginning in 1873 and lasting for approximately twenty years, the .45-caliber Model 1873 Springfield rifle and carbine were standard issue for soldiers on the Western frontier.

Q: What were General George Crook's troops doing when they were attacked by Sioux and Cheyenne warriors on June 17, 1876, in what became known as the Battle of the Rosebud?

A: Crook's one-thousand-man force was marching north from Wyoming's Fort Fetterman during the 1876 Sioux Campaign and had broken ranks for a coffee break when the Indians attacked.

Q: What American Army general—winner of the Congressional Medal of Honor—led campaigns against the Kiowas, the Comanches, the Cheyennes, the Sioux, the Nez Percé and the Apaches and received Geronimo's final surrender in 1886?

A: General Nelson A. Miles.

Q: When was the Battle of the Washita, and who was the highest-ranking officer killed in the action?

A: On November 27, 1868, the U.S. Seventh Cavalry under General George A. Custer destroyed Chief Black Kettle's Cheyenne village at the Battle of the Washita in what is now western Oklahoma. During mopping-up operations Major Joel H. Elliott was surrounded and killed, and Elliott's friends blamed Custer for not doing enough to rescue the major—a charge Custer bore until he suffered a similar death eight years later.

FACT: Two weapons usually left behind when the soldiers of the West marched off to battle Indians were the cavalryman's saber and the infantryman's bayonet. In campaigns against the Indians of the West, troops were seldom close enough to use either weapon. Despite all the artworks depicting saber-wielding cavalrymen in action against the Indians, saber and bayonet attacks were extremely rare in the Old West.

Q: What did the U.S. Ninth and Tenth Cavalry regiments have in common with the Twenty-fourth and Twenty-fifth Infantry regiments on the Western frontier?

A: All were composed of black enlisted men and noncommissioned officers, although commanded by white officers.

Q: Almost every Army post in the Old West had a "suds row." What was it?

A: The name was commonly applied to the quarters of noncommissioned officers (NCOs), whose wives often served the troops of the post as hired laundresses. In 1878 Congress eliminated the role of company laundress—much to the chagrin of the troops.

Q: What U.S. officer was known to the Sioux as "the Hornet," "the Wasp," "the Big Chief Who Swears," and "the Butcher"?

A: General William S. Harney received these names after he decisively defeated Chief Little Thunder's Brule Sioux at the Battle of Ash Hollow on September 3, 1855.

Q: In what battle, fought on September 17, 1868, did fifty frontier scouts and a U.S. Army major stand off more than seven hundred Sioux and Cheyenne warriors?

A: At the Battle of Beecher's Island, fought on this date, Major George A. Forsyth and a company of hand-picked frontiersmen withstood repeated attacks by Indians and were eventually rescued by black soldiers of the Tenth Cavalry. The battle was named for one of the soldiers who died there—Lieutenant Frederick Beecher—who was a nephew of abolitionist preacher Henry Ward Beecher and novelist Harriet Beecher Stowe.

Q: In the shrunken Army of the post–Civil War era, how long would it typically have taken a new second lieutenant to reach the rank of colonel?

A: Thirty-seven years.

Q: Who was the only regular Army general killed by Indians in the Indian Wars of the West, and who replaced him?

A: On April 11, 1873, General Edward R. S. Canby, commander of the U.S. Army's Department of the Columbia, was assassinated by Modoc Indians at a peace conference during California's Modoc War, becoming the only regular Army general killed in the Indian Wars. He was replaced by General Jefferson C. Davis.

Q: What fort, established in 1862 at Apache Pass in southern Arizona, was the site from which the Apache leader Geronimo and his followers were sent to Florida for imprisonment?

A: Fort Bowie.

Q: During a confrontation with Army officers at Fort Sill, Oklahoma, in 1871, a Kiowa chief named Stumbling Bear shot an arrow at an Army officer and narrowly missed. Who was the fortunate soldier?

A: The errant missile was aimed at General William T. Sherman, the commanding general of the Army, who had come to Fort Sill on an inspection.

Q: What was the "Horsemeat March" conducted by General George Crook in 1876?

A: At the conclusion of an unsuccessful campaign against the Indians who had defeated the Seventh Cavalry at the Little Big Horn, Crook led a large, poorly rationed army on a fruitless final march that ended with the soldiers subsisting on horseflesh. A photographer visiting Crook's army made this rare photograph of soldiers butchering a mount while sentries stand guard.

Q: In what battle, fought on December 21, 1866, was an entire command of the U.S. Army wiped out by Sioux warriors?

A: At the Fetterman Massacre near Wyoming's Fort Phil Kearny, Captain William J. Fetterman and his command of eighty men were surrounded and killed by an estimated fifteen hundred Sioux on this date. Ironically, Fetterman had boasted that he could wipe out the entire Sioux nation with eighty men.

Q: What was a "barrel jacket," and why was it often worn by soldiers of the West?

A: Soldiers convicted of drunkenness or other minor infractions were forced to parade around their post wearing a barrel jacket—a barrel cut with holes for the arms and head.

Q: What experimental mode of transportation did the U.S. government acquire from Alexandria, Egypt, for use by the Army in the West?

A: In 1855 U.S. Secretary of War Jefferson Davis ordered the purchase of thirty-four camels from the Mideast for use in the arid West. Although the animals could go for days without water, they bit, spit and displayed such bellicose behavior that the Army eventually discontinued the experiment.

Q: Who served as chief Army scout for three generals over two decades in numerous campaigns against the Apaches, and how did he die?

A: Respected by his Apache adversaries, who called him Old Gray Head, frontiersman Albert Sieber served as the Army's chief of Indian scouts for generals George Crook, O. O. Howard and Nelson Miles from 1870 to 1890. Although he survived approximately thirty combat wounds, he was killed by an accidental rock slide while supervising road construction in 1907.

Q: What did the battles of White Bird Canyon, Clearwater, Big Hole, Camas Creek, Canyon Creek, Cow Island and Bear Paw Mountains have in common?

A: All were primary engagements in the 1877 Nez Percé War.

Q: What unusual mode of transportation did General George Crook employ in his campaigns against the Apaches?

A: While most commanders supplied their forces in the field from wagons, Crook established an efficient, well-managed mule train that allowed his troops to operate in terrain too rugged for vehicles.

Q: What were the "hog ranches" established near many Western Army posts?

A: So called by soldiers, hog ranches were crude dives that offered cheap whiskey, fast cards and loose women for the entertainment of troops.

Q: In what battle, fought on December 28, 1872, did U.S. troops overwhelm a large body of Yavapai Indians besieged in a cave in Arizona?

A: On this date approximately a hundred Yavapais were trapped inside a cave in Salt River Canyon during General George Crook's Tonto Basin Campaign. Less than one-third of the Indians survived the action, which became known as the Battle of Skull Cave.

Q: Who was Second Lieutenant George N. Bascom, and how did he make history in 1861?

A: In an attempt to rescue the kidnapped son of an Arizona rancher in 1861, Lieutenant Bascom invited the Apache chief Cochise and six other Indians into the Army camp, then tried to take them captive. Cochise escaped and retaliated by launching the Apache Wars, which lasted for years and claimed many lives.

Q: Why was the U.S. Fifth Infantry under Colonel Nelson A. Miles unable to measure the temperature during Miles's winter march against Sitting Bull's Sioux in the winter of 1876?

A: The weather was so cold that the mercury froze in the thermometers.

FACT: The U.S. Army, which numbered more than two million troops at the end of the Civil War, was drastically reduced by Congress during peacetime. At the height of the post–Civil War Indian fighting, the U.S. Army had less than twenty thousand troops on duty throughout the nation, including the soldiers posted to the West. Ranks were so thin on some Western posts that the troops found it difficult to perform basic military duties. In 1876 the Twenty-fourth Infantry was so reduced that one company could assemble no more than two men for drill—a captain and a sergeant, who performed the drill anyway.

Q: What were "The Regular Army, O," "The Dreary Black Hills," "Beautiful Dreamer," "La Paloma," "Little Annie Roonie" and "Mother, Kiss Me in My Dreams"?

A: All were songs popular with soldiers in the West.

Q: At what civilian structure did General Patrick E. Connor, commander of Fort Douglas in Utah, keep a cannon constantly aimed during the Civil War?

A: Fearful and suspicious of the Mormon population in Utah, Connor kept a cannon trained on the home of Mormon leader Brigham Young for much of the war.

Q: What Army colonel commanded the troops that drove the Navaho from Arizona's Canyon de Chelly in 1864?

A: Kit Carson, the famous Old West scout, was commissioned as a colonel in the First New Mexico Volunteers during the Civil War and was responsible for the Navaho defeat.

Q: What father and son, both Army officers, had U.S. forts named for them in Colorado and Wyoming?

A: Colorado's Camp Collins (later Fort Collins) was named for Lieutenant Colonel William O. Collins, whose son, Lieutenant Caspar W. Collins, was honored by the naming of Fort Caspar in Wyoming.

Q: Who commanded the U.S. troops involved in the 1890 Wounded Knee Massacre, and what Army regiment participated in the bloody encounter?

A: On December 29, 1890, Colonel James Forsyth and the Seventh Cavalry engaged a large band of dissatisfied Sioux encamped on Wounded Knee Creek on South Dakota's Pine Ridge Indian Reservation. Army losses included 25 killed, while the Sioux lost more than 150, including numerous women and children.

Q: What engagement between the U.S. Army and the Cheyennes on July 11, 1869, ended serious Indian hostilities in western Kansas and eastern Colorado?

A: On this date a force of three hundred U.S. troops and Pawnee scouts led by General Eugene A. Carr attacked a Cheyenne village at the Battle of Summit Springs in northeastern Colorado, defeating the Cheyennes and reducing Indian resistance on the Central Plains.

Q: How were cavalry soldiers summoned to the routine duty of water-
      ing and grooming their horses?
A: When encamped at their posts in the Old West, the cavalry was
      governed by bugle calls like the stable-call, which summoned
      troops to horse duty.

Q: How much basic training did Army recruits usually receive before
      they were assigned a post in the West?
A: Recruits usually received no more than three or four weeks of basic
      instruction at a training depot before they were posted to the West.
      When assigned to a regiment, they would often receive additional
      training, like this soldier of the Sixth Cavalry, who learned to use
      his horse as a breastwork in training at Fort Bayard, New Mexico
      Territory, in 1885.

Q: What prominent general of the West was nicknamed "the Praying General"?

A: The nickname belonged to General Oliver Otis Howard, a devout Christian, who often led his troops in hymn singing. The Nez Percé called him "One-Arm Howard."

Q: In what battle, fought in the Texas Panhandle on September 28, 1874, did Colonel Ranald S. Mackenzie rout a large force of hostile Indians?

A: Mackenzie's victory was the Battle of Palo Duro Canyon, which helped end the 1874 Red River War between the Army and hostile Kiowas, Comanches and Southern Cheyennes.

Q: Who commanded the famous U.S. Tenth Cavalry—composed entirely of black soldiers—which conducted much of the roughest campaigning of the Indian Wars?

A: Colonel Benjamin H. Grierson, who led Federal troops on Grierson's Raid in the Civil War, assumed command of the Tenth Cavalry in 1866 and made it into one of the most efficient regiments of the Indian-fighting Army.

Q: What did these men have in common: "Yellowstone" Kelly, "Lonesome" Charlie Reynolds, "California Joe" Milner and "Buffalo Bill" Cody?

A: All served at various times as scouts for the Army in the West.

Q: What was the biggest killer of troops on the Western frontier?

A: Disease was the worst killer, causing eight deaths for every five from wounds or injuries.

Q: How did Army surgeons usually remove an Indian arrowhead from the body of a wounded soldier?

A: A common method of extracting the soft iron arrowhead used by Western tribes was to fish it out with a piece of wire fashioned into a loop.

Q: What article of equipment was invented for the Army of the West by Lieutenant Samuel McKeever of the U.S. Seventeenth Infantry?

A: The lieutenant invented the McKeever cartridge box, a hinged device fixed with enough loops for twenty cartridges. Troops were supposed to wear two of the boxes, but most soldiers chose to wear nonregulation looped belts.

Q: What occupation was held by General Nelson A. Miles, a major military figure in the Indian Wars, prior to his military career?

A: He was a clerk in a glassware shop.

Q: What battle, fought on September 9, 1876, ended the 1876 summer campaign against the Sioux, and what were the Army's casualties in the engagement?

A: On this date troops under General George Crook engaged Sioux warriors led by Chief American Horse at the Battle of Slim Buttes, fought in what is now western South Dakota. Although the battle was costly for the Sioux, the Army recorded minimal casualties.

Q: What part of the Army uniform in the West was despised by the troops, who called it a "useless, uncouth rag"?

A: Receiving such disdain was the black wide-brimmed 1872 campaign hat, which often disintegrated after the first hard rain and was usually discarded in favor of nonregulation headgear.

Q: What was the desertion rate in the U.S. Army during the primary era of Indian fighting in the West?

A: Desertion from the Army ranged from a high of almost 33 percent in 1871 to a low of about 6 percent in 1891, with the average rate of desertion between 1867 and 1890 at about 30 percent.

Q: What did Fort Richardson, Fort Griffin, Fort Concho, Fort Stockton and Fort Davis have in common?

A: All were military posts built to protect the Texas frontier.

FACT: At the 1867 Hayfield Fight the U.S. troops engaged in the battle were commanded by a civilian. On August 1 of that year twelve civilians were mowing hay near Fort C. F. Smith in Montana Territory, protected by a force of twenty soldiers, when they were attacked by more than five hundred Sioux and Cheyenne warriors in what became known as the Hayfield Fight. When the commanding officer, Lieutenant Sigismund Sternberg, was killed, a civilian hay cutter named Al Colvin took command. Under his leadership the soldiers and civilians withstood repeated Indian attacks until they were rescued six hours later by reinforcements.

Q: What did *Harper's Weekly*, *Galaxy*, *Police Gazette*, the *New York Herald*, the *Salt Lake Tribune* and *The Army and Navy Journal* have in common?

A: All were popular periodicals read by officers and some enlisted men at Western posts during the Indian Wars.

Q: Where were soldiers convicted of serious crimes in the Old West imprisoned during the post–Civil War era?

A: Troops convicted of minor infractions were normally punished at their posts, but after 1874 soldiers convicted of major crimes were usually placed in the military prison built at Fort Leavenworth, Kansas, that year. Prior to its construction, serious offenders were placed in civilian prisons.

Q: What major battle of the Nez Percé War was fought on August 9–10, 1877, at a site near the present-day border of Montana and Idaho?

A: The Battle of Big Hole.

Q: What Western Army fort, begun with purchase of an old trading post in 1849, was a key site on the Oregon Trail and an anchor for Army operations in the West?

A: Fort Laramie, located in southeast Wyoming, was established on the Laramie River at the site of a trading post built by mountain men William Sublette and Robert Campbell. The fort served the Army of the West for more than forty years.

Q: When a soldier of the Western Army found a piece of salt pork and a couple of hardtack crackers in his bunk or wrapped in his blankets, what did it mean?

A: It meant he had been judged and condemned by his fellow soldiers for some unsoldierly act.

Q: What battle was fought between U.S. troops and Comanche and Kiowa warriors on the North Fork of the Red River on Christmas Day, 1868?

A: On this date Major Andrew W. Evans and a large force of the U.S. Third Cavalry defeated Comanche and Kiowa Indians and destroyed their village at the Battle of Soldier Spring.

Q: In 1848–49 more than half the soldiers stationed in northern California deserted. Why?

A: The troops succumbed to gold fever: they could not resist the temptation to join the newly erupted California Gold Rush.

Q: What milestone military campaign against Indians of the West culminated in battle on August 10, 1823?

A: On this date a large force of U.S. troops and Sioux allies assaulted an Arikara Indian village on the upper Missouri River in retaliation for a bloody surprise attack by the Arikaras on a group of trappers. Most of the Arikaras escaped, but the battle was the first major military campaign against the Indians of the West.

Q: What was the pay for an Army private fighting Indians in the West between 1866 and 1891?

A: During much of the era of the Western Indian Wars, a U.S. Army private earned $16 a month. One dollar was deducted monthly to be saved for mustering-out pay, and 12½ cents was subtracted for a mandatory donation to the Soldier's Home, leaving the Indian-fighting soldier with monthly pay of $14.87½. In 1870 base pay for a private was reduced to $13. Above, troops of the Twenty-second Infantry were photographed earning their pay in the field near Fort Keogh, Montana, in 1889.

Q: How did General William T. Sherman, the commanding general of the U.S. Army, react to the continued disputes between his command and Secretary of War William W. Belknap in 1869?

A: In response to the clash with Belknap, Sherman moved his headquarters from Washington, D.C., to St. Louis.

Q: Who were the "dog robbers" found on every Army post in the West?

A: Dog robbers were enlisted men detailed to act as servants for post officers.

Q: What battle was fought on January 8, 1877, between Sioux and Cheyenne forces led by Chief Crazy Horse and the Fifth and Twenty-second Infantry led by Colonel Nelson A. Miles?

A: At the Battle of Wolf Mountain, fought along Montana's Tongue River on this date, Miles repelled repeated attacks launched by Crazy Horse's forces.

Q: General Ranald S. Mackenzie, highly regarded for his successes in the Western Indian Wars, received an early retirement from the Army in 1884. Why?

A: Mackenzie was retired early because of insanity.

Q: What firearm replaced the single-shot Model 1873 Springfield as the primary firearm of the U.S. Army?

A: In 1892 the Springfield was replaced by the Krag-Jorgensen magazine rifle, which became the Army's standard weapon in the West and elsewhere.

Q: What was the length of enlistment for cavalry troops during the post–Civil War Indian Wars?

A: In 1866 cavalry enlistments were set at five years.

Q: What were "Josh," "Guts," "Soapy," "Brigham," "Brute," "Tinker Bill" and "Crazy Jim"?

A: Many soldiers in the Western Army used aliases to escape their pasts, and almost all were assigned nicknames, like these given to troopers of the Seventh Cavalry in 1876.

Q: Where and when did General George Crook die?

A: Crook, the famous Indian fighter, died of heart failure while exercising with dumbbells at his Chicago headquarters on March 21, 1890.

Q: What was "bucking and gagging," and how was it used in the Army of the West?

A: Bucking and gagging was a method of punishment in which a gagged victim's legs and arms were bent and tied tightly to a heavy piece of wood or a rifle, leaving the offender in a cramped and painful sitting position. Although forbidden by regulations, the punishment was practiced frequently on Western Army posts.

Q: As the Seventh Cavalry launched its dawn surprise attack on Chief Black Kettle's village at the Battle of the Washita, why did the soldiers hear music?

A: The Seventh's commander, Lieutenant Colonel George A. Custer, had brought the Seventh's band on the campaign and ordered it to play the regimental marching song, "Garry Owen," as the cavalrymen charged the village.

Q: At what 1867 Indian fight did thirty-two soldiers and civilians successfully withstand assault by an estimated one thousand Sioux and Cheyenne warriors?

A: At the Wagon Box Fight on August 2, 1867, Captain James W. Powell, a company of the Twenty-seventh Infantry and four civilian woodcutters—all armed with breechloading rifles—barricaded themselves behind a corral of wagon boxes and for more than four hours repelled Indian assaults until they were rescued by reinforcements from nearby Fort Phil Kearny.

Q: What rank was held by the senior officer of a U.S. Army regiment in the post–Civil War Army of the West?

A: Regiments were commanded by a colonel, with a lieutenant colonel as second-in-command; companies or troops were commanded by a captain.

FACT: Few Army posts in the Old West were protected by the log stockades so familiar in Hollywood movies. Direct attacks on forts by Indians were so rare that only a handful of posts in the most dangerous country were defended by stockades. Most forts in the West sprawled over several acres, with no more protection necessary than posted sentries and the firepower of the garrison.

Q: In May of 1885 the assistant surgeon of the U.S. Fourth Cavalry carried military dispatches on a hazardous trek through hostile Apache country, an act that earned him the Medal of Honor. What was his name, and what famous military unit did he later command?

A: The plucky surgeon was Leonard Wood, who rose to command the Rough Riders during the Spanish-American War.

Q: What was unusual about the unsuccessful Apache attack on Fort Apache in Arizona Territory in 1881?

A: It was one of the extremely rare direct Indian attacks on an Army fort.

Q: What was the most common civilian profession of the men who wore the Army blue in the Old West?

A: Military duty in the isolated West attracted recruits from innumerable civilian professions, but according to Army records for 1882 the largest number of recruits listed their civilian profession as "laborers." A much smaller percentage were professional soldiers, and an equally small number of recruits were farmers. Here, a force of cavalry leaves Fort Bowie, located at infamous Apache Pass, in Arizona Territory.

Q: What three frontier forts on the Bozeman Trail did the U.S. Army
    abandon in 1868 after an inconclusive period of hostilities with the
    Sioux?
A: After a series of unsuccessful confrontations with the Sioux and
    after railroad development lessened the importance of the Bozeman
    Trail, the Army abandoned three forts built to protect the route:
    Fort Reno, Fort C. F. Smith and Fort Phil Kearny. All were later
    burned by Indians.

Q: What did Captain Anson Mills do with his Army-issue equipment,
    and how did his act make him wealthy?
A: In 1866 Mills discarded his awkward Army cartridge box and at-
    tached cartridge loops to his belt to carry his ammunition. An
    improved version of his invention became standard issue for the
    Army in 1881 as the popular webbed belt—a patented invention
    that eventually produced a fortune for the captain.

Q: What Missouri-born teacher-turned-soldier, a lieutenant in the
    U.S. Sixth Cavalry, helped set up a series of Army heliograph
    stations through Arizona's Apache country in 1886—and later be-
    came one of the most famous men in the world?
A: The young trooper, who later became a Rough Rider in the Span-
    ish-American War and also led a border expedition against Fran-
    cisco ("Pancho") Villa, was John J. Pershing, who eventually
    gained international fame as General Pershing, commander of the
    American Expeditionary Force during World War I.

FACT: U.S. troops battling Indians in the West were notorious for
      collecting battle souvenirs—a practice that was also popular
      with the Indians. On November 25, 1876, five months after
      the Custer Massacre, troops led by General Ranald S. Mac-
      kenzie defeated a force of Cheyennes and destroyed their en-
      campment at the Dull Knife Battle in Wyoming. In the cap-
      tured village Mackenzie's soldiers found weapons and
      equipment the Cheyennes had taken from the Seventh Cav-
      alry at the Battle of the Little Big Horn. Among the Indian
      trophies was a Seventh Cavalry guidon that some Indian war-
      rior had claimed as a souvenir—and had made into a pillow-
      case.

Q: What educational institution was founded by General Oliver O. Howard, who directed campaigns against the Nez Percé, the Bannocks, the Paiutes and the Apaches during his service in the West?

A: Howard, a staunch promoter of civil rights for blacks, played a major role in the establishment of Howard University in Washington, D.C.

Q: What percentage of the soldiers of the West were foreign-born, and from what countries did most of them come?

A: Between 1865 and 1874 approximately fifty percent of all Army recruits were born in a foreign country. The largest group was from Ireland, followed by those from Germany.

Q: Who described the U.S. troops fighting the Modoc War of 1872–73 as "cowardly beef-eaters"?

A: After suffering a series of costly defeats by the Modoc warriors, the battle-weary soldiers engaged in the Modoc War were so described by their new commanding officer, General Jefferson C. Davis, who assumed temporary command after the Modocs killed General Edward R. S. Canby.

Q: What did cavalrymen on the Western frontier often wear on the seats of their trousers for service in the field?

A: Canvas.

Q: What was Major George A. Forsyth doing when reinforcements arrived to assist him and his small command following the Battle of Beecher's Island in 1868?

A: Although badly wounded, Forsyth was found reading a battered copy of *Oliver Twist* when his rescuers arrived.

Q: Who were the "Custer Avengers"?

A: Following the 1876 Custer Massacre, the numerical strength of cavalry companies in the U.S. Army was raised by congressional decree, and the men recruited to fill the expanded ranks were known as Custer Avengers.

Q: What Indian fighter was mourned aloud at his death in 1890 by Apaches on the reservation?

A: The Apaches "wept and wailed like children" upon learning of the death of General George Crook, who was waging a political battle to have long-time Apache prisoners-of-war moved from imprisonment in Alabama to a reservation in Oklahoma.

Q: What was the pay for a first sergeant defending the Western frontier in the 1870s?

A: A first sergeant in this era earned twenty-two dollars a month.

Q: On August 19, 1854, Second Lieutenant John L. Grattan took a force of thirty men from Wyoming's Fort Laramie, went into a nearby Sioux village, confronted Sioux Chief Conquering Bear and engaged in an exchange of gunfire that killed the chief and resulted in the massacre of Grattan and his command. What prompted the confrontation?

A: Grattan marched on the village because an Indian reportedly had taken a trail-weary cow left by a passing wagon train.

Q: What was a soldier's "bunky"?

A: A soldier's bunky was his best friend, with whom he shared blankets on campaigns, helped prepare rations in the field and faced combat during engagements with the enemy.

Q: What was the most unpopular duty in the Army of the West?

A: Soldiers of the West spent much of their time in "fatigue duty," performing unsoldierly jobs like gardening, roofing, post maintenance and minor repairs. Probably the most loathsome chore for soldiers of the Old West was the routine under way by the soldiers pictured here—cutting ice in the worst of winter for use in warmer weather.

Q: What was unusual about the method of attack used by U.S. troops under Colonel Edwin V. Sumner at the Battle of Solomon River on July 29, 1857?

A: Sumner launched a saber charge against his Cheyenne opponents, a rare method of battle in the Western Indian Wars.

Q: What famous Old West figure was dismissed from South Carolina's College of Charleston in 1831 for "incorrigible negligence" as a student?

A: The dismal display of discipline was recorded by explorer and soldier John C. Fremont, who became famous for establishing the paths later followed by the great wave of Western emigrants.

Q: How did General Nelson A. Miles die?

A: A Civil War veteran and winner of the Medal of Honor, Miles led aggressive campaigns against the Sioux, the Nez Percé, the Apaches and other tribes, becoming a general in 1880. On May 15, 1925, he died of a heart attack while attending a circus in Washington, D.C.

5 | Pioneers, Sodbusters and Town Raisers

Q: What historic strip of Old West geography bore these landmarks: Big Vermilion, Court House Rock, Chimney Rock, Scott's Bluff, Poison Spider Creek, Independence Rock, the Devil's Gate, South Pass, Fort Bridger, Soda Springs, American Falls, the Columbia River and Fort Vancouver?

A: All were landmarks on the Oregon Trail.

Q: How did pioneers commonly make butter on the long, demanding trail westward?

A: Most emigrants herded at least one milk cow over the continent with them, and cow's milk, when poured into a bucket and hung under a jostling wagon, would automatically be churned into butter by day's end.

Q: What violent act at the hands of Indians did railroad worker William Thompson survive?

A: In 1867, while taking a handcar through Indian country in Nebraska, Thompson was attacked and scalped by Cheyenne warriors, who thought they had killed him. He survived, found his discarded scalp on the prairie and walked back to civilization carrying it in a bucket of water, hoping it could be restored to his head—which it could not. He then moved to England.

Q: With what did the early settlers of the Old West commonly treat a cold or a fever?

A: Isolated from civilization and commercial medical products, Western pioneers usually treated colds and fevers with an improvised remedy: an ointment of goose grease and turpentine.

Q: What milestone in the history of the Old West occurred on September 15, 1858?

A: On this date the newly created Overland Mail Company sent its stagecoaches on the first delivery of the U.S. mail overland between the East and the Pacific Coast.

Q: At what time of year did emigrant wagon trains usually depart on the two-thousand-mile journey to California or Oregon?

A: Most emigrants tried to leave Missouri in late April or early May. Leaving too soon would put the train on the prairie before adequate grazing would be available for stock, and leaving too late could cause the pioneers to be trapped in the mountains by early snows. This pioneer family pauses beside a loaded wagon, accompanied by one of the numerous soldiers sent West to protect settlers.

Q: What did Ben Hur, Jenny Lind, Yankee Jims, You Bet and Poke Flat have in common?

A: All were nineteenth-century California mining camps during the Gold Rush, and all became ghost towns.

Q: What item was known to homesteaders of the Old West as "prairie coal"?

A: Prairie coal was a popular Old West nickname for buffalo and cow chips, which homesteaders, like the Indians, mountain men and pioneers before them, found useful as a substitute for firewood on the treeless prairie.

Q: From August to October 1868 how many settlers were killed by Indians on the southern plains of the Old West?

A: According to Army reports for 1868, Indian raids on the southern plains during the three-month period resulted in the deaths of seventy-nine settlers.

Q: How many gambling establishments and saloons were located in little Abilene, Kansas, in 1871?

A: At the height of its days as a railhead for Texas cattle drives, Abilene boasted sixty-four gambling houses and saloons in what became known as "the Devil's Half-Acre." The showiest barroom was the Alamo Saloon, which was decorated with a wall of mirrors, lewd paintings and glass doors.

Q: What did Ferdinand B. Hayden, a respected scientist with the U.S. Geological Survey, propose as a method of producing increased rainfall in the arid Great Plains?

A: Hayden officially expressed the mistaken notion that active plowing and planting increased rainfall—a popular theory that caused plows to turn over thousands of acres of Western sod—without any effect on the weather.

FACT: The federal Homestead Act became law on May 27, 1862. For a ten-dollar filing fee a homesteader could claim 160 acres of public land in exchange for agreeing to live on the homesite for five years. The remarkable legislation sent thousands of Americans westward in search of a better life.

Q: Who was James Wilson Marshall, and how did he influence the development of the Old West?

A: Marshall, the boss at John Sutter's sawmill near Coloma, California, was the man who discovered gold in the American River in 1848 and launched the California Gold Rush.

Q: How long did the famous Pony Express operate?

A: The Pony Express was in operation for only nineteen months, from April 1860 through October 1861. Established by the freight company of Russell, Majors and Waddell, the Pony Express carried almost 35,000 pieces of mail over more than 650,000 miles during those nineteen months—and lost only one mail sack.

Q: What historic highway, connecting Independence, Missouri, to Santa Fe, New Mexico, was the main route of commerce to and from the American Southwest in the early nineteenth century?

A: The famous route was known as the Santa Fe Trail, and at its peak, between 1822 and 1843, goods amounting to as much as $450,000 a year moved along this highway.

Q: What were the primary commercial products exported from California prior to the California Gold Rush?

A: Cowhides and tallow.

Q: How was the name selected for Bismarck, North Dakota—the site of Fort Abraham Lincoln?

A: Executives of the Northern Pacific Railroad named the railroad town after Germany's Otto von Bismarck, in an attempt to please a group of German investors who helped bankroll the railroad's expansion.

Q: Homes on the Western frontier were usually floored with what substance?

A: Most cabins or sod houses had dirt floors; those near a supply of wood sometimes had split log floors chinked with mud.

Q: How was California stagecoach driver Charlie Parkhurst different from most stage drivers of the Old West?

A: A well-known figure in California in the 1860s and 1870s, Charlie drove stage routes throughout northern California, survived numerous mishaps and developed a reputation as one of the hardest-driving expressmen in California. Upon his death in 1879 Charlie was found to have been a woman in disguise.

Q: How many miles were walked or ridden on horseback by Father Pierre Jean De Smet in the thirty-two years he spent ministering to the Indians of the Northwest?

A: A well-known Catholic missionary to the Flathead and Coeur d'Alene tribes, De Smet trekked an estimated 100,000 miles back and forth through the wilds of the Northwest.

Q: What heroic act was performed by eleven-year-old Merton Eastlick during Minnesota's 1862 Santee Sioux Uprising?

A: After his father and three brothers were killed by the Sioux and his mother was taken prisoner, young Merton carried his baby brother approximately forty miles to safety, walking barefoot, hiding from Indians en route and keeping himself and his baby brother alive by picking and eating wild berries.

Q: On the early Western frontier, where matches were in short supply, how did settlers start the day's fire?

A: Coals were banked in the fireplace each night for the next day's fire. If no coals were available, a settler might hike over to the nearest neighbor to borrow some. If available, flint was sometimes used to kindle a blaze.

Q: Who were the first white women to cross the Rocky Mountains en route to Oregon?

A: Narcissa Prentiss Whitman, wife of missionary Marcus Whitman, and Mrs. Henry H. Spalding, wife of another missionary, traveled with their husbands overland to Oregon in 1836, becoming the first white women to cross the Rocky Mountains to Oregon by a route to be followed by thousands more.

Q: What familiar euphemism originated with a Dodge City brothel?

A: Known for a front door made of red glass, which produced a rosy glow when illuminated at night, Dodge City's Red Light bordello lent its name to the cow town's brothel district and reportedly produced the term "red-light district."

Q: What famous Old West character worked at various times as a wash woman, a stage performer and a prostitute; once rode a bull down the main street of Rapid City, South Dakota; achieved notoriety in the mining town of Deadwood and was born with the name Martha Jane Canary?

A: Calamity Jane.

Q: What was the mysterious "fever and ague" that struck and debilitated so many residents and travelers in the Old West, and what caused it?

A: The "fever and ague" was really malaria, which doctors then believed originated from bad air and only later was found to be borne by mosquitoes.

Q: What was the most popular musical instrument among settlers in the Old West?

A: The fiddle.

Q: What town was both the site of Montana's first major gold strike and the first capital of Montana Territory?

A: Montana's first important gold rush occurred on Grasshopper Creek in 1862 and led to the establishment of the town of Bannack, Montana, which became the territorial capital—until it was overshadowed by nearby Virginia City.

Q: What were the Schutler, the Bain, the Studebaker and the Conestoga?

A: Each was a different type of wagon used extensively in the Old West.

Q: In 1878 prospectors August Rische and George Hook shoveled into a mountainside near Leadville, Colorado, and struck a gigantic vein of silver that eventually produced more than $20,000 a week. How did the miners select the digging spot that led them to paydirt?

A: According to mining lore, the two picked the site that made them rich simply because it lay in the shade.

Q: What was the record for the most track laid in one day during the building of the transcontinental railroad across the West?

A: In April of 1869, while track crews of the Union Pacific and Central Pacific railroads raced each other to complete the transcontinental route, Chinese laborers of the Central Pacific placed 4,037 rails and 31,000 ties and drove 120,000 spikes, laying a record 10.6 miles of completed track in one day.

Q: What was the most famous pass through the Rocky Mountains and the approximate halfway point on the Oregon Trail?

A: South Pass, a relatively easy crossing through the Rockies and a major landmark of the Old West, was located in what is now Wyoming, at the approximate halfway mark on the Oregon Trail.

Q: Where was "home" for the estimated 100,000 Chinese laborers living in the West in 1880, and how were they different from the typical nineteenth-century emigrant?

A: The majority of Chinese emigrants who came to the American West in the 1880s were from the Pearl River Delta in south China. Unlike the typical emigrant, most Chinese left their families behind and did not plan to remain in the United States permanently; instead their goal was to return to China with enough money to provide prosperity for their families.

Q: Who was the primary manufacturer of the famous Concord stage-coach, familiar throughout the Old West?

A: Produced by Abbot, Downing & Company of Concord, New Hampshire, the popular Concord stagecoach had a frame made of straight-grained white ash; side panels were made of poplar; and the running gear was made of ash or white oak. The Concord stage weighed about 2,500 pounds and cost approximately $1,000. Here, a Concord stage protected by a military guard delivers the mail to Fort Wallace, Kansas, in 1867.

FACT: The cool ceilings of the sod homes constructed by settlers on the prairie were attractive to a variety of snakes, which made their homes in crevices among the sod bricks. Occasionally the snakes would surprise the human occupants of the "soddies" by falling onto the dinner table or plopping into an occupied bed at night. However, settlers consoled themselves with the knowledge that the snakes at least eliminated any mice in the house.

Q: William Jayne, the governor of Dakota Territory in 1861, was appointed to his post by President Abraham Lincoln. What was Jayne's relationship to the President?

A: He was Lincoln's family doctor. A former mayor of Springfield and a former state senator, he had also served as Lincoln's campaign manager in Illinois.

Q: What Western mining community boasted "the Richest Hill on Earth"?

A: Butte, Montana, which produced more than five thousand tons of copper in 1882 alone, could rightfully make this boast as the largest producer of copper in the United States during the late nineteenth century.

Q: Why was sourdough bread so named?

A: The yeast used to "start" baked bread on many Old West homesteads was part of a meticulously hoarded lump of dough left from previous bakings, and was often "sour" from its long storage. During wintertime some Western cooks took the jar of "starter" dough to bed with them to protect it from freezing.

Q: How did Western homesteaders protect their beds from the bedbugs that often infested log cabins on the prairie?

A: Bedbugs were barred by placing each leg of the bed in a tin can of coal oil.

Q: What pioneer trail began at Santa Fe, New Mexico, scaled the Rockies in modern-day Colorado, crossed the Great Basin of the Southwest and ended in Los Angeles?

A: The Old Spanish Trail.

Q: Who was Olive Oatman, and what gave her national fame in the mid-nineteenth century?

A: Olive Oatman was a pioneer's daughter captured and enslaved by Indians in 1851 at age fourteen. She was rescued after five years of harrowing captivity in the Southwest and eventually drew large crowds on the lecture circuits, perhaps because her attractive face bore permanent tattoos inscribed by her captors.

Q: What was the favorite game of chance in the Old West?

A: Gambling was popular and commonplace in the Old West, and many games were favored by the Western gambler. The most popular game of chance was probably faro, in which players bet on cards drawn from a dealing box. Anxious faro players await the next card in this photograph made in a saloon in Bisbee, Arizona.

Q: What important Missouri community rivaled Independence as the jumping-off place for thousands of emigrants making the long trek westward in the nineteenth century?

A: Westport Landing, Missouri, established by trapper François Chouteau in the early 1830s, was a major embarkation point for the Santa Fe Trail and the Colorado and California gold fields. As the migration westward shifted to the railroads, Westport shrank in importance and by 1899 had become a Kansas City suburb.

Q: Who was the first man to take wagons over the Santa Fe Trail?

A: In 1822 trader William Becknell took some pack animals and three wagons from Missouri to Santa Fe. His route became the famous Santa Fe Trail and was followed by countless wagon trains.

Q: Why were Leland Stanford, Collis P. Huntington, Charles Crocker and Mark Hopkins called the "Big Four," and what was their primary contribution to the Old West?

A: All were founders and builders of the Central Pacific Railroad.

Q: What famous Old West hotel opened in San Francisco in 1875 with 755 rooms, more than 300 private baths and a glass-roofed parlor—at a cost of six million dollars?

A: The San Francisco Palace.

Q: Who was Erastus Beadle, and how did he forever affect the Old West?

A: Beadle was a New York publisher of cheap songbooks who, in 1860, launched the first successful mass-produced series of dime novels. The books' dramatic, glorified Western heroes created a romantic image of the Old West that persists even today. In his first five years of publishing Beadle sold more than five million dime novels.

FACT: The first large group of miners to enter California for the Gold Rush came from Hawaii. Seamen from San Francisco carried the news of the gold discovery to the Hawaiian Islands, and in response to the announcement nineteen shiploads of miners set sail for the gold fields of California, getting there much sooner than those who had to cross the continent or sail from the East.

Q: Who were Philip Arnold and John Slack, and what famous hoax did they engineer in the Old West?

A: The two were cousins from Kentucky who staged the "Great Diamond Hoax" in 1872, when they "salted" a remote site in Wyoming with $35,000 worth of rough, uncut and low-grade diamonds. The "discovery" of the top-secret diamond field enabled the two to fleece $600,000 from eager San Francisco and New York tycoons before the hoax was revealed.

Q: What major Western city was established under the name New York–Someday?

A: In 1852 American emigrants from the ship *Exact* gave this hopeful name to their settlement, which was later renamed Seattle in honor of a local Indian leader.

Q: Who was "King of the Thimbleriggers," and what happened to him?

A: King of the Thimbleriggers was Jefferson R. ("Soapy") Smith, a professional gambler who made a fortune in saloons of the Old West by playing the "shell game"—hiding a pea under one of three thimbles. In 1898 he was killed by an irate vigilante in Skagway, Alaska.

Q: What massacre occurred in Rock Springs, Wyoming, on September 2, 1885?

A: On this date approximately 150 white coal miners and residents of Rock Springs attacked the town's Chinese laborers, who had declined to join the other workers in a coal mine strike against the Union Pacific coal department. Twenty-eight Chinese were killed in the attack, fifteen more were wounded, and hundreds of others were driven out of town.

Q: Who were the "heart and hand women" of the Old West?

A: Westerners applied this name to the mail-order brides who came West to yield hearts and hands to unseen correspondents.

Q: What happened to the countless objects discarded along the Oregon Trail by overpacked emigrants?

A: Everything from clothes to food to furniture was left along the trail; much of the abandoned material was picked up by other emigrants as a substitute for inferior goods; some objects were carried off by Indians; the rest rotted or rusted at trailside.

Q: What was a "butcher knife" wagon, and why was it called by that
     name?
A: "Butcher knife" wagon was the name cowboys applied to the wag-
     ons used by Western farmers. The name was derived from the
     vehicle's narrow tires, which left ruts on the prairie that resembled
     slices made by a giant butcher knife.

Q: How many sheep could be hand-sheared by an expert shearer in
     the Old West?
A: Some shearers could hand-shear as many as 150 sheep in one day.

Q: At what point did westward-bound emigrants consider themselves
     to be "across the Rocky Mountains"?
A: Although rugged and challenging mountain terrain still faced
     them, emigrants bound for Oregon or California expressed relief at
     being "across the Rocky Mountains" when they crossed the Conti-
     nental Divide—the mountaintop line that separates the waters
     that flow toward the Pacific from those that drain toward the At-
     lantic.

Q: What railroad connected Denver, Colorado, with Salt Lake City
     in 1883—after thirteen years of track-laying competition and court
     battles?
A: The Denver and Rio Grande Western Railroad.

Q: Who was Margaret Tobin Brown, and what famous disaster did she
     survive?
A: The wife of millionaire miner James J. Brown, Margaret survived
     the sinking of the *Titanic* and became famous as the "Unsinkable
     Molly Brown."

Q: What was the occupation of these Old West characters: "Curly
     Dan," "Buffalo Jim," "Dutch John," "Old Shalcross," "Uncle Jim
     Miller" and "One-eyed Charlie"?
A: All were stagecoach drivers of the Old West.

Q: In April, 1876, in a circuslike atmosphere, more than seven thou-
     sand residents of the frontier assembled in Fort Smith, Arkansas.
     Why did they come?
A: The cheerful crowd came to town to witness the hanging of five
     outlaws—a public exercise that drew giant crowds every year until
     it was restricted in 1881.

Q: Where was the first gold strike in the Old West?

A: In 1832 gold was discovered by José Ortiz south of Sante Fe, New Mexico, in what would quickly become the boom town of Delores, site of the Old West's first recorded gold strike.

Q: Who founded Wells, Fargo and Company, the express firm that became a legend in the Old West?

A: On March 18, 1852, Henry Wells, a former New York City steamboat operator, and William George Fargo, a former New York mailman, established Wells, Fargo and Company to serve the California gold fields during the Gold Rush. Although not the first express company to operate in California, Wells, Fargo expanded and outlived all competitors from the Gold Rush era.

Q: Why did some emigrants prefer oxen instead of mules in making their trek west to Oregon or California?

A: Mule teams were surefooted, smarter and faster than oxen, but a mule's temper and stubbornness were legendary. Oxen, like these photographed in Arizona in 1883, were much slower than a mule team, but oxen ate less, were easier to care for and could pull heavier loads. In addition, oxen cost about fifty dollars each in the mid-nineteenth century, while a mule cost ninety dollars.

Q: Who were the first American migrants to reach California by an overland route?

A: In 1841 a group of thirty-one settlers led by John Bartleson and John Bidwell left the Oregon Trail at Soda Springs, in what is now southern Idaho, and crossed the Sierra Nevada mountains into California, becoming the first American settlers to reach California by an overland route.

Q: How frequently did residents of the Old West encounter attacks from mountain lions and wolves?

A: Mountain lions—also called cougars, panthers, pumas, catamounts and "painters"—were extremely shy of human contact, and attacks in the Old West were almost unheard of; wolves, though feared by many in the Old West, rarely, if ever, attacked humans.

Q: What historic Old West landmark included these important sites: Round Grove, Black Jack Point, Switzer's Creek, Council Grove, the Arkansas River, Pawnee Rock, Chouteau Island, Round Mound, Rio Gallinas and San Miguel?

A: All were key points on the famous Santa Fe Trail.

Q: What sporting event in Old California left a lasting impact of sorts on the American financial community?

A: A favorite diversion in Old California was the bull-and-bear fight, which pitted a captive grizzly bear against a mean-tempered bull. Inspired by a visit to one of the bloody contests, New York newspaper publisher Horace Greeley reportedly applied the terms "bear" and "bull" to the activities of New York's Wall Street.

Q: Was there ever a real "Grizzly" Adams?

A: Yes. His real name was James Capen Adams, and he operated a commercial "zoo" in California that specialized in grizzly bears—a profession that led the dime novelists of his day to dub him Grizzly Adams. In 1860, during a ten-week tour jointly staged with showman P. T. Barnum, Adams was severely mauled while trying to ride a "tame" grizzly.

Q: What Old West landmark was called the Great Register?

A: Independence Rock, 838 miles westward on the Oregon Trail, was known as the Great Register because hundreds of emigrants traveling the Oregon Trail carved their names into the base of the towering rock.

Q: Who founded California's Fort Ross, and how was it different from most forts of the Old West?

A: It was established as a Russian colony in California. In 1812 a large group of Russian settlers from Alaska, led by I. A. Kuskov, established Fort Ross as the site for production of food for the Russians in Alaska and as a center for harvesting sea otters. Both enterprises failed, forcing the Russians to sell the property to Americans in 1841.

Q: How did the stagecoach driver of the Old West normally hold his coach reins?

A: He would hold the reins of the lead team between the middle fingers and forefingers of each hand; the reins for the middle team between the middle and third fingers; and the reins for the wheel team between the third and little fingers.

Q: What was the "dogtrot" so common in the Old West?

A: A dogtrot was a popular style of frontier cabin that featured two rooms connected by a breezeway—the dogtrot from which the name came.

Q: For what purpose were buffalo bones gathered from the prairie, and how much money did the "bone pickers" who gathered them earn for their skeletal harvests?

A: Buffalo bones, which were strewn across the Great Plains after the mass buffalo hunts of 1870–1883, were bought by Eastern firms for the production of fertilizer and bone china. The "bone pickers" usually earned eight dollars a ton for the bones.

Q: What landmark on the Oregon Trail was called Gate of Death, Devil's Gate and Massacre Rocks, and why?

A: At a point on the Oregon Trail near what is now American Falls, Idaho, the emigrants had to pass through a narrow gap between a large outcropping of rocks. So many emigrants were ambushed and killed by Indians that the site was given these grisly names.

FACT: Glass window panes were scarce luxuries for most early homesteaders in the Old West. Until they were prosperous enough to afford glass, many settlers fitted their windows with panes made of greased paper.

Q: What eventually happened to John M. Bozeman, the explorer who established the Bozeman Trail from Wyoming to the Montana gold fields?

A: He was later killed by Blackfeet Indians while traveling the trail named in his honor.

Q: How much did it cost to buy the wagon, team and equipment that was necessary to outfit a family of emigrants going West in the 1840s?

A: A typical family spent approximately one thousand dollars going West by wagon.

Q: What infamous massacre occurred on November 29, 1847, at a site in present-day Washington State called "Place of the Rye Grass" by local Indians, and what major political event did the massacre influence?

A: On this date Presbyterian missionaries Marcus and Narcissa Whitman and twelve others at Whitman's Waiilatpu mission were killed by Cayuse Indians, who blamed the missionaries for a measles epidemic that had struck the tribe. The massacre prompted the organization of the Oregon Territory by the U. S. Congress in order to provide military protection for settlers.

Q: The population of San Francisco was less than five hundred in 1845. What was it seven years later, at the height of the California Gold Rush?

A: Thirty-six thousand.

Q: How long was the Oregon Trail?

A: From Independence, Missouri, to Fort Vancouver in modern-day Washington State, the Oregon Trail measured 2,020 miles.

Q: What was the average age of a Pony Express rider, and how much salary did he earn?

A: The typical Pony Express rider was nineteen years old and made $100 to $150 a month, plus room and board. In 1861 off-duty expressman Frank Webner struck this pose while astride a well-equipped mount. When on a mail run, Webner and the other riders would save weight by arming themselves with nothing heavier than two pistols and a knife.

Q: Who invented the barbed wire that fenced in the Old West, and where was the wire manufactured?

A: The inventor of the first mass-produced barbed wire was Joseph Farwell Glidden, an Illinois farmer who perfected and patented a popular barbed wire based on a type developed by Henry M. Rose. Glidden's invention, produced in thousands of miles, ended the open range and opened the West to mass homesteading by small farmers. The wire was manufactured at Glidden's Barb Fence Company in DeKalb, Illinois.

Q: What famous Old West town boasted these establishments: Julius Caesar's New York Coffee House, Eagle Brewery, Capitol Saloon, The Grotto and the Oriental Saloon?

A: Tombstone, Arizona.

Q: Who was Lansford W. Hastings, and why was the haze in one section of the Rockies named in his honor?

A: Hastings was an early promoter of Western settlement whose controversial 1845 guidebook for emigrants, *The Emigrants' Guide to Oregon and California,* sent numerous emigrants over an arduous, dangerous route through the mountains. Later emigrants claimed the blue haze over the mountains along this route—the Hastings Cutoff—was created by all the curses uttered against Hastings by frustrated emigrants.

Q: How did pioneer women pack eggs to prevent breakage in the jostling wagons on the way West?

A: A common practice among emigrant homemakers was to pack the eggs in the family barrel of cornmeal, protecting the eggs and allowing them to be cooked at the same time bread was baked.

FACT: The Pony Express set a record for its best time in March of 1861, when its riders delivered the text of President Lincoln's inaugural speech to California. Pony Express delivery of mail between St. Joseph, Missouri, and Sacramento, California, normally took ten days, but the riders delivering Lincoln's address covered the 1,966 miles between the two points in seven days and seventeen hours.

Q: What two rival Western settlements bore the name of a territorial governor of Kansas and eventually merged to become a major Western state capital?

A: The settlements of Auraria and Denver City, which faced each other and competed for growth during the Colorado gold rush, merged in 1860 and with the name of Kansas Governor James W. Denver became famous as Denver, Colorado.

Q: What caused the deadly "milk sick," which killed countless settlers on the Western frontier in the nineteenth century?

A: The mysterious milk sick, which sometimes wiped out whole families, was actually toxic poisoning caused by consumption of milk or butter from cows that had grazed on white snakeroot or rayless goldenrod plants, which contained the poison tremetol.

Q: What unusual cargo was imported to Seattle, Washington, in 1865 by Asa Mercer, who was then president of the fledgling University of Washington?

A: To combat a shortage of marriageable females, Mercer organized a scheme to import Civil War widows to Seattle as potential wives for the local male population. Later unable to meet the constant demand for mates, Mercer was forcefully encouraged to leave town by the area's unhappy loggers and miners.

Q: What decorated the walls of the typical settler's cabin?

A: Old newspapers were the most common wallpaper in the Old West. Not only were they inexpensive wall covering, but they also provided the entertainment of wall-reading on long winter nights.

Q: What was the Raft River Turnoff, which was known to every pioneer on the Oregon Trail?

A: At the Raft River in what is now Idaho, emigrants bound for California would leave the Oregon Trail, travel south to the Hudspeth Cut-Off and take that route into California.

Q: What convinced California landowner John A. Sutter that the object found on his property by employee James W. Marshall was really gold?

A: Marshall's discovery, which ignited the California Gold Rush, was examined and tested by Sutter at his home. What finally convinced him of its authenticity was an article he read in *Encyclopedia Americana*.

Q: What peculiar Old West tool was perfected by Wyoming black-smith James Candlish?

A: In 1884 Candlish took an old wagon from behind his Cheyenne blacksmith shop and converted it into a sheep wagon, a vehicle that became a standard tool for sheepherders.

Q: What important Western city was launched in 1841 by John N. Bryan, who established a frontier farm on the banks of the Trinity River that year?

A: Dallas, Texas.

Q: What was unusual about the burial of an unknown family of emi-grants who were killed by Indians on the Oregon Trail near Soda Springs, Idaho Territory, in 1861?

A: The pioneers who found the bodies of the slain parents and their five children reportedly buried them all in the wagon box in which they had traveled West.

Q: What prompted a Pueblo, Colorado, newspaper to make this an-nouncement in 1876: "The biggest drunk of the present century will occur here on the 7th of March"?

A: The newspaper's prediction welcomed the coming of the Atchison, Topeka and Santa Fe Railway, which reached Pueblo that year.

Q: How many passengers could be seated inside the stagecoaches op-erated by the Overland Mail Company between St. Louis and Cal-ifornia; how much was the fare; and how much luggage could each passenger carry?

A: The company's Concord coaches seated nine passengers inside, although more could ride atop the vehicle. The fare was normally two hundred dollars for the entire route, and each passenger could carry up to forty pounds of luggage.

Q: Who was Dr. John Sappington, and what were his famous Anti-Fever Pills designed to cure?

A: A physician on the Missouri frontier in the early nineteenth cen-tury, Sappington developed an experimental "Anti-Fever Pill" made from a derivative of Peruvian tree bark, which was designed to cure the mysterious fever that sickened or killed many people on the frontier. The fever was later found to be malaria, and Sapping-ton's bark derivative was quinine, eventually found to be an effec-tive treatment for the fever.

Q: What was the death rate for emigrants on the Oregon Trail, and what was the most common killer?

A: Of the estimated 350,000 emigrants who took the Oregon Trail, at least 20,000 died en route—one out of seventeen—and the most common cause of death was cholera.

Q: What Old West occupation was known as "the jehu," or "the whip"?

A: The nicknames were applied to the reinsmen who drove the stagecoaches of the Old West.

Q: What was the most popular fiddling tune of the Western frontier?

A: Although candidates for this distinction are numerous, the most popular tune on the Western frontier was probably "The Arkansas Traveler." Other favorites were "Turkey in the Straw," "Irish Washer Woman," "Dinah Had a Wooden Leg," and "Give the Fiddler a Dram."

Q: How long did it normally take passengers to reach California from St. Louis aboard one of the stagecoaches of the Overland Mail Company?

A: The trip normally took about three weeks, if the traveler remained aboard the coach day and night for the entire journey. If he chose to stay at the way stations at night, the trip could take much longer.

FACT: The infamous Donner tragedy occurred because the Donner party took the advice of an ill-informed emigrant guidebook. In 1846 brothers Jacob and George Donner led a wagon train of pioneers across the rugged Sierra Nevada Mountains toward California on a shortcut recommended in a travelers' guide published by Lansford Hastings, a California real estate promoter eager to lure settlers to the West Coast. High in the Sierra the Donner party was snowed in by an early winter storm and remained trapped in the mountains until rescued in February of 1847. When rescuers reached the starving emigrants they found only forty-four of the eighty-nine pioneers alive, and most of the survivors had lived through the winter by resorting to cannibalism.

Q: How was the famous Conestoga wagon normally painted?
A: Originally produced by Pennsylvania Dutch craftsmen and used by thousands of emigrants to the West, the Conestoga's wagon box was frequently painted blue and its running gear red. Topped by a white canvas canopy, the distinctively designed red, white and blue vehicle became a familiar feature of the trails West.

Q: How did a barroom brawl in the Brahma Bull Saloon of Richmond, Texas, lead to the closing of bars and saloons throughout the nation?
A: In 1889 barroom toughs in the Brahma Bull Saloon beat up a visitor from Kansas named David Nation, whose incensed wife, Carry A. Nation, began attacking illegal Kansas saloons with a hatchet, thus fueling the temperance movement throughout the nation.

Q: What milestone in the history of the Old West was reached in 1890?
A: That year the U.S. Superintendent of the Census officially announced that due to population expansion, the Western frontier no longer existed. Soon remote regions of the West that had been inhabited mainly by buffalo and Indians a few years before would boast civilized developments, like this sod schoolhouse with its students, photographed in Oklahoma in 1895.

Q: What became of the famous Elizabeth ("Baby Doe") Tabor, who
     was the wife of multimillionaire silver baron Horace Tabor?

A: Owner of Colorado's famous Matchless Mine, Horace Tabor struck
     it rich as a poor prospector, enjoyed an immense fortune, divorced
     his wife Augusta and married lovely Baby Doe, who became the
     belle of Denver's mining elite. Her husband eventually lost his
     fortune, wound up as the postmaster of Denver and at his death in
     1899 left Baby Doe nothing but the played-out Matchless Mine.
     For the rest of her life she lived in a shack at the Matchless, where
     she died during a winter freeze in 1935 at age eighty.

Q: How often did a Pony Express rider change horses, and how much
     did it cost to send a letter by Pony Express?

A: The goal of Russell, Majors and Waddell, the freighting firm that
     created the Pony Express, was to deliver the U.S. mail between St.
     Joseph, Missouri, and Sacramento, California, within ten days.
     The company built 190 relay stations over a distance of 1,966 miles
     so riders could change horses every fifteen miles. The initial cost of
     sending a letter by Pony Express was ten dollars an ounce, but was
     reduced to one dollar an ounce in July of 1861. Russell, Majors and
     Waddell lost $200,000 on the Pony Express and eventually de-
     clared bankruptcy.

6 | Wranglers, Rustlers and Roundups

Q: Why were cowboys sometimes called "cowpunchers"?

A: Cowboys who drove the Texas herds to railhead markets in Kansas often used long poles to prod cattle into the railroad cars, an act that earned them the nickname cowpunchers.

Q: What was the last act of the day for the cook while on a cattle drive?

A: On a cattle drive directions were usually taken from the North Star. The cook's final job of the day was to point the chuck wagon tongue toward the north, so the herd could "follow the tongue" the next morning.

Q: What cattle trail began in southeastern Texas, crossed what is now eastern Oklahoma, passed through eastern Kansas and ended in Kansas City?

A: Known primarily as the Shawnee Trail, this route was also called the Texas Road and the Osage Trace.

Q: Why did so many cowboys wear vests?

A: In their day few shirts had pockets, and most of the work season was too warm for coats, so cowboys wore vests as a lightweight source of pockets.

Q: Which was the largest ranch in the Old West: the XIT Ranch, the Goodnight Ranch or the King Ranch?

A: The Goodnight Ranch was the largest. Although much of the land it used was public range, Charles Goodnight's huge ranch sprawled over twenty million acres and was much larger than the one-million-acre King Ranch or the three-million-acre XIT. However, the XIT Ranch ran more cattle—160,000 head—than the Goodnight Ranch, which claimed 100,000 at most.

Q: When a cowboy had his "Arbuckle's" in his hand, what was he doing?

A: He was savoring a cup of coffee. Arbuckle's preroasted coffee with its flying-angel trademark was produced by Arbuckle Brothers in Pittsburgh and was so popular in the Old West that "Arbuckle's" became a generic name for coffee.

Q: How old was the typical Old West cowboy?

A: Cowboys of the Old West, like these photographed on the range, varied in age from teenagers to old-timers. However, the demanding work and sometimes grueling conditions made riding the range primarily a young man's profession. The largest age group of working cowboys was composed of men who were between ages twenty and twenty-five.

Q: What vital tool was called a "John B." by cowboys and why?

A: Cowboys commonly referred to their hats by this name, in honor of John B. Stetson, who developed the famous, beloved Stetson cowboy hat.

Q: Why did Texas rancher S. Burk Burnett brand his cattle "6666"?

A: The novel brand was a reminder of how the once-poor Burnett acquired his ranch and herd—with four sixes in a Fort Worth poker game.

Q: What was a "Judas steer"?

A: Used at almost every slaughterhouse during the days of the Old West, a Judas steer was an animal trained to lead other cattle to slaughter. As long as he performed, he escaped the meathook.

Q: What kind of lariat did most cowboys prefer?

A: Some ropers preferred a lariat made from the Mexican maguey plant; others chose a rope made from sisal (a derivative of the *Agave* plant); some liked rawhide lariats; many used lariats made of American or Russian hemp; but the most popular lariat in the Old West was made from imported Manila hemp, a product of the Philippine banana plant.

Q: How many head of cattle were sent East to market during the prime years of cattle driving?

A: Between 1866 and 1886 more than ten million head of cattle were shipped from the West to markets in the East.

Q: Besides saloons, gambling halls and brothels, what other diversions did Kansas cattle towns offer trail-driving cowboys?

A: Some cow towns were also equipped with bowling alleys and roller-skating rinks.

Q: What were cowboys referring to when they used the term "brand artist"?

A: In cowboy slang brand artists were livestock rustlers, who sometimes demonstrated artistic ability when altering an animal's brand.

Q: What two primary types of grass grew wild on the Western range during the era of the American cowboy?

A: The Old West's main varieties of wild grass—buffalo grass and grama grass—fattened millions of buffalo, which were later replaced by millions of cattle.

Q: When a cowboy was "airin' the lungs," what was he doing?
A: Cowhands so referred to their frequent practice of cursing.

Q: What famous Old West animal was described by those familiar with
    the beast as "tall, bony, coarse-headed, coarse-haired, flat-sided,
    thin-flanked . . . three-fifths horn and hooves and the rest hair"?
A: Westerners familiar with the breed so described the Texas longhorn
    steer.

Q: Why did so many cattlemen hate sheep?
A: Sheep competed for the open range and water holes, destroyed the
    range grass with their eating habits and sharp hooves and emitted
    a distinctive odor many cattlemen found unpleasant.

Q: Who was the "cattle king" of Colorado, and what common cowboy
    equipment did he usually leave at home?
A: Cattle baron John Wesley Iliff, who came West with $500 in the
    1850s, eventually became known as the cattle king because of his
    huge ranching interests, which sprawled across much of Colorado.
    Iliff was known throughout the state as a man who never wore a
    gun.

Q: Name at least five common uses for the cowboy's kerchief.
A: It was used to mask dust when trailing cattle; it served as an earmuff
    in cold weather; it protected the cowboy's neck from sunburn; it
    served as a towel for rain or sweat; it was an insulator for hot pot
    handles and branding irons; it could prevent snow blindness in
    winter; and it was used as a tourniquet or sling in an emergency.

Q: Who owned the Swan Land and Cattle Company, which held title
    to more than 60,000 head of cattle and ranched on more than
    600,000 acres of Wyoming and Nebraska rangeland?
A: Cattleman Alexander H. Swan, a part-owner, operated the com-
    pany, which was financed by investors in Scotland.

FACT: Cowboys really *did* sing to their cattle at night, to calm ner-
vous animals and to prevent stampedes. Some favorite cowboy
tunes were: "Old Dan Tucker," "The Texas Lullaby," "Nearer
My God to Thee," "The Old Time Religion," "In the Sweet
By and By" and "Jesus, Lover of My Soul."

Q: Why did cowboys prefer boots with pointed toes and high heels?

A: The heels were designed to lodge securely in the stirrup, and the pointed toes enabled a horseman to slip his foot easily in and out of the stirrup.

Q: In what year were the most cattle driven north to railheads from Texas?

A: The biggest year for Texas cattle drives was 1871, when more than 700,000 cattle were driven up the trails from Texas.

Q: When a cowboy put on his "Justins," what was he wearing?

A: Most Old West cowboys believed in going first-class when buying tools, so many bought their boots from the premier bootmaker of the Old West: Justin's of Texas. Cowboys called their footwear Justins and were properly dressed when they wore their Levi's, Stetson, Justins and Colt.

Q: Who was Theobald Smith, and what famous discovery of his made a major impact on the Old West?

A: In 1889 Dr. Theobald Smith, a medical researcher in Washington, D.C., discovered the cause of the deadly Texas fever spread by longhorn cattle to market states like Kansas, where it killed short-horn cattle by the thousands. The infamous fever, Smith discovered, was caused by ticks native to the South and Southwest, which were borne by the immune longhorns. Cattle dipping eradicated the disease.

Q: Who owned South Dakota's huge 73 Ranch, and what creature of the Old West did he try to rescue?

A: Scottish immigrant James ("Scotty") Philip was owner of 73 Ranch, which ran more than twenty thousand head of cattle. Married to a Cheyenne woman and the father of ten children, Philip feared the bison would be hunted to extinction, so he captured five buffalo calves and from them eventually built a herd of more than a thousand buffalo.

FACT: Despite dramatic episodes to the contrary in books and movies, a veteran cowboy never tried to stop a cattle stampede by firing his gun into the air—a futile act that would have been ignored by terrorized, stampeding cattle.

Q: On which side were cattle normally branded?
A: Most cattle were branded on the left hip.

Q: What major cattle trail was established in 1866 between Fort Belknap, Texas, and Fort Sumner, New Mexico, who established it and what happened to them?
A: The trail was established that year by cattlemen Charles Goodnight and Oliver Loving and became known as the Goodnight-Loving Trail. Loving was later killed by Indians on the trail bearing his name; Goodnight, on the other hand, died a wealthy man in his nineties in 1929.

Q: What cowboy occupation was known among cowpunchers as "gut robber," "dough-boxer," "Sallie," "greasy belly," "bean-master," "belly-cheater" and "biscuit shooter"?
A: All these names—and some less complimentary—were applied to ranch-house and trail-drive cooks. Above, a cowboy cook prepares supper at his chuck wagon. Dutch ovens await use in the foreground, sacks of flour are propped handily against a wagon wheel and bedrolls are stacked neatly atop the wagon.

Q: What was the standard recipe for cowboy coffee?
A: "A handful of coffee and a cup of water" were the normal ingredients.

Q: What were "the backhand slip," "forefooting," "heeling," "the pitch" and "the hoolihan"?
A: All were cowboy rope throws.

Q: Who was the most successful Texas trail driver?
A: John T. Lytle, a rancher and trail driver from Medina County, Texas, probably deserves this title. In fifteen years of trail driving he moved almost a half-million head of livestock from Texas to Kansas, Montana and Colorado—property worth an estimated nine million dollars.

Q: What was a "Little Mary" on a cattle drive?
A: A Little Mary was the driver of the calf wagon, a vehicle taken on some cattle drives to transport newborn calves.

Q: The bark of what Western tree was used by ranchers as horse feed?
A: Bark from the cottonwood tree, a favorite food of deer and elk, was shaved and cut up for horse feed by Western ranchers who claimed it was superior to other feed. When frozen in wintertime, however, the bark's edges would become razor sharp, making it too dangerous for consumption.

Q: What indispensable cowboy tool was produced by the Plymouth Cordage Company in Plymouth, Massachusetts?
A: The Plymouth Cordage Company was the principal supplier of rope to the Old West following the Civil War.

Q: Why were cattle dehorned by ranchers, and how was it done?
A: Horned cattle, especially the famed Texas longhorn, could be dangerous to man and horse and could also injure each other. For safety they were often dehorned by sawing off the horns, clipping the horns with store-bought mechanical dehorners or applying a chemical solution to the heads of calves.

Q: Which Kansas cattle town had the longest life as a boom market for Texas cattle drives?
A: The longest record as an active trail-driving market probably belongs to Baxter Springs, which lay on the Kansas end of the Shawnee Trail, and enjoyed ten years as a boom market.

Q: Why were unbranded cattle called "mavericks"?

A: According to the most popular theory, a South Carolinian named Samuel A. Maverick moved to Texas in the 1830s, acquired a large herd of cattle and neglected to brand the animals. As his unbranded cattle roamed over the Texas prairie, they became known as maverick cattle—a term that eventually was applied to all unmarked cattle.

Q: How did empty flour sacks contribute to healthy hygiene in the cowboy bunkhouse?

A: Flour sacks were commonly used as face and hand towels.

Q: Who owned the famous King Ranch of Texas, and how large was it?

A: The King Ranch belonged to Texan Richard King, who, by the end of the nineteenth century, owned more than one million acres on the Texas Gulf Coast, with more than 65,000 head of cattle and more than three hundred employees.

Q: What was a "jaw cracker," whose arrival sometimes sent shivers of dread through even the cockiest cowboy?

A: A jaw cracker was an itinerant dentist who traveled from ranch to ranch, practicing a crude form of dentistry on tooth-sore cowboys.

Q: What was the most common cause of stampedes on Old West cattle drives?

A: Thunder and lightning.

FACT: The .44-caliber Model 1873 Winchester repeating rifle—the successor to the popular 1866 Winchester—was the most popular saddle gun and shoulder arm among cowboys. The Winchester's distinctive lever-action design was patented in 1860 by B. Tyler Henry of New Haven, Connecticut, who produced the first model of the weapon as the Henry repeater. In 1867 Oliver F. Winchester founded the Winchester Repeating Arms Co. in New Haven, acquired Henry's patent and began manufacturing an improved model of the firearm as the Winchester repeating rifle. His Model 1873 Winchester was the weapon of choice in the West for more than twenty years.

Q: What was the lethal enemy of cattle that was borne by Western blowflies?

A: Cowboys constantly surveyed their herds for evidence of screw worms, which were laid in open wounds by blowflies and which caused the eventual death of large numbers of cattle in the Old West.

Q: How many head of cattle were driven from Texas to Kansas by Jesse Chisholm, the man for whom the famous Chisholm Trail was named?

A: None. Chisholm was not a cattleman; he was a trader. A Tennessee native of Scottish and Cherokee ancestry, Chisholm came West in the 1820s, established several Indian trading posts in what is now Kansas and cut a rutted wagon road that ran between Kansas and Texas—a trail that was later followed by countless cattle drives.

Q: How long was Dodge City, Kansas, a wild and woolly cattle town?

A: Dodge City's boom period as a cattle market for Texas drovers lasted barely nine years, from 1877 to 1885. An Old West photographer recorded this image during the town's boom years.

Q: What common cattle-drive device was known as "the possum belly" or "the coonie"?

A: The nicknames referred to a rawhide apron fastened underneath the chuck wagon and used to store dried cow chips or wood for use as emergency fuel.

Q: If a cowboy spent his time in the "hoosegow," where would he be?

A: In jail. "Hoosegow" was derived from the Spanish word *juzgado*, which referred to a court of justice and was cowboy slang for the jailhouse.

Q: When cattle shipped by rail to market were let off the railroad cars for their daily feed and water, what was the first thing steers would normally do—and why would cowboys not let them do it?

A: Cattle packed into railroad cars did not have room to lie down and rest, so when let off to feed they would usually lie down. Vigilant cowboys prodded them to their feet so they would not be trampled to death.

Q: In the parlance of the Old West cowman, what was a "mail-order cowboy"?

A: The derogatory phrase was applied to tenderfoot "cowboys" from the East, who came West attired in custom-designed Western finery.

Q: What was the first railhead cattle market established in Kansas to receive Texas cattle drives?

A: Abilene became first when it received a herd of Texas beef in 1867 and shipped the animals East by rail.

Q: What Western city was touted as the richest city in the world in 1884, based on per capita income?

A: Cheyenne, Wyoming, which had a population of seven thousand in 1884, acquired this reputation due to its large population of millionaire cattlemen.

Q: Where was the famous Stetson cowboy hat first produced?

A: In 1865, after a stint in the arid West to improve his health, New Jersey hat maker John B. Stetson began manufacturing the famous Stetson hat, which was designed for wear on the Western range. By the end of the nineteenth century Stetson's 3,500 employees were producing two million hats a year, but in 1865, when he made his first order, Stetson produced the hats himself in a Philadelphia shop.

Q: What prominent Dakota Territory rancher eventually became governor—of New York?

A: Theodore Roosevelt, who also became vice-president and president, was elected governor of New York in 1898, eight years after he ended his three-year stint as a rancher in what is now North Dakota.

Q: What creature of the range was known to cowboys as a "nice kitty," a "piket," a "wood pussy" or a "pole cat"?

A: The skunk.

Q: If a cattleman hired 165 cowboys and used a thousand horses to move 45,000 cattle from Texas to Montana in 1884—with expenses of approximately $45,000 and a 3 percent loss of stock—how much profit could he expect to make from the cattle drive?

A: Given this typical overhead, a cattleman could expect to realize a profit of $125,000 from such a cattle drive.

Q: Where and when was the first Old West rodeo?

A: From California to the Mississippi, numerous communities lay claim to the "original" Western rodeo. Prescott, Arizona, claims it was first; Pecos, Texas, staged an American-style rodeo on July 4, 1883; Payson, Arizona, did likewise the following year and claims the oldest consecutive annual rodeo; but Santa Fe, New Mexico, may hold the record with a history of roping and throwing contests dating back to 1847.

Q: Where did cowboy artist Charles Russell receive his art training?

A: Russell was a self-taught artist who rose from the stature of a gifted hobbyist to become perhaps the most revered of all Western artists.

Q: What settlement was the last stop for supplies and mail for cattle drives going from Texas to Dodge City on the Western Trail?

A: Located at a crossing of the Red River on the southwest border of present-day Oklahoma, Doan's Store was the last chance for the cattle companies to stock canned goods and for cowpokes to receive letters from home.

Q: Why did cowman R. O. Watkins of Texas choose the brand "3" for his cattle?

A: Watkins, who ranched in Texas in the 1850s, was also a preacher, and he chose "3" as his brand to honor the Holy Trinity: God the Father, God the Son and God the Holy Spirit.

Q: What cowboy left a bloodstained account of his battle with hired gunmen in the 1892 Johnson County War, which pitted Wyoming's large ranchers against the territory's nesters and settlers?

A: Accused of rustling by the cattlemen and besieged by their hired gunmen, cowboy Nate Champion penned what would become a memorable diary moments before he was burned out of his cabin and shot to death in the 1892 conflict.

Q: How fast could prairie fires travel?

A: The speed of prairie fires was affected by the condition of the grass and the strength of the wind, so speeds varied. Aided by strong winds, prairie fires were known to have overtaken men on horseback traveling at a gallop.

Q: What was the "Montana Pinch," which was so common among cowboys of the northern plains in the 1880s?

A: The Montana Pinch was a style of cowboy hat with a distinctive pointed crown pinched in on four sides, much like a twentieth-century Army drill instructor's hat.

Q: Who invented the chuck wagon, which became standard equipment on cattle drives?

A: The origin of the chuck wagon is obscure, but the likeliest inventor was Texas ranching giant Charles Goodnight, who reportedly converted an old government-issue wagon to his specifications—which included iron axles and a chuck box in the rear for foodstuffs.

Q: When a cowboy "tailed" a steer, what was he doing?

A: To stop a wild steer, a cowboy would sometimes ride alongside the animal, grab its tail and turn the animal head over heels. The practice, called tailing, would usually knock the wind from the beast and leave it docile.

Q: What was a cowboy's "apple"?

A: His saddle horn.

Q: When Abel Head "Shanghai" Pierce, a self-made millionaire cattleman from Texas, learned that no rooms were available in the Arkansas hotel he visited one year, how did he react?

A: He wrote a $15,000 check for half-interest in the hotel, evicted one of his guests, and checked into one of his newly purchased rooms.

Q: What Abilene, Kansas, establishment did cowboys declare to be the best hotel on the plains in 1868?

A: Built at a cost of $15,000, the Drovers Cottage earned this reputation with forty rooms, a billiard parlor, a restaurant and a barroom —all designed to serve trail-worn cowboys.

Q: What was a "die-up"—feared by cattle ranchers throughout the West?

A: A die-up was the mass death of cattle during a brutal Western blizzard or a prolonged drought, calamities that sometimes wiped out entire herds.

Q: What were the "wreck pan" and the "squirrel can" found in every cowboy chuck wagon?

A: On cattle drives the company cook produced a wreck pan in which the trail hands would put their dirty dishes, and a squirrel can in which food scraps were tossed.

Q: What were the "makin's" carried by most Old West cowboys?

A: Makin's were cigarette paper and tobacco, the ingredients of the "roll-your-own" cigarettes used by most cowboys.

Q: What region became known as Arizona's "dark and bloody ground" and why?

A: Pleasant Valley, in Arizona's Tonto Basin, acquired this name from the bloody Pleasant Valley War of the 1880s, which pitted three of the area's ranching families against each other in a deadly family feud.

FACT: In 1850 a San Francisco merchant who was left with an unsold surplus of canvas converted the material into work pants, which he sold with surprising success to the prospectors pouring into San Francisco during the California Gold Rush. Demand for more of the durable trousers led the merchant to produce britches made of tough blue denim strengthened with copper rivets. The product was perfected just in time for the cowboy era and became standard wear in the West. The innovative San Francisco merchant, Levi Strauss, became rich, and his tough trousers—"Levi's"—became an American legend.

Q: When a cowboy toted his "war bag," what was he carrying?

A: A cowboy's war bag was the sack in which he stored his meager personal possessions: an extra set of clothes, extra ammunition, spare parts for equipment repairs, playing cards, maybe a harmonica, the bill of sale for his horse, cigarette paper, tobacco and maybe some worn letters from his mother or a faraway young lady.

Q: At what time of year were cattle driven north from Texas to the railhead markets in Kansas?

A: The first herds usually arrived in Kansas in early June, and cattle continued to arrive throughout the summer, with the final herd usually appearing in mid-September.

Q: What was rancher Richard King's profession before he became the owner of the giant King Ranch, and what was his place of birth?

A: King was born in New York City and was a steamboat captain before becoming a rancher.

Q: What were cowboys talking about when they referred to the "doghouse," the "dive," the "shack," the "dump," the "dicehouse" or the "ram pasture"?

A: All were names cowboys applied to the ranch bunkhouse. These cowpunchers near Holbrook, Arizona, pose in front of a better-than-average bunkhouse.

Q: What Old West rancher was known to Indians as "Big Heart White Man" and ran a ranch cowboys called the "Headquarters for Hospitality"?

A: Andrew Voigt, a German immigrant who became one of North Dakota's premier ranchers, earned tributes from red men and white men alike for his unequaled generosity.

Q: What was the first thing a cowboy did with a new pair of spurs?

A: Ranchers were quick to fire cowboys who injured the stock with sharp spurs, so cowboys usually blunted the rowel points on a new pair of spurs before wearing them. A good horseman used a light touch to control his mount and carefully avoided injuring the animal.

Q: What was the "jinglebob" method of identifying cattle?

A: A jinglebob was a type of earmark in which a steer's ear was sliced deeply enough to leave half of it flopping—a distinctive earmark easily spotted by drovers but disliked by many cattlemen for humane reasons.

Q: What public structure in Texas was built in exchange for three million acres of rangeland?

A: The Texas state capitol in Austin, which was finished in 1888, was built by the Chicago contracting firm Taylor, Babcock and Company in exchange for three million acres of Texas rangeland, on which the company established the giant XIT Ranch.

Q: What was the difference between a blizzard and a "norther" to cowboys of the Old West?

A: The only difference was geographical: what was known as a blizzard in most of the West was called a norther in the Southwest because most blizzards came from the north.

Q: What bizarre event temporarily stopped the shooting at the Tewksbury ranch on September 2, 1887, during Arizona's infamous Pleasant Valley War?

A: On this date the bloody feud among the Tewksbury, Graham and Bleven families resulted in the death of John Tewksbury at his ranch in a shootout with a party of Grahams. The shooting temporarily stopped when Tewksbury's widow left her ranch house to chase away hogs that were rooting around her late husband's body. After she buried him, the shooting resumed.

Q: Who was Jacob Karotofsky, and what did he do for cowboys?

A: A German immigrant who had come West to make his fortune, Karotofsky operated a huge Western-wear store—Karotofsky's Great Western Store—in Abilene, Kansas, during its boom years as a cattle town. He sold hats, boots, clothes and general merchandise to cowboys, and as the cattle market shifted to other towns, he moved his store accordingly.

Q: What was the "night hawk" on a cattle drive?

A: The night hawk was the luckless cowboy whose job was guarding the drovers' saddle horses during the night.

Q: What were the "swallow fork," the "steeple fork," the "underslope," the "overslope," the "undersharp," the "oversharp," the "bit," the "split" and the "crop"?

A: All were earmarks used to identify cattle in the Old West. Cutting the cattle's ears reinforced the owner's brand and made identification easier when cattle were in a herd or in brush where the brand could not be seen. Here Oklahoma cowboys halt their herd beside a water hole.

FACT: The first successful long-range American cattle drive from Texas occurred in 1866, when veteran frontiersman Nelson Story recruited a well-armed company of cowboys to move 2,500 head of Texas beef from the Lone Star State to western Montana. Despite Indians, outlaws, badlands, distance and snowstorms, Story got his herd through—and made cowboy history.

Q: How long was the famous Chisholm Trail in use as a cattle-driving route?

A: The favored trail from Texas to Kansas, the Chisholm Trail was in steady use for less than twenty years, becoming an established cattle trail in 1868 and seeing continued use until 1885, by which time most cattle were shipped by rail.

Q: Who was Richard Grant, and how was he a pioneer in the cattle industry of the Old West?

A: A fur trader at Fort Hall on the Oregon Trail, Richard Grant traded provisions for weary cattle brought up the trail by emigrants between 1843 and 1855. After acquiring a herd of more than six hundred cattle, Grant sold them and retired, becoming perhaps the first successful cattle rancher on the northern plains.

Q: What were "woollies" and "shotguns" and why did cowboys use them?

A: Both were styles of chaps or *chaparejos*—leather britches or wrap-around leggings that cowboys wore in dense thickets to prevent injuries to their legs while chasing cattle.

Q: What was the most common cause of death among working cowboys?

A: Only a slim minority of cowpunchers died from violent acts; the largest single cause of death was horse-related accidents.

Q: What was the cowboy job of "grub-line riding," and when was it performed?

A: During the winter, when little work was available, unemployed cowboys drifted from ranch to ranch, working at odd jobs or doing chores for meals, a seasonal practice cowboys called grub-line riding.

Q: What were the "ring," the "curb," the "half-breed" and the "spade"?

A: All were types of horse bits used by cowboys of the Old West. The curb bit, which was easier on the horse's mouth, was one of the most common.

Q: Over what trail were more than a quarter-million cattle driven *east* to market between 1869 and 1875?

A: Although seldom thought of as a cattle trail, the Oregon Trail moved at least 250,000 cattle during these years from eastern Oregon to southeastern Idaho, where the animals were turned north to be marketed to Montana's miners.

Q: What cattlemen's clubhouse, erected in 1881 in Wyoming, boasted fine wines, paintings by famous artists, billiard tables for its patrons, professional servants from the East and a library stocked with journals ranging from the *Breeder's Gazette* to the *New York Tribune*?

A: Restricted to wealthy cattlemen, the Cheyenne Club of Cheyenne, Wyoming, boasted all these amenities in the 1880s.

Q: Where did the rodeo practice of "bulldogging" originate, and why was it so named?

A: Cowboy Bill Pickett, a rodeo star with the 101 Ranch Wild West Show, is said to have introduced bulldogging by jumping from his horse and grabbing the horns of a running steer, which he would bring to a sudden stop by biting the animal's lip. Pickett apparently was influenced by reports of bulldogs controlling cattle by chomping on the creatures' lips; therefore he reportedly dubbed his unusual technique bulldogging.

FACT: Abel Head "Shanghai" Pierce, a prominent Texas cattleman, searched for years for a breed of cattle that would be immune to tick fever. His hunt for immune animals led him to examine breeds from Texas to Europe to the Far East. Finally, just prior to his death and about the same time a cure for tick fever was found, Pierce located a breed of cattle that met his criteria and imported them into the West. His candidate for the best all-around feverless cattle came from India, and he is today credited with introducing the Brahman breed into America.

Q: What disaster befell the cattle industry on the northern plains in 1886–87?

A: A savage winter, the worst in memory, destroyed hundreds of thousands of cattle and put countless cattlemen out of business.

Q: What federal post was held by affluent Montana rancher Granville Stuart, and what was his first job in the West?

A: In 1894 Stuart left his huge ranch holdings to become U.S. minister to Uruguay and Paraguay. He had come to Montana in 1858 as a gold prospector.

Q: How much money did cowboys earn on trail drives?

A: While the trail boss might earn $125 a month, cowboys like this one could expect to draw between $25 and $40 a month for driving cattle to market.

Q: Cattle rancher C. C. Slaughter, once the largest single landowner in Texas, was named for what famous figure?
A: Owner of a Texas ranch that measured fifty miles by eighty miles, Slaughter was known by the initials C. C., which stood for Christopher Columbus.

Q: What development ended the famous cattle drives from Texas to Kansas and also ended the wild and lawless atmosphere that brought notoriety to prairie hamlets like Dodge City and Abilene?
A: In 1885 the Kansas legislature barred Texas longhorns from Kansas because the beasts transmitted the deadly Texas fever to the native shorthorn stock, killing the Kansas cattle by the thousands. By the time a cure for the disease was discovered several years later, most Texas cattle were being shipped to market by rail, bypassing the once-booming cow towns of Kansas.

Q: Why did cattle-drive cooks throw their dirty dishwater under the chuck wagon?
A: The practice was designed to discourage drowsy cowhands from sneaking under the wagon for a nap in the shade, and protected the cook's hallowed domain.

Q: With what kind of plumbing were cowboy bunkhouses equipped?
A: Plumbing was rare in the Old West. Most bunkhouses were supplied with water from a nearby well, spring or creek, so bathing was occasional and was performed in a tub near the fire in winter or in a creek in warm weather. Toilet facilities were usually located in a wooden privy a discreet distance from the bunkhouse, and a well-equipped ranch might boast a four-seater outhouse.

Q: What was meant when a cowboy was said to have "sold his saddle"?
A: The phrase was a cowboy colloquialism that meant the cowboy in question had finally retired from the range.

7 | Words from the West

Q: What circumstances prompted this observation: "Floors are a luxury here, and I noticed yesterday a member of our family making up his bed with a hoe"?

A: An Old West homesteader made this observation upon surveying the interior of her sod house one day.

Q: Who offered this inducement: "Forward! If any man is killed, I will make him a corporal"?

A: Captain Adna R. Chaffee made this promise to his troops as they prepared to do battle with Cheyenne, Comanche and Kiowa warriors during the Red River War of 1874–75.

Q: Who said, "You damn dirty cow thief, if you're anxious to fight, I'll meet you!"?

A: Wyatt Earp issued this challenge to cowboy Ike Clanton shortly before Earp, Clanton and others shot it out in the famous gunfight at the O.K. Corral.

Q: About what Western tool was it said, "It will take on weight with age and get to the point where you can smell it across the room, but you can't wear it out"?

A: A Western traveler so described the proverbial cowboy hat.

Q: What Old West figure was described this way by a companion: *"Le fou,* the fool, is the name by which he is commonly known. No sooner does the boat touch the shore than he leaps out, and when his attention is arrested by a plant or flower everything else is forgotten"?

A: Thomas Nuttall, the famous naturalist, was the object of this critique, expressed by a member of the 1811 expedition that took Nuttall up the Missouri River to gather samples of Western flora.

Q: What Old West tool was advertised with the boast that it "takes no room, exhausts no soil, shades no vegetation, is proof against high winds, makes no snowdrifts, and is both durable and cheap"?

A: Barbed wire.

Q: What Old West business establishments were so described by an observer: "The lumber used often warped badly, being more or less green. The structures stood propped up one or two feet above ground. Each had a front flare on which the owner boldly printed the name of his place"?

A: The businesses so described were the typical cow-town saloons, like these photographed in Hazen, Nevada.

Q: Who said, "I never want to leave this country; all my relatives are lying here in the ground, and when I fall to pieces I am going to fall to pieces here"?

A: The Sioux leader Wolf Necklace so expressed his opposition to moving to a reservation away from traditional Sioux territory.

Q: Who said, "Boys, I believe I've found a gold mine"?

A: James W. Marshall, whose discovery of gold launched the California Gold Rush, reportedly uttered this understatement to skeptical workers at the sawmill where Marshall plucked a nugget from the American River.

Q: What Old West community rated this description: "Money and whiskey flowed like water downhill, and youth and beauty and womanhood and manhood were wrecked and damned in that valley of perdition"?

A: Abilene, Kansas, and its red-light district were so condemned by one of its law-abiding citizens during Abilene's heyday as a cattle market.

Q: Members of what Indian tribe were said to be "almost as awkward as a monkey on the ground, without a limb or branch to cling to, but the moment he lays his hands upon his horse his face even becomes handsome, and he gracefully flies away like a different being"?

A: Noted for their remarkable horsemanship, the Comanches of the southern plains were remembered with these words by an early-nineteenth-century traveler.

FACT: When railroad czar Grenville M. Dodge was building the Union Pacific Railroad across the West, his crewmen were beset by an army of gamblers, thugs and prostitutes that followed the railroad across the Western wilds in search of profits. Union Pacific official Jack Casement, who supervised the track laying in the field, was ordered to clamp down on the offenders and responded by hanging several of them. When Dodge inquired if the gamblers and thugs were quiet, Casement replied, "You bet they are, General. They're out in the graveyard."

Q: What famous Old West figure was so recalled by his wife: "He wore troop-boots reaching to his knees, buckskin britches fringed on the sides, a dark navy blue shirt with a broad collar, a red necktie whose ends floated over his shoulder. . . . On the broad felt hat that was almost a sombrero was fastened a slight mark of his rank"?

A: General George Armstrong Custer was so remembered by his wife, Elizabeth ("Libbie") Custer.

Q: Who was so described: "He is universally despised by all the officers of his regiment excepting his relatives and one or two sycophants"?

A: General George Armstrong Custer was so remembered by a member of his command.

Q: These words by explorer Meriwether Lewis described what Western animal: "They appear to be of excellent race, elegantly formed, active, and durable"?

A: Lewis so praised the carefully bred Appaloosa horses, which were a tribal trademark of the Nez Percé Indians.

Q: To whom did Geronimo make this statement: "There are many men in the world who are big chiefs and command many people, but you, I think, are the greatest of them all. I want you to be a father to me and treat me as your son. . . . I am now in your hands"?

A: With these words Geronimo surrendered to General George Crook in 1883.

Q: Who delivered this critique of Apache leader Geronimo: "I don't want to hear anything from Geronimo. He is such a liar that I can't believe anything he says"?

A: General George Crook, to whom Geronimo twice pledged his surrender, offered this opinion prior to a meeting with the old warrior in 1890.

Q: What event prompted this observation: "In whatever direction we go, we see nothing but melancholy wrecks of human life. The tents are still standing on every hill, but no rising smoke announces the presence of human beings, and no sounds but the croaking of the raven and the howling of the wolf, interrupt the fearful silence"?

A: A visitor to the northern plains so described the region after the smallpox epidemic of 1837 swept through the area, decimating the Indian population.

Q: Where and by whom was this offer made: "I now want every man who is determined to stay here and die with me to come across this line"?

A: Colonel William B. Travis, commander of the Texans defending the Alamo, reportedly issued this invitation to his troops—and all but one chose to stay and fight.

Q: Who said, "I did not intend that any of the band would get the drop on me if I could help it"?

A: This thoughtful explanation was delivered by Wyatt Earp in a post-action analysis of the gunfight at the O.K. Corral.

Q: What nature of work was solicited with these words: "The subscriber wishes to engage one hundred young men to ascend the Missouri River to its source, there to be employed for one, two, or three years"?

A: With this advertisement in a St. Louis newspaper, fur merchant William H. Ashley recruited trappers for the 1822 expedition that helped launch the golden era of the American mountain men.

Q: What prompted this desperate message: "Came to these hills in 1833. All ded but me Ezra kind. Killed by [Indians] beyond the high hill. Got our gold. 1834 . . . I hav lost my gun and nothing to eat and indians hunting me"?

A: On March 14, 1887, South Dakota stonecutter Louis Thoen discovered a sandstone slab inscribed with these words at the foot of Lookout Mountain near Spearfish, South Dakota. The slab, which became known as the Thoen Stone, apparently recorded the fate of a party of early gold miners killed by Indians in 1834.

▶

Q: Who issued this angry statement and why: "The Great Father sends us presents and wants us to sell him the road, but White Chief goes with soldiers to steal the road before Indians say yes or no"?

A: Chief Red Cloud of the Oglala Sioux used these words in 1866 to angrily denounce the U.S. government, which posted troops on the Bozeman Trail in Sioux country while negotiating with the Sioux for a right-of-way. Red Cloud went to war over the issue and forced the Army to temporarily abandon its forts on a long stretch of the trail.

Q: Who said, "We are rough men and used to rough ways"?

A: Old West outlaw Bob Younger stated this creed to a newspaper
     reporter following the famous 1876 Northfield, Minnesota, Raid.

Q: Who said, "Men jumped off the train at every stop and all the
     others wanted to"?

A: A recruit to the Seventh Cavalry following the Custer Massacre
     later recalled how some would-be soldiers escaped the appalling
     conditions on trains taking the new soldiers west in 1876.

Q: For whom was this verse penned?
                      Over the Rocky Mountains' height,
                      Like ocean in its tided night,
                      the living sea rolls onward, on!

A: An 1858 guidebook for emigrants to the West included this poem
     as an encouragement to pioneers.

Q: Who voiced this exasperated plea: "Leave me alone and let me go
     to hell by my own route"?

A: The sentiment was expressed by the notorious Calamity Jane
     shortly before her death in Deadwood, South Dakota, in 1903.

Q: What river of the Old West was described by nineteenth-century
     observers as "a thousand miles long and six inches deep—the most
     magnificent and the most useless of rivers"?

A: The Platte River, which crossed a great swath of the Old West,
     was a mile wide in some places at flood stage and yet was riddled
     with sand bars and shallows. Its unique personality rated this de-
     scription.

Q: Under what circumstances was this offer made: "Here's one, lady,
     that's already saucered and blowed"?

A: A proper matron from the East entered a Western train station and
     demanded a quick cup of coffee during a ten-minute train stop. She
     was dismayed to receive a cup of boiling-hot coffee, Western-style,
     but an obliging cowboy seated nearby issued this generous offer.

Q: About whom was it said that he "will sigh to lose his friend, groan
     if his wife dies, but if his dog is lost by death, his grief is over-
     whelming"?

A: A sheepherder of the West and his devotion to his sheepdog were
     so depicted by a nineteenth-century reporter.

Q: Who said, "The Seventh can handle anything it meets"?

A: General George A. Custer made this ill-fated prediction while declining reinforcements for the U.S. Seventh Cavalry en route to the Battle of the Little Big Horn.

Q: About whom was it said: "They consider their life a servitude, and being beaten at times like animals, and receiving no sort of sympathy, it acts upon them accordingly"?

A: Sioux women were so described by a white woman who had lived with them for a long time as a captive.

Q: Who delivered this cheery, inaccurate opinion: "The route to the mouth of the Columbia is easy, safe, and expeditious"?

A: Virginia Congressman John Floyd, who had never made the trip, so encouraged Americans to go west to Oregon. Thousands of grave sites along the Oregon Trail would give his words a hollow ring.

Q: What infamous character of the Old West was remembered with this profile: "He is, in all, quite a handsome looking fellow, the only imperfection being two prominent front teeth slightly protruding like squirrel's teeth, and he has agreeable and winning ways"?

A: Billy the Kid.

Q: Whose appearance produced this description: "I cannot express my surprise at beholding a small, stoop-shouldered man, with reddish hair, freckled face, soft blue eyes, and nothing to indicate extraordinary courage or daring"?

A: A Western visitor penned this description of Kit Carson after an encounter with the famous scout.

FACT: Chief Washakie of the Shoshones was a leader of his tribe throughout the Western Indian Wars—for more than half a century. He kept his tribe at peace, negotiated a large reservation in Wyoming's Wind River region, led his warriors in campaigns against the Sioux and was eventually honored by the U.S. government by the naming of Fort Washakie in his honor. When he died in his nineties, these were his last words to his people: "You now have that for which we so long and bravely fought. Keep it forever in peace and honor."

Q: Who said, "Carpenter, you have spilled the whiskey!"?
A: This unemotional observation was made by riverman Mike Fink after he killed a friend named Carpenter while attempting to shoot a tin cup of whiskey off the man's head.

Q: About whom was it said, "A man afoot is no man at all"?
A: Dependent on horses for livelihood and survival, cowboys often used this adage to stress the importance of being mounted.

Q: Who said, "You are fools to make yourselves slaves to a piece of fat bacon, some hardtack, and a little sugar and coffee"?
A: With these words Chief Sitting Bull, a leader of the nonreservation Sioux in the 1870s, derided the Sioux who had chosen to live on the reservation.

Q: About what was it said: "They jes' pour off the North Pole with nothin' to stop 'em but barbed-wire"?
A: An old cowhand so described the blizzards that could sweep across the Western range from northern Canada.

Q: "There is no law, no restraint in this seething cauldron of vice and depravity" described what Old West community?
A: A reporter for the *New York Tribune* so described Abilene, Kansas, in its boom years as a cattle town.

Q: Who penned this note in his diary: "Attended the Sabbath school this A.M. and was delighted as it was the most pleasant hour I have spent since leaving home"?
A: An unusually devout cowboy made this entry after rejecting the dance halls and gambling tables of an end-of-the-trail cow town in favor of a morning spent in Sunday school.

Q: Under what circumstances was this statement made: "I see a good many enemies around, and mighty few friends"?
A: Texas gunman Bill Longley, who claimed to have killed thirty-two victims, so expressed himself moments before he was hanged in 1877.

Q: What group of Westerners were described with these words: "They feast, they fiddle, they drink, they sing, they dance, they frolic, and they fight"?
A: An observer so described Rocky Mountain fur trappers enjoying a Rendezvous.

Q: Who made this callous statement and how did it come back to haunt him: "If they're hungry, let 'em eat grass for all I care"?

A: Minnesota Indian trader Andrew J. Myrick commented in this way on the plight of hungry Santee Sioux shortly before they launched the bloody Minnesota Uprising of 1862. Myrick was one of the first killed—he was found later with his mouth stuffed with grass.

Q: What prompted this sentiment: "After some hours occupied in this excursion, I descended to the encampment, much gratified with what I had seen of the works of God"?

A: Samuel Parker, a missionary to the Indians, was moved to express his thoughts in this manner after viewing Wyoming's Grand Teton Mountains in 1835.

Q: What structure was so described by its inhabitant: "The wind whistled through the walls in winter and the dust blew in in summer, but we papered the walls with newspapers and made rag carpets for the floor, and we thought we were living well"?

A: A pioneer homemaker recalled her log home in the wilds of the Old West with these words. These women photographed outside their cabin in New Mexico Territory in 1895 would have understood her sentiments.

Q: Who made this request and why: "As I have spent nearly eight years of the hardest work of my life in this department, I respectfully request that I may now be relieved from its command"?

A: With these words General George Crook resigned command of the Department of Arizona in 1886, after Army officials in Washington overturned the terms of surrender he had offered Apache leader Geronimo.

Q: About whom did a veteran frontiersman so comment: "They laid in an over-supply of bacon, flour and beans, and in addition thereto every conceivable jimcrack and useless article that the wildest fancy could devise or human ingenuity could invent—pins and needles, brooms and brushes, ox shoes and horse shoes, lasts and leather, glass beads and hawkbells, jumping jacks and jews-harps, rings and bracelets, pocket mirrors and pocketbooks, calico vests and boiled shirts"?

A: This catalog was compiled by an observer watching the packing practices of emigrant families heading West by wagon train.

Q: About whom was it said: "Father at times wished that he could see, and only have his eyesight back again, so that he could go back out to see the mountains. I know he at times would feel lonesome, and long to see some of his old mountain friends to have a good chat of olden times back in the fifties . . ."?

A: Mountain man Jim Bridger, old and blind, was so described by his daughter, who witnessed his last years on a farm in Missouri.

Q: Members of what organization were said to be able to "ride like a Mexican, track like a Comanche, shoot like a Kentuckian, and fight like the devil"?

A: The Texas Rangers.

FACT: Mountain man Jim Bridger, like his fellow trappers, enjoyed spinning yarns designed to baffle greenhorns and Easterners. Bridger once told listeners that he had discovered a petrified forest where "a peetrified bird was sitting on a peetrified limb singing a peetrified song." The veteran mountain man's colorful stories—even the true ones—eventually became known as "Bridger's Lies."

Q: Who was so described: "Their blue navy shirts, broad brimmed hats, belts stuffed with cartridges, and loose handkerchiefs knotted around the neck, gave them a wild, bushwhacker appearance, which was in amusing contrast with their polished and gentlemanly manners"?

A: Officers of the U.S. Cavalry were so depicted in 1876 as they arrived at a frontier post from the field, attired as usual in nonregulation dress.

Q: Who was it who said, "A spirit of hatred and revenge took possession of me"?

A: Notorious California bandit Tiburcio Vásquez issued this statement before he was hanged for his crimes in 1875.

Q: Why was it said: "There is no Sunday west of St. Louis—and no God west of Fort Smith"?

A: This familiar frontier adage referred to the irreverent behavior found on the wild Western frontier in general and the widespread lawlessness found particularly in Indian Territory—which later became Oklahoma.

Q: Who delivered this speech and under what circumstances: "I am tired of fighting. . . . The old men are killed. . . . It is cold and we have no blankets. The little children are freezing to death. . . . I am tired; my heart is sick and sad. From where the sun now stands, I will fight no more forever"?

A: Chief Joseph of the Nez Percé spoke these words as he surrendered to Colonel Nelson A. Miles on October 5, 1877, ending the Nez Percé War.

Q: Who said, "No more battles and blood. From this sun, we will have a good time on both sides, your band and mine"?

A: Colonel Nelson A. Miles accepted Chief Joseph's surrender with these words.

Q: About whom did General William T. Sherman observe: "I know no way to satisfy his ambitions but to surrender to him absolute power over the whole Army, with President and Congress thrown in"?

A: Sherman so characterized the aggressive and ambitious Indian fighter Colonel Nelson A. Miles in 1878.

Q: Who said, "So long as there remains a gopher to eat, I will not go back"?

A: Sioux leader Sitting Bull so vowed his determination not to return to the United States after taking his followers to safety in Canada. Eventually starvation forced his people to move onto an American reservation.

Q: Who said, "It was a thing to melt the heart of a man, if it was of stone, to see those little children, with their bodies shot to pieces, thrown naked into the pit"?

A: A white member of the burial detail at Wounded Knee so recalled his feelings while burying the Indian victims of the 1890 Wounded Knee Massacre.

Q: What prompted this recollection: "Dat make me so mad I walk into de herd an' I walk right along wid de sheep, an' I catch up wid de bear. Den I take out my knife an' I cut he's throat!"?

A: With those words, a Basque sheepherder in Montana recalled his anger over the killing of his beloved sheepdog by a bear, an act that prompted the sheepman to attack the bear with a knife.

Q: What Old West professional was so described: "His skin, from constant exposure, assumes a hue almost as dark as that of the Aborigine. . . . His hair, through inattention, becomes long, coarse, and bushy, and loosely dangles on his shoulders. . . . His waist is encircled with a belt of leather, holding encased his butcher-knife and pistols"?

A: A mountain man of the 1830s so recalled the appearance of his fellow trappers.

Q: What experience produced this emotional recollection: "Starting out ahead of the team and my men folks, when I thought I had gone beyond hearing distance, I would throw myself down on the unfriendly desert and give way like a child to sobs and tears, wishing myself back home with my friends"?

A: A young woman who took the trail West with her husband in 1860 so recalled the difficulties of the trek westward.

Q: Under what circumstances was it said: "I believed that I was right. I hoped for the best, and pressed onward"?

A: Old West pioneer Joel Palmer so expressed his determination to go West in 1845.

Q: About what creature was this gruesome observation made: "Unless shot through the lungs or spine, they invariably escape; and even when struck through the very heart, they will frequently run a considerable distance before falling to the ground"?

A: The buffalo.

Q: What beverage was so popular among the men and women of the Old West that a period observer described it as "unfailing and apparently indispensable . . . served at every meal—even under the broiling noonday sun"?

A: The words describe the favored drink of the Old West: coffee— served black and boiling-hot. Here, a well-armed group of Western-ers keeps the coffee warm on an Idaho ranch in 1872.

Q: About what was it said: "They were in a great hurry to get out—
no order at all; every man was for himself"?

A: The retreat of the troops under Major Marcus Reno at the Battle
of the Little Big Horn was so recalled by interpreter F. F. Girard,
who witnessed it.

Q: Who said, "That was a charge, sir"?

A: Major Marcus Reno so described his retreat at the Little Big Horn.

Q: What prompted a Wyoming newspaper to huff: "Some morning we
will wake up to find that a corporation has run a wire fence about
the boundary lines of Wyoming"?

A: The editorial grumbling was a response to the explosive erection of
barbed wire throughout the western plains in the 1880s.

Q: What did these cowboy commands mean: "Grubpile! Come a-
runnin', fellers!" "Boneheads! Boneheads! Take it away!" "Roll
out! Roll out! While she's hot!" and "Wake up, snakes, and bite a
biscuit!"?

A: All were calls used by cattle-drive cooks to summon the hands to
meals.

Q: Who said that "a woman with a party of men is a token of peace,"
and why?

A: Explorer William Clark made the observation upon noting the
success with which the Shoshone guide Sacagawea established
peaceful relations with Indians encountered by the explorers during
the Lewis and Clark Expedition.

Q: What prompted this unnerving memory: "Of all the eerie, dreary
experiences, to be lost at night on the prairie . . . then to hear the
chorus of coyotes, like hyenas, laughing at one's predicament"?

A: An emigrant so recalled her fear when she and her fellow travelers
temporarily lost their bearings while crossing the Great Plains.

FACT: Visitors to an isolated homestead far out on the Great Plains
found this inscription scrawled on the door of the vacant
cabin by the defeated settler who had once lived there: "250
miles to the nearest post office; 100 miles to wood; 20 miles
to water; 6 inches to hell. Gone to live with wife's folks."

Q: What adventure provoked this outburst: "All I hope for is to get home, alive, as soon as possible, so that I can forget it"?

A: A disenchanted Forty-niner, his visions of treasure gone, expressed this sentiment after striking out in the California Gold Rush.

Q: Whose obituary was so put: "No one left his home cold or hungry"?

A: Trader Jesse Chisholm, founder of the famous Chisholm Trail, was so remembered by an inscription on his tombstone.

Q: Whose words were these: "If any young man is about to commence in the world . . . we say to him publicly and privately, go to the West. There your capacities are sure to be appreciated and your industry and energy rewarded"?

A: Horace Greeley, editor of the *New York Tribune*, so urged young men to go West in the 1850s.

Q: What jurist reportedly called court into session thusly: "Hear ye! Hear ye! This honorable court's now in session. If any galoot wants a snort before we start, let him step up and name his pizen!"?

A: Heralded as "the law west of the Pecos," Judge Roy Bean of Langtry, Texas, was said to have used these words to open court in the barroom-turned-courtroom where he dispensed justice and whiskey.

Q: Who held this view of womanhood: "He felt that a man was pretty low that would bring a woman in contact with dirt. . . . He wanted to look up to her. He wanted her feminine with frills and fluffs all over. He had no use for those he-women who wore pants and tried to dress like a man"?

A: The cowboy of the Old West held to this philosophy, according to an observer of Western customs.

Q: What advice was offered by this Old West slogan: "Keep your ear to the ground," and where did it originate?

A: The line referred to the veteran plainsman's practice of listening to the ground to hear distant sounds such as hoofbeats, and it was the Westerner's way of advising the listener to keep alert.

Q: Who said, "One does not sell the earth upon which the people walk"?

A: The Oglala Sioux leader Crazy Horse reportedly so expressed his opposition to government plans for moving the Sioux to a distant reservation in 1875.

Q: About what beast did a Westerner observe: "They don't walk. They plod"?

A: A veteran emigrant to the West Coast so described the pace of a team of oxen, which were usually dependable but which were also maddeningly slow.

Q: What famous figure of the Old West was so described in this 1826 newspaper ad: "a boy sixteen years old, small for his age, but thick set, light hair, ran away from the subscriber . . . to whom he had been bound to learn the saddler's trade"?

A: This notice in the *Missouri Intelligencer* vainly sought to locate young Kit Carson following his hasty departure from apprenticeship.

Q: About whom was it said, "The adulations heaped on him by a grateful nation for his supposed genius turned his head, which, added to his natural disposition, caused him to bloat his little carcass with debauchery and dissipation which carried him off prematurely"?

A: Indian fighter George Crook delivered this unusual obituary in memory of General Philip Sheridan, whose alleged favoritism as commander of the Military Division of the Missouri earned him the dislike of many Army officers in the West.

Q: What Old West figure regularly proclaimed: "I am a Salt River roarer, and I love the wimmin, and now I am chock full of fight!"?

A: This was the favorite boast of riverman Mike Fink.

Q: What was the last official dispatch known to have been sent by General George Armstrong Custer?

A: Moments before riding to his death at the Battle of the Little Big Horn in 1876, Custer sent this dispatch to Captain Frederick W. Benteen, one of his troop commanders, ordering him to bring reinforcements and extra ammunition into the battle. Custer gave the order verbally and his adjutant, Lieutenant W. W. Cooke, scrawled the message on a note pad, tore out the sheet and gave it to an orderly. The last recorded message from Custer, it was believed lost for years until it turned up in a private collection. It is now on display in the U.S. Military Academy Museum at West Point.

Benteen:

Come on. Big Village,
Be quick. Bring Packs.

P.S. Bring Pack.

W. W. Cooke

Q: Who said, "Have I any apology to make for loving the Indians? The Indians have always loved me, and why should I not love the Indians?"?

A: Western artist George Catlin, whose early-nineteenth-century depiction of Western Indians made him famous, so responded to Eastern critics who denounced him as the "Indian-loving Catlin."

Q: About whom was it said, "Most of those he did kill deserved what they got"?

A: A Lincoln County, New Mexico, resident so expressed one opinion of the violence wrought by Billy the Kid.

Q: Who posted these rules for employees: "You can't drink whiskey and work for us. You can't play cards and work for us. You can't curse or swear in our camps or in our presence and work for us"?

A: Devout and disciplined cattleman Dudley H. Snyder, whose ranching empire was one of the largest in Texas, used these rules to control hard-drinking, fast-playing, loud-swearing cowpokes.

Q: Who said, "As far as you see I am chief here and the people look up to me. There I would be a poor half-breed Indian"?

A: Comanche Chief Quannah Parker, the son of a full-blooded Comanche chief and a captive white woman, delivered this analysis when encouraged to join his white relatives back in civilization.

Q: Who penned this final epistle: "I have but a few minutes to write, as we move at twelve, and I have my hands full of preparations for the scout. Do not be anxious about me. . . . I hope to have a good report to send you by the next mail"?

A: With these words General George Armstrong Custer concluded his last letter to his wife, written June 22, 1876—three days before "Custer's Last Stand."

Q: About whom was it said: "Small salaries are best for young officers who know little of the real value of money"?

A: The statement was made during a Congressional debate by a supporter of a proposal to reduce the meager pay of infantry second lieutenants in the West and elsewhere.

Q: Who said, "Are you from California or heaven?"

A: A survivor of the tragedy-stricken Donner party, a group of emigrants trapped by winter in the Sierra Nevada Mountains, so greeted her rescuers in 1847.

Q: What Plains Indian practice was defended with this statement: "Eight wives could dress 150 skins in the year, whereas a single wife could dress only ten"?

A: A Blackfoot chief used this argument to defend the polygamy practiced by many Plains tribes.

Q: Who said: "Kill and scalp all Indians—big and little; nits make lice"?

A: This statement was uttered in a public speech by Colonel J. M. Chivington, who directed the Colorado volunteer militia in its controversial 1864 attack on Chief Black Kettle's Cheyenne village in the Sand Creek Massacre.

Q: Who issued this command: "The bodies of the dead, even of a savage enemy, shall not be subjected to indignities by civilized and Christian men"?

A: The order was issued by Colonel Henry H. Sibley, commander of troops battling the Santee Sioux in the 1862 Minnesota Uprising, and it was designed to prevent the scalping of Indians killed in battle.

Q: About whom was it said, "He could find water quicker than any man I ever knew"?

A: Mountain man and explorer Joseph Walker was remembered thusly by a contemporary.

Q: Who was so described: "He can be made a firm friend, but no mercy can be expected from him as an enemy"?

A: The Apaches, who were among the last of the tribes to end their resistance to encroaching civilization, were so described by a Westerner who knew them.

FACT: Mountain man Jim Bridger was wounded by a Gros Ventre arrow at the Battle of Pierre's Hole in 1832 and carried the arrowhead in his back for almost three years. Finally, in 1835 the old arrowhead was surgically removed by Dr. Marcus Whitman, the famous missionary physician, who was en route to Oregon. When Whitman expressed his surprise that the old wound had not become infected over the years, Bridger replied, "Meat don't spoil in the Rockies."

Q: Who said this under what circumstances: "I like the command just
    as it stands—'go ye into all the world'—and no exceptions for poor
    health"?
A: Eliza Spalding, wife of missionary Henry Spalding, quoted Jesus
    Christ in Matthew 28:19 as evidence that she should continue the
    rugged journey to Oregon following a difficult childbirth on the
    trail.

Q: Who delivered this eulogy about whom: "He, at least, never lied
    to us. His words gave the people hope. He died and their hope died
    again"?
A: General George Crook was so eulogized upon his death by Sioux
    Chief Red Cloud.

Q: About whom was it said: "It is good. He has looked for death, and
    it has come"?
A: A friend of Sioux Chief Crazy Horse so commented moments after
    Crazy Horse was killed in a scuffle with troops and Indian police at
    Fort Robinson, Nebraska, in 1877.

Q: Under what circumstances was this pledge made and by whom: "I
    give you my word I'll be back tonight"?
A: Cowboy Butch Cassidy, soon to become a famous Western outlaw,
    made this promise to law enforcement officials after being con-
    victed of rustling in 1894. The lawmen granted Cassidy one more
    night of freedom, and he returned to serve a two-year jail sentence
    as promised.

Q: What commodity deserved this description by a frontier resident:
    "It smells like gangrene starting in a mildewed silo, it tastes like
    the wrath to come, and when you absorb a deep swig of it you have
    all the sensations of having swallowed a lighted kerosene lamp"?
A: Frontier corn whiskey.

Q: Who said, "The Indian is a peculiar institution. You cannot tell by
    their looks whether there is honey or vinegar inside. . . . But all
    the time he is reading you as if you were an open book"?
A: Veteran campaigner General George Crook made this observation
    after years of warring with the Indians of the West.

Q: Who said, "I regard myself as a woman who has seen much of life"?
A: Horse thief and outlaw Belle Starr so described her life shortly
    before she was murdered in 1889.

Q: About whom was it said: "He was a good man; he was my friend; he was murdered"?

A: Indian agent A. G. Boone delivered this informal eulogy in memory of Cheyenne Chief Black Kettle, who was killed in a surprise attack on his village by Custer's troops at the Battle of the Washita in 1868.

Q: What Old West character received literary fame by proclaiming, "Paint her up, Bonner! Paint her up!"?

A: With these words former mountain man James Beckwourth encouraged journalist and drinking companion T. D. Bonner to produce a colorful reminiscence about Beckwourth's adventures in the wilderness.

Q: What Old West establishment was targeted by this critique: "Here you may see young girls not over sixteen drinking whiskey, smoking cigars, cursing and swearing until one almost loses respect for the weaker sex. . . . Plenty of rotten whiskey and everything to excite the passions were freely indulged in"?

A: An Old West journalist so reported the conditions of a typical cow town bordello.

Q: Who made this statement: "Your victories are lasting and, unlike mine, are not purchased at the expense of the lifeblood of fellow creatures, leaving sorrow, suffering and desolation in their track"?

A: General George Armstrong Custer so expressed himself in a private letter to a sculptress he admired in 1871.

Q: Who said, "I hate all the white people. You are thieves and liars"?

A: Sitting Bull made this public statement in ceremonies at the opening of a railroad. His embarrassed interpreter transformed the words into a complimentary speech that produced applause from the white audience—to Sitting Bull's surprise.

Q: When a trapper said he had "made wolf meat" of an adversary, what did he mean?

A: He meant he had fought and killed an opponent in the wilderness, leaving his remains for the wolves.

Q: Who said, "Sometimes I feel like a leaf on a stream. It may whirl about and turn and twist, but it is always carried foward"?

A: Daniel Boone, who helped extend the frontier into the Far West, thus evaluated his wanderlust near the end of his life.

Q: Whom did shootist Wyatt Earp describe as "the most skillful gambler and the nerviest, speediest, deadliest man with a six-gun I ever knew"?

A: Doc Holliday.

Q: About whom was it said: "Some men loved their horses more than they loved their wives"?

A: Although a similar observation would later be applied to the American cowboy, this statement referred to the Comanche warrior, who was famous for his equestrian skills.

Q: About what profession did Western outlaw Henry Starr observe: "I love it. It is wild with adventure"?

A: Shortly before he was shot to death in a gunfight in Arkansas, Starr so described the life of banditry in the Old West.

Q: About whom was it said: "There is no use trying to be overbearing with them, for they will not stand the least assumption of superiority"?

A: An Eastern visitor to the West recorded this generalized assessment of the American cowboy. Equipped with tin plates and cups, these Texas cowpunchers interrupt their lunch to pose for a visiting photographer.

Q: To whom was it said: "What the hell you doing in here afoot anyhow?"?

A: A horseless dude from the East was so addressed by an indignant cowboy who was surprised to see the Easterner patronizing a favorite cowboy bar.

Q: About whom was it said: "Oh, how white they look! How white!"?

A: The exclamation was made by one of the Army officers who discovered the stripped bodies of General Custer's command lying on the field of battle at the Little Big Horn.

Q: Who said: "I do not want to settle down in the houses you would build for us. I love to roam the wild prairie. There I am free and happy"?

A: White Bear, a Kiowa chief, so expressed his people's reluctance to become "civilized" Indians. Less than a decade later he was dead, a victim of suicide in prison.

Q: Who said, "I have no more stomach for it"?

A: Hired gunman Tom Horn used these words to resign his position as a lawman.

Q: Who reportedly made this admission: "I'm not ashamed to say that I have been so frightened that it 'peared if all the strength had gone out of my body, and my face was white as chalk"?

A: Famed shootist Wild Bill Hickok was said to have expressed this recollection of self-doubt to an Eastern writer in 1867.

Q: What were the last words spoken by the Oglala Sioux leader Crazy Horse?

A: Mortally wounded during his arrest for alleged subversion on Nebraska's Red Cloud reservation, Crazy Horse died near midnight on September 5, 1877. His last words: "Tell the people it is no use to depend on me anymore now."

FACT: Old West outlaw Sam Bass, who robbed trains, banks and stagecoaches from South Dakota to Texas, was finally cut down by lawmen in a shootout in Round Rock, Texas, in 1878. His dying words were: "Let me go. The world is bobbing around."

Q: What act prompted this description from a Western traveler: "Away across the endless dead level of the prairie a black speck appears against the sky. . . . In a second or two it becomes a horse and rider . . . and the flutter of the hooves comes faintly to the ear —another instant . . . a man and horse burst past our excited faces, and go winging away like a belated fragment of a storm!"?

A: An observer so recalled the fleeting moment when he witnessed the passing of a Pony Express rider galloping across the prairie with the mail.

Q: Under what circumstances was this prediction made: "Our country has become very small, and, before our children are grown up, we shall have no more game"?

A: A Sioux chief issued this complaint while studying the steady passage of emigrants through Sioux country.

Q: Who said, "No! Give me the five hundred dollars and let me go West!"?

A: This earnest plea was made by young John Wesley Iliff, who declined his father's offer of $7,500 to remain home in Ohio and chose instead to take $500 and go West—where he eventually became one of the West's most successful cattlemen.

8 | Custer and the Little Big Horn

Q: On what date and day of the week did Custer's Last Stand occur?

A: The Custer Massacre occurred on Sunday, June 25, 1876, on the Little Big Horn River in Montana Territory.

Q: What Seventh Cavalry officer graduated from West Point with a record-setting 1,031 demerits?

A: Major Marcus A. Reno, held back from graduation for two years because of demerits, was finally graduated in 1857—with the highest number of demerits ever acquired by a West Pointer at that time.

Q: By what name was the Little Big Horn River known to the Sioux and Cheyenne?

A: The Greasy Grass.

Q: How much did the U.S. government have to pay for an 1873 Springfield carbine like that issued to the soldiers of the Seventh Cavalry?

A: $10.50.

Q: What was Custer's date of birth, and where was he born?

A: George A. Custer was born in New Rumley, Ohio, on December 5, 1839.

Q: What horse did Custer ride into combat at the Little Big Horn?
A: On the march to the Little Big Horn Custer alternated riding two
     mounts: Dandy and Vic. He went into battle mounted on Vic, a
     Kentucky-born bay known for its white-stockinged feet and a white
     blaze on its forehead.

Q: What insignia decorated the collar lapels of the dark blue military
     blouses worn by many officers of the Seventh Cavalry at the time
     of the Battle of the Little Big Horn?
A: The blouse collar points were adorned with the regimental "7" and
     a design of crossed sabers, stitched in white or yellow silk.

Q: How many troops did Custer take with him to the Battle of the
     Little Big Horn, and how many Indian warriors did they face?
A: The Seventh Cavalry numbered approximately 650 men when en-
     gaged at the Little Big Horn, where the troops attacked 10,000 to
     12,000 Indians, including a force of 2,500 to 4,000 warriors.

Q: Where were Custer and his command last seen by any Army survi-
     vor of the battle?
A: Custer was last seen leading his command off the riverside bluffs
     and down Medicine Tail Coulee toward a ford across the Little Big
     Horn. Presumably he planned to cross the river and attack the
     Indian village.

Q: What kind of headquarters flag did Custer's color-bearer take into
     battle at the Little Big Horn?
A: Custer's headquarters flag was a red and blue forked guidon deco-
     rated with white sabers in a crossed position.

Q: **What was George Armstrong Custer's rank at the time of the Battle
     of the Little Big Horn?**
A: **He was a lieutenant colonel. He had risen to the rank of major
     general in the volunteer Army of the Civil War, but, like most
     volunteer officers, his rank was reduced in the regular Army after
     the war. Custer rose from the regular Army rank of captain to lieu-
     tenant colonel, but because it was customary to address an officer by
     his highest rank, Custer was normally referred to as "General" Cus-
     ter. At the time of his death he appeared as he does in this photo-
     graph, made shortly before the Battle of the Little Big Horn.**

Q: Where was Captain Frederick W. Benteen when the Battle of the
     Little Big Horn began?
A: Custer had sent Benteen and three companies of troops on a scout-
     ing mission away from the battlefield, so Benteen was absent when
     the fighting began. He rejoined Reno's force in a defensive position
     on Reno Hill above the river, where the combined force was be-
     sieged by Indians on June 25 and 26. Unknown to Reno and Ben-
     teen, Custer and his command had all been killed.

Q: What was the first name of Captain Benteen's wife, and what
     personal tragedy did she and her husband endure?
A: Benteen's wife was named Catherine—he called her "Katie"—and
     four of the five Benteen children died of spinal meningitis.

Q: How long was Custer's hair at the time of the battle?
A: Although long hair was a Custer trademark, it could be uncomfort-
     able and troublesome during a long summer campaign. Custer had
     received a closely cropped haircut and went into battle with short
     hair.

Q: Who was Isaiah Dorman, and what was his role in the Battle of the
     Little Big Horn?
A: Isaiah Dorman, the only known black participant in the Battle of
     the Little Big Horn, was taken on the expedition by General Custer
     as an interpreter. He was killed in the battle while under Major
     Reno's immediate command.

Q: Who was Lieutenant W. W. Cooke, and what was his nickname
     among the enlisted men of the Seventh Cavalry?
A: Cooke, who was Custer's adjutant, was known to the troops as
     "Cookie." He was killed with Custer at the Battle of the Little Big
     Horn.

FACT: George Armstrong Custer was known by a variety of nick-
      names during his lifetime. As a child, he was called "Curly";
      West Point classmates dubbed him "Fanny" and "Cinnamon";
      his wife called him "Autie"; his troops privately referred to
      him as "Iron Butt"; and the Indians knew him as "Long Hair"
      and "Son of the Morning Star."

Q: What was unusual about the time of day Custer attacked the Indian village at the Little Big Horn, and what was odd about the state of his horses?

A: In Indian fighting it was customary to attack Indian villages at dawn with fresh men and horses. Custer attacked at midday after a forced all-night march that tired his mounts and men.

Q: What foreign nations produced the largest number of enlisted men at the Little Big Horn—and which produced the fewest?

A: Approximately 30 percent of the Seventh Cavalry was foreign-born. The largest number of foreign-born soldiers at the battle were from Ireland, followed closely by German natives. Greece, France and Russia each had one native son in the battle—and one cavalryman was born aboard ship "on the high seas."

Q: Who was Custer's commander at the Little Big Horn, and what was his occupation before joining the Army?

A: Senior commander of the 1876 Sioux Campaign was General Alfred H. Terry, who had received national acclaim for the capture of Fort Fisher near Wilmington, North Carolina, during the Civil War. Before joining the Union Army at the beginning of the Civil War, he was Clerk of Superior Court in New Haven, Connecticut.

Q: Name the rocky summit from which Custer's Indian scouts first sighted the hostile village on the Little Big Horn.

A: From the Crow's Nest, a rocky hill about fifteen miles from the site of the Battle of the Little Big Horn, Custer's scouts reported sighting the Indian village and warned Custer of its huge size. Custer said he could not see the village through the haze and ordered his force forward.

Q: What did these Indian warriors have in common: Hawk Man, Red Face, Elk Bear, Long Dog, Cloud Man, Flying-By, Swift Cloud, Owns-Red-Horse, Young Skunk, Many Lice and Bad-Light-Hair?

A: All were killed in action at the Battle of the Little Big Horn while assaulting Custer's position.

Q: What mechanical problem sometimes affected the Springfield carbines carried by the Seventh Cavalry at the Little Big Horn?

A: After repeated firing in battle, the Springfield's copper cartridges sometimes jammed in the carbine breech, leaving the user of the inoperable weapon in a difficult combat position.

Q: Where was Custer's body found, and how had he been wounded?

A: Stripped and propped against two dead soldiers, Custer's body was found with members of his staff on a knoll of the battlefield known thereafter as Custer Hill. He had been shot in the left chest near the heart and in the left temple, but he had not been scalped; however, Indian survivors of the battle claimed to have snipped off one of Custer's fingertips and to have pierced his eardrums with a sewing needle.

Q: The bodies of what three Seventh Cavalry officers were never found following the Battle of the Little Big Horn?

A: The three officers missing and presumed dead were First Lieutenant James E. Porter, Second Lieutenant James G. Sturgis and Second Lieutenant Henry M. Harrington.

Q: Who told Elizabeth Custer about her husband's death, and where was she when she received the news?

A: Shortly before 7 A.M. on July 6, 1876, Captain William S. Mc-Caskey, Lieutenant C. L. Gurley and Dr. J. V. D. Middleton—the post surgeon—went to the Custer home on officers' row, above, at Fort Abraham Lincoln to break the news to Elizabeth Custer. Lieutenant Gurley knocked on the back door and summoned the family maid, who awakened Mrs. Custer. Joined by other Army widows, she received the officers in the parlor of her home, where she was told of her husband's death.

Q: Who was regimental commander of the U.S. Seventh Cavalry at
    the time of the Battle of the Little Big Horn?
A: Although George Custer exercised field command of the regiment,
    the Seventh Cavalry's official commander was Samuel D. Sturgis,
    who was on a recruiting assignment in St. Louis at the time of the
    battle.

Q: How did the Army horse Comanche, the famous survivor of the
    Battle of the Little Big Horn, receive his name?
A: In 1868, shortly after Captain Myles Keogh bought the horse from
    an Army quartermaster at Hays City, Kansas, the animal was
    wounded in a skirmish with Comanche Indians, an event that
    prompted Keogh to name the horse Comanche.

Q: At the time of his death how old was George Armstrong Custer,
    how tall was he and how much did he weigh? What color were his
    eyes?
A: Custer was thirty-six years old at the time of his death and was
    described by widow Libbie Custer as being "nearly six feet tall,"
    although his West Point file records his height as 5 feet 8⅛ inches.
    At the time of the Battle of the Little Big Horn, he weighed
    approximately 170 pounds. His eyes were blue.

Q: What two melodies did the Seventh Cavalry's regimental band
    perform as the men of the Seventh left their post on the march
    toward the Little Big Horn?
A: The band played "Garry Owen," the regiment's battle tune, as the
    Seventh paraded out of Fort Abraham Lincoln, then performed
    "The Girl I Left Behind Me" as the regiment marched away to the
    west.

Q: Who was the last soldier to hear Custer's voice—and live to tell
    about it?
A: The last surviving trooper to hear Custer speak was a Seventh
    Cavalry trumpeter, Private Giovanni Martini, who was dispatched
    by Custer with a final message moments before Custer's command
    engaged the Indians. An Italian immigrant who had served as a
    drummer boy with Garibaldi in Italy before joining the Seventh
    Cavalry in 1873, Martini survived the battle and remained in the
    Army until 1904, when he retired as sergeant. He died of natural
    causes at his home in the Italian quarter of Brooklyn, New York,
    on December 24, 1922.

Q: What was unusual about the horses ridden by the troopers of the Seventh Cavalry at the Little Big Horn?

A: Custer had the regiment's various companies assigned horses of the same color: Company A had blacks; Companies B, D, I and L rode bays; Company H was mounted on blood bays; Companies C, G and K rode sorrels; Company E rode grays; Company M rode mixed colors and piebalds; and Company F rode chestnuts.

Q: How many members of the Custer family died at the Battle of the Little Big Horn?

A: Five. Killed in the battle were General Custer; his brother, thirty-one-year-old Captain Thomas W. Custer; a civilian brother, twenty-seven-year-old Boston Custer; a brother-in-law, thirty-year-old Lieutenant James Calhoun; and an eighteen-year-old nephew, Harry Armstrong ("Autie") Reed.

Q: Who led the Indian defense that annihilated General Custer and his command at the Battle of the Little Big Horn?

A: Although the Hunkpapa Sioux chief Sitting Bull was the principal Sioux leader of the Indians encamped at the Little Big Horn, he was a medicine man who probably did not fight in the battle. The principal Indian war leaders at the battle were Chief Gall of the Hunkpapa Sioux, Chief Crazy Horse of the Oglala Sioux and Chief Lame White Man of the Southern Cheyenne—who have all received credit for leading the successful Indian defense.

Q: How many companies of the Seventh Cavalry were wiped out with Custer at the Little Big Horn, and what were they?

A: Under Custer's immediate command at the Little Big Horn were five companies—C, E, F, I and L—all of which were wiped out. Downriver from Custer, seven other companies under Major Marcus Reno survived bloody fighting with moderate casualties.

FACT: General Alfred H. Terry, Custer's commanding officer in the 1876 Sioux Campaign, was promoted to major general in 1886 but was forced to retire two years later because of Bright's disease. He returned to his home in New Haven, Connecticut, where he died of heart failure at 4 A.M., Tuesday, December 16, 1890, at age sixty-four.

Q: How far was Reno Hill, where Reno and Benteen's troops were besieged, from the site where Custer and his command were killed?
A: Approximately four and a half miles.

Q: Why was Major Marcus Reno dishonorably discharged from the Army?
A: In 1880 Reno was court-martialed, convicted and dishonorably discharged for excessive drunkenness; for breaking a billiard stick over another officer's head; and for peeping in a window at the daughter of his commanding officer. Although he declared himself innocent, Reno was cashiered from the service.

FACT: The oldest soldier to die at the Battle of the Little Big Horn is believed to have been forty-five-year-old Benjamin Brandon, a farrier for the Seventh Cavalry. The youngest soldiers killed in the battle were probably Private Henry C. Voight and Trumpeter George A. Moonie, who were twenty-one years old.

Q: What was notable about the score Seventh Cavalry Surgeon James M. DeWolf recorded on the Army Medical Board examination?

A: DeWolf, who held an M.D. degree from Harvard Medical School, failed the Army Medical Board exam. He was serving as a private physician under Army contract at the time of the Battle of the Little Big Horn and was killed on Reno Hill.

Q: What headgear was Major Marcus A. Reno wearing when he attacked the Indian camp at the Little Big Horn?

A: When he launched the attack on the village Reno was wearing a straw hat like many soldiers of the Seventh Cavalry, who had bought them from a trader earlier in the campaign. Reno lost his hat in the fighting and tied a handkerchief around his head.

Q: Who carried Custer's battle flag in the Battle of the Little Big Horn?

A: Custer's battle flag was carried by Sergeant Robert Hughes of Company K, who was killed in the fighting on Custer Hill near the general.

Q: Where is the Seventh Cavalry's Captain Myles Keogh buried?

A: Keogh was born in Ireland on May 25, 1840; served in Africa as a soldier of fortune; was decorated as a soldier in the Papal army; and fought as a Union major in the American Civil War. Killed with Custer's command at the Little Big Horn and buried in a shallow grave on the field, he was later reburied by friends in a cemetery in Auburn, New York.

Q: What kind of scouts did Custer use at the Little Big Horn, and who was his chief of scouts?

A: Custer used Arikara and Crow scouts, commanded by Lieutenant Charles Varnum. The lieutenant was assisted by a half-breed Sioux, Minton ("Mitch") Bouyer, who served as a guide for the expedition.

Q: What prominent casualty at the Little Big Horn was known as White-Hunter-Who-Never-Goes-Out-for-Nothing to Indians and as "Lonesome Charley" to whites?

A: Both nicknames were borne by Charles A. Reynolds, Custer's chief guide, who was killed during Reno's retreat at the Battle of the Little Big Horn. A doctor's son, Reynolds was born in Warren County, Illinois, on March 20, 1842, and attended Abingdon College in Virginia.

Q: When the Seventh Cavalry went into battle at the Little Big Horn, how many of the regiment's forty-three officers were actually present?

A: Due to detached service, sick leave and ordinary leave, only twenty-eight of the regiment's officers were present when the Seventh went to the Little Big Horn.

Q: From what did these words come?
> We'll break windows, we'll break doors
> The watch knock down by threes and fours;
> Then let the doctors work their cures,
> And tinker up our bruises.

A: These boisterous lines are some of the lyrics from "Garry Owen," the regimental theme song of the U.S. Seventh Cavalry when led by General George A. Custer.

Q: What connection did Gray Goat, Wild Bill and Puff have with the Seventh Cavalry and the Battle of the Little Big Horn?

A: All were Army horses slain in the battle.

FACT: Following the Battle of the Little Big Horn, Custer's superior officer, General Alfred H. Terry, drafted two reports on the battle: one designed for public release and a second report, critical of Custer, meant only for the Army high command. In Washington, General-in-Chief William T. Sherman sent the private report to the Secretary of War by a civilian "messenger" who turned out to be a newspaper reporter in disguise. Before delivering Terry's critique, the newsman read it, and his paper—the Philadelphia Inquirer—printed the controversial report.

Q: Why was George Custer court-martialed and suspended from rank and command without pay for a year in 1867?

A: That year Custer led a contingent of troops on a punishing forced march through Kansas' Indian country, sustained several casualties, made a controversial decision to shoot deserters and later left his troops for an unauthorized visit to his wife. A court-martial suspended him from rank and command without pay for one year—a sentence that was later reduced.

Q: What officer left Reno Hill and made a vain attempt to join Custer during the battle?

A: Captain Thomas Weir, who was a friend of Custer's, left the hill with a small force without permission, rode toward the Custer battlefield, but was forced to retreat back to Reno Hill because of hostile fire.

Q: What newspaper reporter accompanied the Seventh Cavalry to the Little Big Horn at Custer's invitation, and why was he selected to go?

A: Reporter Mark Kellogg of the *Bismarck Tribune* accompanied the Seventh Cavalry on the 1876 Sioux Expedition. The *Tribune's* editor, Clement A. Lounsberry, originally planned to go on the campaign, but because of illness in his family, he sent Kellogg, his assistant, who was killed with Custer's command.

Q: Who was the most prominent Indian killed in the Battle of the Little Big Horn?

A: The highest-ranking Indian leader to die in the battle was the Cheyenne chief Lame White Man, who was shot to death in the fighting, then scalped by a Sioux warrior who mistook the chief for an Army scout.

Q: How was Custer dressed at the Battle of the Little Big Horn?

A: According to his orderly, Trumpeter Giovanni Martini, General Custer went to his fatal engagement wearing "a blue-gray flannel shirt, buckskin trousers, and long boots." Custer had a fringed buckskin jacket, but presumably because of the June heat, he went into battle with it tied to his saddle.

Q: What was Custer's class standing at the time of his graduation from West Point?

A: He was last in his class.

FACT: After the Battle of the Little Big Horn, the Seventh Cavalry's wounded were placed on the steamboat *Far West* for transportation back to Fort Abraham Lincoln. The boat's captain, a veteran riverman named Grant Marsh, brought the wounded and the first full account of the battle back to the fort so quickly that he set a speed record on the Yellowstone and Missouri rivers—seven hundred miles covered in fifty-four hours.

Q: During the march from Fort Abraham Lincoln, what event caused the Seventh Cavalry and the other troops of the expedition to interrupt their advance on June 1–2, 1876?
A: Despite the season, the troops were struck by a freak June snowstorm that left two inches of snow on the plains and delayed the march for those two days.

Q: How many soldiers were awarded the Congressional Medal of Honor for action at the Battle of the Little Big Horn?
A: Twenty-four Medals of Honor were awarded to soldiers who fought under Reno and Benteen. Most of the medals were awarded to soldiers who braved Indian fire to get water from the river for wounded comrades.

Q: What indoor game did Custer enjoy playing with his wife Libbie and his brother Tom while he was posted at Fort Abraham Lincoln?
A: One of Custer's favorite indoor pastimes was playing tag with his wife and brother, chasing each other through the Custer home and up and down the stairs.

Q: What was found underneath General Custer's body following the Battle of the Little Big Horn?
A: When Custer's body was moved for burial, the supervisor of the burial detail, Sergeant John Ryan, discovered five brass cartridge cases under Custer's body.

Q: George Armstrong Custer had a scar on his forehead at the time of his death. How did he get it?
A: As a child, Custer was placed on a cow by his sister, Lydia-Ann, and was bucked off, gashing his forehead.

Q: Who was Custer's favorite scout, and what happened to him?

A: Custer's favorite scout was said to be the Arikara warrior Bloody
    Knife, who had served with Custer on earlier expeditions. Bloody
    Knife accompanied Reno in the attack against the Indian village, was
    shot between the eyes and killed and was reportedly later beheaded
    by two Sioux girls. Two years before their deaths, Bloody Knife and
    Custer posed for this photograph while on a campaign in the West.

Q: Why was Frederick Benteen suspended from the Army without pay for a year and a half in 1887?

A: Benteen was court-martialed and convicted of sustained drunkenness and "unsoldierlike conduct" while serving as post commander at Fort Du Chesne, Utah. Specifically, he was charged with cursing the post's civilian employees while in a drunken state and urinating near a group of women.

Q: What did the soldiers of the Seventh Cavalry eat on the march that ended at the Little Big Horn?

A: Although officers ate better, the troops received standard Army fare: hardtack, bacon and coffee for breakfast; hardtack while in the saddle; and hardtack, cooked beef and coffee for supper. The evening meal was sometimes supplemented with wild game.

Q: What newspaper was first to report the Custer Massacre?

A: The *Bozeman Times* of Montana Territory broke the story with an extra edition on July 3, 1876, which was followed by an extra published by the *Helena Herald* on July 4 and the *Salt Lake Tribune* on July 5. The first full account of the disaster appeared in an extra published by the *Bismarck Tribune* on the morning of July 6 in Bismarck, Dakota Territory.

Q: With whom was General Custer first buried?

A: An Army burial detail buried Custer in a shallow grave with his brother Tom and covered the grave site with about a foot and a half of dirt, a discarded Indian travois and a pile of stones. The Custer brothers remained buried there until their remains were separately reinterred a year later.

Q: Who commanded each of the five companies wiped out with Custer in the Last Stand?

A: Company C was commanded by Custer's brother, Captain Thomas W. Custer; Company E was commanded by First Lieutenant Algernon E. Smith; F Company was led by Captain George W. Yates; I Company's commander was Captain Myles W. Keogh and Company L was commanded by First Lieutenant James Calhoun.

Q: What did these Crow warriors have in common: White-Man-Runs-Him, Goes Ahead, Hairy Moccasin and Curly?

A: All were scouts for Custer. They took him to the Little Big Horn River and to within sight of the Indian village, where they were dismissed—and thus survived the battle.

Q: How many rounds of ammunition were expended by the Seventh Cavalry at the Little Big Horn?

A: According to Army records, the troops in General Custer's immediate command and those under Captain Benteen and Major Reno fired or lost 38,030 carbine rounds and 2,954 pistol rounds for a total of 40,984 rounds of ammunition. An estimated 10,000 rounds of "lost" ammunition were captured by the Indians.

Q: Where and when did the Reno Court of Inquiry meet to investigate the conduct of Major Marcus A. Reno at the Little Big Horn, and what was the court's verdict?

A: Requested by Reno and ordered by President Rutherford B. Hayes, the Court of Inquiry convened at the Palmer House in Chicago on Monday, January 13, 1879, and cleared Reno of blame for the disaster—a verdict approved by the president on March 5, 1879.

Q: If Custer was buried on the battlefield at the Little Big Horn, why is his grave located at West Point?

A: On July 2, 1877, a detachment of troops under Lieutenant Colonel Michael V. Sheridan reburied the enlisted men killed in the Custer massacre and removed the remains of officers for burial elsewhere. General Custer's remains were placed in a pine box and taken by the steamer *Fletcher* to Fort Abraham Lincoln, from which they were shipped eastward for reburial at West Point. The general's remains were stored in a vault at Poughkeepsie Cemetery in Poughkeepsie, New York, for two months until reburied in West Point Cemetery.

Q: When were the survivors of the Battle of the Little Big Horn rescued?

A: The survivors under Major Reno and Captain Benteen, who were under siege by Indians on June 25 and 26, saw the Indians withdraw on the afternoon of June 26 and were rescued by troops under Generals Terry and Gibbon on June 27.

Q: Who was the last soldier to fall in the Custer Massacre?

A: No one knows. However, Cheyenne veterans of the battle said that as they stripped the dead on the hill where Custer's body was found, a large, bearded soldier suddenly sat up and waved his pistol. Although they were momentarily frightened, the warriors quickly killed the lone survivor—who probably was the last of Custer's command to fall.

Q: What became of Captain Thomas B. Weir, the Seventh Cavalry officer who led a futile attempt to rescue Custer and his command but was forced back to Reno Hill?

A: A graduate of the University of Michigan and a veteran of the Civil War, Weir was posted to New York City following the Custer massacre. His behavior became erratic after the battle, however, and on December 9, 1876, the thirty-eight-year-old officer died at his New York home of "congestion of the brain."

Q: What happened to Custer on February 9, 1864?

A: On this date he married Elizabeth Bacon in Monroe, Michigan.

Q: What decoration did Captain Tom Custer wear on one arm?

A: Unlike his brother George, Tom wore elaborate tattoos on one arm, which was adorned with an image of the goddess of liberty, an American flag and his initials. The tattoos were used to identify Tom Custer's body after he was slain in the battle.

Q: How were the graves of Custer and the officers of his command initially marked?

A: When an officer was identified, his name was written on a small slip of paper and stuffed into an empty rifle cartridge, which was then jammed onto a stick marking the soldier's burial site.

Q: How many wagons accompanied the 1876 Sioux Campaign when it left Fort Abraham Lincoln?

A: Approximately 150.

Q: Who was the last Indian survivor from the Battle of the Little Big Horn?

A: The last surviving warrior from the battle is believed to have been a Minniconjou Sioux named Iron Hail, who fought in the engagement and lived until November 1955. The last Indian witness to the battle is thought to have been Charles Sitting Man, who saw the battle as a child and who lived until 1962.

Q: When, where and how did Elizabeth Custer die?

A: Elizabeth Bacon Custer, the widow of George A. Custer, died of a heart attack in her apartment at 71 Park Avenue in New York City at 5:30 P.M. on Tuesday, April 4, 1933. She was ninety-one years old; had survived her husband by more than a half century; and two days after her death she was buried beside him at West Point.

FACT: In an attempt to explain the death of Custer and the defeat of the Seventh Cavalry at the Battle of the Little Big Horn, some Eastern journalists proposed the fanciful theory that Chief Sitting Bull had graduated from West Point under an alias and was thus equipped to successfully oppose Custer and the Seventh.

Q: Why was Custer detained at West Point after his class had graduated?

A: A few days after graduation Custer was arrested and court-martialed for failing to break up a cadet fistfight while serving as officer of the guard at summer camp. He was detained for trial when the rest of his class left for duty, and he was convicted. However, due to the wartime demand for officers, he was allowed to report for active duty.

Q: What confusion surrounded the reinterment of General Custer's remains?

A: When a Seventh Cavalry burial detail arrived at the Little Big Horn to rebury the enlisted men and disinter the officers, they found General Custer's grave disturbed and were surprised to find the grave's skeletal remains lying on a corporal's blouse. After some confusion they removed the remains they thought were General Custer's. Said Sergeant M. C. Caddle of the burial detail: "I think we got the right body the second time."

Q: What was the original name of Fort Abraham Lincoln, the Dakota Territory post from which Custer and the Seventh Cavalry marched to the Little Big Horn?

A: When first established in 1872, the post was named Fort McKeen. It was located near what is now Bismarck, North Dakota, and was later renamed in honor of the sixteenth president.

Q: Who assumed field command of the Seventh Cavalry following Custer's death at the Little Big Horn?

A: Major Marcus A. Reno assumed field command of the remnants of the regiment on June 26, 1876—the day after Custer's death—and held field command until October 18, 1876, although he was acting under the direction of superior officers for most of the time.

Q: What military honor was twice bestowed on Captain Tom Custer
     but was never given to his famous brother, George Armstrong Cus-
     ter?
A: For deeds of valor as a Union soldier in the Civil War, Tom Custer
     had twice received the Congressional Medal of Honor. His higher-
     ranking brother never received the award and sometimes referred to
     Tom Custer's medals as "baubles." In this photograph, made shortly
     before the Battle of the Little Big Horn, Tom Custer wears both
     decorations. He was killed, scalped and terribly mutilated on Custer
     Hill near his famous brother.

Q: When did Captain Frederick Benteen die, and where is he buried?

A: In 1888 Benteen received a disability discharge from the Army and retired to Atlanta, Georgia, where he spent the rest of his life with his wife and son. On June 22, 1890, Benteen died of a stroke and was buried in Atlanta. In 1902 his body was reinterred in Arlington National Cemetery.

Q: What weapons did George A. Custer personally carry into battle at the Little Big Horn?

A: Custer armed himself with Remington's .50-caliber Sporting Rifle, a hunting knife and two British-made revolvers—probably Webley's Royal Irish Constabulary pistols.

Q: When and where was George A. Custer's funeral and who conducted it?

A: Custer's funeral was held at 2 P.M., October 10, 1877, in the U.S. Military Academy Chapel at West Point and was conducted by Dr. John Forsyth, the chaplain of West Point. Custer's widow, Elizabeth, was accompanied by the West Point commandant, General John M. Schofield, and the West Point Cadet Choir recited the nineteenth and thirty-ninth Psalms.

Q: Who was John M. Carnahan, and what part did he play in Custer's Last Stand?

A: Carnahan was the telegraph operator at Bismarck, Dakota Territory, who was rushed from bed the night of July 5, 1876, to telegraph a lengthy account of the battle to the East. Carnahan stayed at his key for twenty-two hours, at a cost of more than $3,000, and while waiting for more Custer copy he retained possession of the telegraph line by dispatching Scripture passages from the New Testament.

Q: Was Captain Myles Keogh's horse Comanche the only Army survivor of Custer's command?

A: No. Many Army mounts were captured by Indians, and others, badly wounded, were destroyed by troops after the battle. Some of the dogs that were seen on the field after the battle also may have accompanied Custer's troops into action; however, Comanche was the only surviving Seventh Cavalry horse in Army possession. Despite seven wounds, Comanche became a regimental mascot until the rugged animal died on November 6, 1891, at the age of twenty-nine.

Q: What happened to John Burkman, Custer's long-time horse handler, following Custer's death at the Little Big Horn?

A: Burkman, who was with the pack train on Reno Hill during the Battle of the Little Big Horn, survived the famous battle and eventually retired to Billings, Montana, near the site of the Custer fight. In 1925 he committed suicide with his pistol.

FACT: On the day of his funeral George Armstrong Custer's remains were removed from temporary storage in a Poughkeepsie, New York, cemetery vault and were taken in a casket by hearse to the Hudson River, passing a crowd of ten thousand lining Poughkeepsie's streets. The Custer casket was then placed on a boat, the *Mary Powell,* and was ferried to West Point for funeral services. The casket was adorned with a two-foot-long arrangement of geraniums fashioned into the shape of an Army shoulder strap, decorated with two large general's stars made of tuberoses.

Q: Where, when and how did Major Marcus A. Reno die?

A: Reno died at Providence Hospital in Washington, D.C., on March 30, 1889, following an operation for mouth cancer.

Q: What states produced the largest number of enlisted men at the Battle of the Little Big Horn and what states produced the fewest?

A: The largest number of troops in the battle were Pennsylvania natives, followed closely by New Yorkers. Iowa, North Carolina, Texas, Wisconsin, Kansas, Delaware, Connecticut and Georgia each had one native son fighting in the Seventh Cavalry at the battle.

Q: Who was the last Army survivor of the Battle of the Little Big Horn?

A: Sergeant Charles Windolph, who was in the fighting on Reno Hill, died in Lead, South Dakota, on March 11, 1950—the last Army survivor of the Little Big Horn.

9 | Hollywood's Wild West

Q: What was cowboy actor Marion Morrison's screen name, and where did he get it?

A: Morrison was better known to moviegoers as John Wayne—so named by film director Raoul Walsh, who claimed to have named Wayne in honor of the eighteenth-century general "Mad" Anthony Wayne.

Q: What did Walter Brennan lose to a poker-playing Indian in the 1948 epic *Red River?*

A: His false teeth.

Q: Who said, "There's no living with a killing"?

A: Gunfighter Alan Ladd, bleeding from a victorious shootout with the bad guys, delivered this memorable line to Joey, the homesteader's son, at the conclusion of the 1953 movie *Shane.*

Q: How did early cowboy star Tom Mix die?

A: Mix, who claimed to have been a real cowboy at one time, starred in his last Western in 1935 and was killed in an automobile accident near Florence, Arizona, in 1940.

Q: What was the first Zane Grey Western to be made into a movie?

A: *The Vanishing American* (1927), *Riders of the Purple Sage* (1918, 1925, 1931 and 1941), *The Rainbow Trail* (1918, 1925, 1932), *To the Last Man* (1933) and *The Last Roundup* (1934) were all based on novels by Zane Grey, the prolific writer of Western fiction. The first movie adapted from a Zane Grey book was *Fighting Blood,* made by D. W. Griffith in 1911.

Q: What three films made up director John Ford's "Cavalry Trilogy," and when were they released?

A: Ford's three-film vision of the U.S. Cavalry in the West was expressed in *Fort Apache* (1948), *She Wore a Yellow Ribbon* (1949) and *Rio Grande* (1950). All starred John Wayne. Here, Wayne pauses in tribute to a fallen comrade in a scene from *She Wore a Yellow Ribbon.*

Q: Who played young George Armstrong Custer in the 1940 Western tale *The Santa Fe Trail,* which also starred Errol Flynn, Olivia de Havilland and Raymond Massey?

A: Ronald Reagan.

Q: What famous leading man began his film career with a walk-on part in the Hopalong Cassidy film *Hoppy Serves a Writ,* released in 1943?

A: Robert Mitchum.

Q: Where was the first Western movie filmed?

A: *The Great Train Robbery,* the first Western movie complete with plot, featured the story of a train holdup in the Old West and was shot on location near Dover, New Jersey.

Q: In what 1969 film did Paul Newman and Robert Redford portray the ringleaders of the Wild Bunch, the notorious turn-of-the-century outlaw gang?

A: Newman and Redford held the title roles in *Butch Cassidy and the Sundance Kid.*

Q: Who played the Apache leader Cochise opposite Jimmy Stewart's Tom Jeffords in the 1950 film *Broken Arrow?*

A: Jeff Chandler.

Q: What 1972 movie was based on the life of mountain man John Johnson?

A: "Crow Killer" John Johnson's life was depicted by movie star Robert Redford in the 1972 film *Jeremiah Johnson,* in which Redford battled Crow Indians—without any of the real Johnson's alleged cannibalistic tendencies.

FACT: Silent cowboy star William S. Hart grew so fond of his movie horse Fritz that he offered to buy the animal from the studio, but studio officials refused. Finally, after repeated attempts to purchase the horse, Hart volunteered to star in a movie without salary in exchange for Fritz. The studio heads agreed, and Hart was finally united with his beloved movie mount—in a deal he claimed cost him $40,000.

Q: How did Maine native Sean O'Feeney affect the film legend of the Old West?

A: O'Feeney created one of Hollywood's most enduring images of the West through the many Westerns he directed under his professional name—John Ford.

Q: In what 1952 Western did Gary Cooper play Marshal Will Kane, an Old West lawman deserted by his fellow townsmen in his hour of need?

A: *High Noon.*

Q: Who directed the 1953 classic *Shane?*

A: George Stevens.

Q: Who was it who said, "All right, Dude, this time right between the eyes"?

A: Villain Lee Marvin delivered this final threat of his life to mild-mannered Jimmy Stewart seconds before being gunned down by vigilante John Wayne in the 1962 Western *The Man Who Shot Liberty Valance.*

Q: In what Hollywood Western did John Wayne appear in his first leading role?

A: The Duke's first film lead was the role of wagon-train scout Brick Coleman, the hero of the 1930 Western *The Big Trail.*

Q: What was the first Western film to use an American Indian language on screen?

A: The 1930 Western *The Indians Are Coming* included dialogue in Sioux and became the first feature film to use an Indian language.

Q: What Old West character was portrayed in various films by Johnny Mack Brown, Robert Taylor, Paul Newman and Kris Kristofferson?

A: Billy the Kid.

Q: What was the first film directed by John Ford in Monument Valley, Utah?

A: Ford "discovered" Monument Valley for his 1939 *Stagecoach* and returned to the location repeatedly for future films.

Q: What actor played the lead in these Westerns: *Destry Rides Again* (1939), *Broken Arrow* (1950), *Winchester '73* (1950), *The Naked Spur* (1953) and *The Man from Laramie* (1955)?

A: James Stewart.

Q: In what 1970 film did Dustin Hoffman play a character named Jack Crabb, who was trapped between white and Indian cultures?

A: Hoffman was Jack Crabb in *Little Big Man,* a dramatization of George Custer and the Battle of the Little Big Horn.

Q: Who made the first screen version of *The Virginian,* and what actor played the lead?

A: Cecil B. DeMille released the original silent film based on the Owen Wister novel in 1914, and it featured silent film star Dustin Farnum.

Q: The 1952 Western classic *High Noon* was nominated for an Academy Award as Best Picture but lost. What movie was judged superior to *High Noon?*

A: Although Gary Cooper won an Oscar for the lead in *High Noon,* the famous Western lost in the best-picture category to Cecil B. DeMille's circus story *The Greatest Show on Earth.*

Q: Who swallowed hard and made this admission in what popular Western: "I didn't know who you were when I said you were cheating"?

A: A cowed gambler used these words to back down from a confrontation with Robert Redford as the Sundance Kid in *Butch Cassidy and the Sundance Kid.*

Q: Why were "B" Westerns so named?

A: In the 1930s double features became a national fad as the film industry struggled to keep the Depression-afflicted moviegoer in the theater. "B" pictures developed during this era and were so named because they occupied the bottom half of the double-feature billing.

Q: How many locomotives and railroad cars did Cecil B. DeMille assemble for his 1939 saga *Union Pacific?*

A: *Union Pacific* starred Barbara Stanwyck, Joel McCrea, six locomotives and fifty-five railroad cars.

Q: On what common source were these Western movies based: *Frontier Marshal* (1934 and 1939), *My Darling Clementine* (1946) and *Powder River* (1953)?

A: In 1928, a year before his death, Wyatt Earp shared his memoirs with writer Stuart Lake, who later recorded Earp's story in the 1931 book *Wyatt Earp: Frontier Marshal.* All these movies were based on Lake's book.

Q: What frequent star of Westerns was born in Helena, Montana, in 1901 and once worked as a guide in Yellowstone National Park?

A: Gary Cooper.

Q: To whom was this screen observation directed: "I call that bold talk for a one-eyed fat man!"?

A: Outlaw Ned Pepper, played by Robert Duvall, delivered this critique in his final showdown with John Wayne's Rooster Cogburn in the 1969 film *True Grit*.

Q: What film dilemma provoked this exasperated comment: "It's no good. I've got to go back. They're making me run. I've never run from anybody before"?

A: Gary Cooper as Marshal Will Kane so expressed his determination to face the badmen gunning for him in *High Noon*.

Q: Who was the star of the first version of the frequently repeated Western movie entitled *The Squaw Man?*

A: Dustin Farnum.

Q: Who played the lead in the 1929 original sound version of *The Virginian?*

A: Gary Cooper.

Q: In what famous Western movie does this wishful thinking occur: "I think we lost 'em! Do you think we lost 'em? [Pause.] Neither do I!"?

A: Butch Cassidy (Paul Newman) expresses his hopes and fears to a stoic Sundance Kid (Robert Redford) as the two bandits try to outrun a persistent posse in the 1969 hit *Butch Cassidy and the Sundance Kid*.

Q: What three Italian-made Westerns propelled Clint Eastwood from a career as a television supporting actor to that as an international film star?

A: Eastwood, who played trail drover Rowdy Yates on TV's "Rawhide," saw his film career blast off after starring in the Italian films *A Fistful of Dollars*, *For a Few Dollars More* and *The Good, the Bad and the Ugly*.

Q: What 1963 John Wayne Western was reportedly based on William Shakespeare's *The Taming of the Shrew?*

A: *McLintock!*

Q: By what screen name did cowboy star William Boyd become famous after playing leading roles in prominent silent films like *The Volga Boatman* (1926) and *King of Kings* (1927)?

A: In 1935 William Boyd rescued a waning film career and gained instant cowboy stardom when he played the lead in *Hop-a-Long Cassidy*, which was a role that he would repeat in more than sixty sequels.

Q: What motion picture marked Errol Flynn's first appearance in a Western?

A: The swashbuckling Flynn's first Western was *Dodge City*, which appeared in 1939.

Q: What Academy Award did *Shane* win?

A: Although nominated in a parade of categories, *Shane* was awarded but a single Oscar—for Best Color Cinematography. The film judged Best Picture of the Year was *From Here to Eternity*. In this scene, Shane (Alan Ladd) comforts Joey, the farmer's son (Brandon de Wilde).

Q: Who was David Horsely, and how did he affect the film industry's vision of the West?

A: David Horsely was the head of Nestor Films, which in 1911 established its studio in the Los Angeles suburb of Hollywood—the first film studio to do so. Horsely's act prompted other film companies to do likewise, and soon the American film industry had shifted from New York to Hollywood, where the availability of Western scenery made pictures about the Old West attractive.

Q: Who played the reckless Lieutenant Colonel Owen Thursday opposite John Wayne in director John Ford's *Fort Apache?*

A: The role was performed by Henry Fonda, who leads his cavalry command into a fatal ambush in the movie's climax.

Q: Name the character played by John Wayne in the 1939 classic *Stagecoach.*

A: The Ringo Kid.

Q: In what 1965 Western did actor Lee Marvin win an Academy Award for playing a double part?

A: Marvin won the Oscar for his performance as a drunken has-been and as a deadly gunfighter in the movie *Cat Ballou.*

Q: How long did it take Edwin S. Porter to shoot *The Great Train Robbery,* the 1903 movie that became father to all Westerns?

A: Two days.

Q: What 1959 Western depicted a team of lawmen that included John Wayne, Walter Brennan, Dean Martin and Ricky Nelson?

A: The odd coupling was orchestrated by director Howard Hawks in *Rio Bravo.*

FACT: Famed Hollywood director Cecil B. DeMille made his first movie in Hollywood because he did not like Flagstaff, Arizona. In 1913 DeMille and a small film crew left his New York headquarters to shoot the original *Squaw Man,* a silent Western, on location in Flagstaff, but upon arrival he decided he did not like the proposed location. Instead he moved on to Hollywood, where he filmed *Squaw Man* and stayed to make many more films.

Q: What 1939 Western included in its cast these famous Hollywood figures: Tyrone Power; Randolph Scott; Lon Chaney, Jr.; and John Carradine?

A: All played in the movie *Jesse James*—with Tyrone Power in the title role—which was released that year by 20th Century-Fox.

Q: What became of early-motion-picture-director Francis Boggs, who directed a string of early Westerns between 1907 and 1910, including *The Bandit King, The Girl from Montana* and *His First Ride?*

A: While directing a movie in 1910, Boggs was shot and killed by a berserk actor.

Q: What was the first Western to win an Academy Award as Best Picture of the Year?

A: The first best-picture Oscar awarded to a Western went to the 1931 motion picture *Cimarron,* which chronicled the history of Oklahoma.

Q: Who played the part of "Singin' Sandy," the singing cowboy, in the 1933 musical Western *Riders of Destiny?*

A: John Wayne.

Q: What notorious Old West figure was depicted by actor Walter Brennan in the motion picture *The Westerner?*

A: Known to a later generation as Grandpa McCoy on television's "The Real McCoys," Brennan played Judge Roy Bean in the 1940 film—and won an Academy Award as Best Supporting Actor.

Q: In what 1946 movie did director John Ford present the legend of the gunfight at the O.K. Corral?

A: *My Darling Clementine.*

Q: What actors played the roles of George Armstrong Custer and Chief Crazy Horse in the 1941 movie *They Died with Their Boots On?*

A: Errol Flynn portrayed Custer and Anthony Quinn played Crazy Horse.

Q: What villain killed John Wayne in the 1972 Western *The Cowboys?*

A: In *The Cowboys* aging rancher John Wayne is done in by villain Bruce Dern, who later gets his just reward at the hands of the young cowboys trained by Wayne.

Q: What Western movie produced this line with effective repetition: "Who *are* those guys?"?

A: Paul Newman, as Butch Cassidy, the affable outlaw, delivered this line as he appraised the persistence of a posse in *Butch Cassidy and the Sundance Kid*. Above, Newman and Redford try to outdistance their pursuers in the 1969 film.

Q: Who delivered this classic line, and in what film: "If you want to call me that—smile"?

A: Cowboy Gary Cooper thus called Trampas's bluff in the 1929 version of *The Virginian*.

Q: What 1935 Western made Gene Autry a national star as America's "singing cowboy"?

A: *Tumbling Tumbleweeds*.

Q: Who played Western badman Whip McCord in the 1939 movie *The Oklahoma Kid?*
A: Humphrey Bogart.

Q: What young Broadway actor starred opposite John Wayne in *Red River?*
A: Montgomery Clift.

Q: What movie recollection began with this line: "I knowed General George Armstrong Custer for what he was . . ."?
A: Jack Crabb, played by Dustin Hoffman, used these words to revive his memory as a 121-year-old survivor of the Battle of the Little Big Horn in the 1970 film *Little Big Man.*

Q: What famous director of Western films was born in Goshen, Indiana, on May 30, 1896, and was a professional race-car driver for a time?
A: Howard Hawks.

Q: Who directed *High Noon?*
A: Fred Zinneman.

Q: Who was the most popular woman in Westerns?
A: Based on her longevity as a Western genre star, the likeliest candidate for this achievement is probably Dale Evans, who co-starred with husband Roy Rogers in numerous "B" Westerns.

Q: What was the first Hollywood version of the Battle of the Little Big Horn?
A: William Selig's 1909 one-reel film, entitled *Custer's Last Stand,* was Hollywood's first attempt to depict the Custer massacre. Others that have followed include *The Scarlet West* (1925), *They Died with Their Boots On* (1941), *Little Big Horn* (1951), *Bugles in the Afternoon* (1952), *The Seventh Cavalry* (1956), *Tonka* (1958), *Custer of the West* (1968) and *Little Big Man* (1970).

FACT: For the 1924 silent epic *The Iron Horse,* which chronicled the building of the transcontinental railroad, director John Ford assembled an unprecedented cast: more than 3,000 railroad workers, approximately 800 Indians, a full regiment of cavalry, an estimated 10,000 cattle and about 1,300 buffalo.

Q: By what name did glove salesman Samuel Goldfish became a famous Hollywood producer of Western movies?
A: Samuel Goldwyn.

Q: For what film performance did John Wayne win his only Oscar?
A: The Duke won his sole Academy Award for his portrayal of Rooster
Cogburn, the "one-eyed fat man" lawman in the 1969 movie *True
Grit.*

Q: What famous star of Western films was the son of an English-born
lawyer and aspired to be a newspaper cartoonist?
A: Born to a British father who became a state supreme court justice
in Montana, Gary Cooper, star of Western classics *The Virginian*
and *High Noon,* worked as a cartoonist for a Montana newspaper
before moving to Hollywood and stardom.

Q: What did Ken Maynard, Buck Jones, Bob Steele, Tim Holt,
Johnny Mack Brown, Donald ("Red") Barry, William ("Wild
Bill") Elliott, Lash LaRue and William Boyd have in common?
A: All were stars of "B" Westerns during the 1930s.

Q: In what 1948 John Ford film did Shirley Temple co-star with John
Wayne, Henry Fonda and John Agar?
A: *Fort Apache.*

Q: What famous American performer played a persecuted Indian
youth in the 1960 Western *Flaming Star?*
A: Elvis Presley.

Q: Who protested his role in a famous Western with these words: "I
don't know if I want to play an old man"?
A: John Wayne so remarked to director Howard Hawks after reading
the script for *Red River.* "You're gonna be an old man soon," Hawks
replied, "so you ought to get used to it."

Q: How much was John Wayne paid to star in the 1969 film *True Grit?*
A: Producer Hal B. Wallis paid Wayne one million dollars plus a large
percentage of the movie's gross.

Q: Who was Max Aronson, and what did he do for Western movies?
A: Aronson, who changed his name to Gilbert M. Anderson, became
famous in the early twentieth century as Bronco Billy Anderson,
Hollywood's first real movie star and the leading man in more than
350 one- and two-reel Westerns between 1908 and 1915.

Q: What was the birthplace of early cowboy star William S. Hart?
A: William Surrey Hart was born in Newburgh, New York, but moved
   to Dakota Territory as a child and claimed to have worked for a
   while as a cowboy. He insisted that the scenery and sets in his
   Westerns look authentic, and he gave his movie horse, Fritz, a screen
   credit.

FACT: After an initial screening of the famous *High Noon*, producer Stanley Kramer felt the film lacked tension. To create a feeling of suspense he inserted shots of a clock interspersed with the action. The clock shots became a trademark of the film, and *High Noon* became famous for its tense countdown to the noon-hour shootout.

Q: In what 1970 Western did Richard Harris portray a rich British sportsman captured by Western Indians?

A: Harris played the role of the captive Englishman mistaken as a beast of burden in the movie *A Man Called Horse*.

Q: What was Roy Rogers's first full-time job in Hollywood?

A: In 1929 Rogers came to California from Ohio and landed a job picking fruit in an orchard near Los Angeles.

Q: Who did Gary Cooper and Jean Arthur portray in the 1936 film *The Plainsman?*

A: Cooper played Wild Bill Hickok and Jean Arthur appeared as Calamity Jane.

Q: Who said, "To talk peace is not hard. To live it is very hard"?

A: The observation was made by the Apache chief Cochise in the 1950 film *Broken Arrow*.

Q: What did the 1970 Western *Monte Walsh* have in common with the 1953 classic *Shane?*

A: Both were based on novels by Western author Jack Schaefer, and both recorded key performances by Jack Palance.

Q: Why was the climactic fistfight between hero and villain in the 1914 original version of *The Spoilers* so realistic?

A: It looked real because it *was* real: actors William Farnum and Tom Santschi agreed not to pull punches, staged a realistic fight and were both hospitalized.

Q: What 1956 John Ford Western included major scenes filmed in Monument Valley; Alberta, Canada; and near Gunnison, Colorado?

A: All were locations for *The Searchers*, which starred John Wayne.

Q: Who played the bride of Marshal Will Kane (Gary Cooper) in *High Noon?*

A: Grace Kelly.

Q: What early cowboy actor played a bit part in the 1963 John Wayne Western *McLintock!?*

A: Bob Steele, once popular as a star of "B" Westerns, played an aging railroad employee in *McLintock!*

Q: Who said, "The larceny of an equine is a capital offense, but a horse thief always gets a fair trial before he's hung"?

A: The law is so misquoted by Judge Roy Bean (Walter Brennan) in the film *The Westerner.*

Q: What 1955 Western was based on a Broadway musical and paired Gordon McCrea with Shirley Jones as singing settlers?

A: *Oklahoma!*

Q: Who played John Wayne's romantic interest in Howard Hawks's 1959 Western *Rio Bravo?*

A: Angie Dickinson.

Q: What popular 1960 Western starring Yul Brynner and Steve McQueen was inspired by a 1954 Japanese movie?

A: *The Magnificent Seven,* which also featured Charles Bronson, James Coburn, Horst Buchholz, Brad Dexter, Robert Vaughn and Eli Wallach, was based on Japan's *Seven Samurai.*

Q: Who issued this threat: "Every time you turn around, expect to see me because one time you'll turn around and I'll be there"?

A: Trail boss John Wayne made this ominous promise to adopted son Montgomery Clift after Clift took over the herd in *Red River.*

Q: What movie-star cowboy of the 1920s was named Edward Richard Gibson in private life?

A: Hoot Gibson.

FACT: Funeral services for Old West lawman and shootist Wyatt Earp were held at 10 A.M., January 16, 1929, at Pierce Brothers' Chapel in Los Angeles. Among the pallbearers at Earp's funeral were cowboy movie stars Tom Mix and William S. Hart, who had known Earp in his last years.

Q: Why did theater audiences shriek at the end of the first Western, *The Great Train Robbery,* which was released in 1903?
A: Moviegoers in 1903 were not prepared for the movie's startling ending, when villain George Barnes faced the camera and blasted away with a handgun.

Q: How long did it normally take to shoot the Roy Rogers and Gene Autry movies of the 1930s?
A: About a week.

Q: What 1962 film, directed by Sam Peckinpah and co-starring Joel McCrea, was Randolph Scott's final appearance as a Western leading man?
A: *Ride the High Country.*

Q: Who made this observation in what 1949 film: "The Army is always the same. The sun and the moon change, but the Army knows no seasons"?
A: John Wayne issued this sentiment as he retired from the Army of the West in *She Wore a Yellow Ribbon.*

Q: What star of Western films began his screen career in the forgettable 1955 movie *Revenge of the Creature?*
A: Clint Eastwood.

Q: What was the running time of *The Great Train Robbery?*
A: The 1903 classic, which was the first theater Western with a plot, ran a total of twelve minutes.

Q: What was the name of Tom Mix's horse?
A: Tony.

Q: What famous Old West scout and frontiersman portrayed himself in a series of early Hollywood Westerns?
A: Buffalo Bill Cody, who had served as a Pony Express rider in 1860, appeared in five early movies between 1909 and 1915, including an autobiographical film: *The Life of Buffalo Bill.*

Q: What famous Western, released in 1914, was based on a popular Broadway play and was produced by a former vaudeville playwright, a glove salesman and a vaudeville producer?
A: *The Squaw Man,* based on the play of the same name, was released that year as the first project by film partners Cecil B. DeMille, Samuel Goldwyn and Jesse Lasky.

Q: Whom did John Wayne describe with these on-camera words: "The pay is $13 a month. The diet—beans and eggs. May be horsemeat before this campaign is over. They fight over cards or rot-gut whiskey, but share the last drop in their canteens"?

A: Wayne offered this pointed tribute to the men of the U.S. Cavalry in the closing moments of *Fort Apache*.

Q: What Old West lawman was depicted on the screen in *Law and Order* (1932), *Frontier Marshal* (1934 and 1939), *My Darling Clementine* (1946), *Wichita* (1955), *Gunfight at the O.K. Corral* (1957), *Hour of the Gun* (1967) and *Doc* (1971)?

A: Wyatt Earp was immortalized in all these films. In a scene from *My Darling Clementine*, above, Earp—played by Henry Fonda—endures a tense moment with his friend Doc Holliday, who was portrayed by Victor Mature.

Q: What film featured this culinary critique: "The specialty of the house and it's still moving"?

A: Butch Cassidy (Paul Newman) so evaluated the cuisine at a Bolivian tavern seconds before coming under fire in *Butch Cassidy and the Sundance Kid.*

Q: Who directed the 1930 motion picture *The Big Trail,* which gave John Wayne his first starring role?

A: *The Big Trail* was directed by Raoul Walsh.

Q: How many films had Montgomery Clift played in when he appeared in *Red River?*

A: Clift, a Broadway actor, had appeared in only one other movie at the time he starred with John Wayne in *Red River.*

Q: Who sang the Academy Award–winning ballad *High Noon?*

A: Tex Ritter.

Q: What was the name of the horse ridden by cowboy star Ken Maynard, and what was wrong with the animal?

A: Maynard's star mount was named Tarzan and his eyesight was so poor he sometimes bumped into objects.

Q: What famous director of Western movies made this observation: "If our ancestors could come back and see us as we are today, they'd vomit"?

A: John Ford.

Q: What waterway was used as the Red River in Howard Hawks's film *Red River?*

A: Although most of the film's story was set in Texas, the movie was actually filmed on the San Pedro River near Tucson, Arizona.

Q: What was John Wayne's last film?

A: In his last film appearance John Wayne played an aging, cancer-stricken gunfighter in the 1976 movie *The Shootist.*

Q: On what location was *Shane* filmed?

A: George Stevens's 1953 classic was shot within sight of the Grand Teton Mountains near Jackson Hole, Wyoming.

Q: What was the destination of the overland stage in the 1939 film *Stagecoach?*

A: Lordsburg, New Mexico.

Q: What was Jimmy Stewart's favorite drink when he visited the Last
Chance Saloon in *Destry Rides Again?*

A: Stewart's character, Thomas Destry, Jr., cleaned up the Western
town of Bottleneck in the 1939 movie after tossing down a glass of
milk in the town saloon.

Q: Of all his Western films, which was John Wayne's favorite?

A: According to son Michael Wayne, the Duke had several favorites.
One was *The Searchers,* in which he played Ethan Edwards, an
embittered former Confederate cavalryman conducting a relentless
search for a niece captured by Indians. Among Wayne's other favorites were *Stagecoach, Red River, She Wore a Yellow Ribbon* and
True Grit. Here he leads a company of Rangers through Monument
Valley in a scene from *The Searchers.*

Q: What poker hand was dealt to badman Liberty Valance in *The Man Who Shot Liberty Valance?*

A: Shortly before his violent demise the bellicose Liberty Valance was dealt the notorious "Deadman's Hand" of aces and eights.

Q: Who was Leonard Slye?

A: A native of Cincinnati gifted with a friendly face and a pleasant voice, Leonard Slye became famous as Roy Rogers, "King of the Cowboys."

Q: On what Western was John Wayne working at the time of his death in 1979?

A: In John Wayne's possession when he died of cancer on June 11, 1979, was a script tentatively entitled *Cattle Drive to the Yukon,* which probably would have been Wayne's next Western. It would have depicted an adventurous cattle drive to Canada's Wild West during the Yukon Gold Rush.

Bibliography

Abbott, E. C., and Helena Huntington Smith. *We Pointed Them North: Recollections of a Cowpuncher.* New York: Farrar and Rinehart, 1939.

Adams, Ramon F. *Come an' Get It: The Story of the Old Cowboy Cook.* Norman: University of Oklahoma Press, 1952.

Adams, Ramon F. *Western Words: A Dictionary of the Range, Cow Camp and Trail.* Norman: University of Oklahoma Press, 1945.

"After the Custer Battle." Edited by Albert J. Partoll. Missoula, Montana: *Frontier and Midland: A Magazine of the Northwest.* Vol. XIX. (No. 4. 1939).

Alter, F. Cecil. *Jim Bridger.* Norman: University of Oklahoma Press, 1962.

America's Fascinating Indian Heritage. Edited by James A. Maxwell. Pleasantville, New York: The Reader's Digest Association, 1978.

Armstrong, Virginia Irving. *I Have Spoken: American History Through the Voices of the Indians.* Chicago: Swallow Press, 1971.

Arnold, Oren, and John P. Hale. *Hot Irons: Heraldry of the Range.* New York: Macmillan Company, 1944.

Beal, Merrill D. *"I Will Fight No More Forever": Chief Joseph and the Nez Percé War.* Seattle: University of Washington Press, 1963.

Bender, Tex. *Ten Years a Cowboy.* Chicago: Rhodes and McClure Publishing Company, 1891.

Berry, Don. *A Majority of Scoundrels.* New York: Ballantine Books, 1961.

The Book of the American West. Edited by Jay Monaghan. New York: Bonanza Books, 1963.

Bourke, John G. *On the Border with Crook.* Lincoln: University of Nebraska Press, 1971.

Brady, Cyrus Townsend. *Indian Fights and Fighters.* Lincoln: University of Nebraska Press, 1971.

Breihan, Carl W. *Great Gunfighters of the West.* San Antonio: The Naylor Company, 1962.

Brininstool, E. A. *Troopers with Custer.* Harrisburg, Pa.: The Stackpole Company, 1952.

Brown, Mark H. *The Flight of the Nez Percé.* Lincoln: University of Nebraska Press, 1982.

Brown, Mark H., and W. R. Felton. *Before Barbed Wire.* New York: Bramhall House, 1956.

Capps, Benjamin. *The Indians.* New York: Time-Life Books, 1973.

Cary, A. Merwyn. *American Firearms Makers.* New York: Thomas Y. Crowell, 1953.

Cary, Lucian. *Lucian Cary on Guns.* New York: Arco Publishers, 1954.

Chandler, Melbourne C. *Of Garryowen in Glory: The History of the 7th U.S. Cavalry.* Annandel, Va.: Turnpike Press, Inc., 1960.

Chappell, Gordon. *The Search for the Well-Dressed Soldier 1865–1890.* Tucson: Arizona Historical Society, 1972.

Chittenden, Hiram Martin. *The American Fur Trade of the Far West.* 2 vols. New York: Francis P. Harper, 1902.

Clapham, Walter C. *Western Movies: The Story of the West on Screen.* London: Octopus Books, 1974.

Cleland, Robert Glass. *This Reckless Breed of Men: The Trappers and Fur Traders of the Southwest.* New York: Alfred A. Knopf, 1963.

Connell, Evan S. *Son of the Morning Star.* San Francisco: North Point Press, 1984.

Cromie, Alice. *Tour Guide to the Old West.* New York: Quadrangle/The New York Times Book Company, 1977.

Custer, Elizabeth. *Boots and Saddles.* New York: Harper and Brothers, 1885.

Custer, Elizabeth. *Following the Guidon.* New York: Harper and Brothers, 1890.

Custer, Elizabeth. *Tenting on the Plains.* New York: Charles L. Webster & Company, 1887.

Custer, George A. *My Life on the Plains.* Edited by Milo Milton Quaife. Lincoln: University of Nebraska Press, 1952.

The Custer Story: The Life and Intimate Letters of General George A. Custer and His Wife Elizabeth. Edited by Marguerite Merington. New York: The Devin-Adair Company, 1950.

Dary, David. *Cowboy Culture: A Saga of Five Centuries.* New York: Alfred A. Knopf, 1981.

DeMattos, Jack. "Gunfighters of the Real West: Billy the Kid." *Real West.* Vol. 26 (August 1983).

Dictionary of American Biography. 20 vols. New York: Charles Scribner's Sons, 1940.

Dobie, J. Frank. *The Longhorns.* Austin: University of Texas Press, 1980.

Dolan, Edward F., Jr. *History of the Movies.* Greenwich, Conn.: Bison Books, 1983.

Drago, Harry Sinclair. *Great American Cattle Trails.* New York: Dodd, Mead & Company, 1965.

Drago, Harry Sinclair. *Outlaws on Horseback.* New York: Bramhall House, 1964.

Dustin, Fred. *The Custer Tragedy.* Ann Arbor: Edwards Brothers, Inc., 1939.

Everson, William K. *A Pictorial History of the Western Film.* New York: The Citadel Press, 1969.

Ewers, John C. *The Blackfeet: Raiders on the Northwestern Plains.* Norman: University of Oklahoma Press, 1982.

The Field Diary of General Alfred H. Terry: The Yellowstone Expedition—1876. Edited by Michael J. Koury. Bellevue, Neb.: The Old Army Press, 1970.

Forbis, **William H.** *The Cowboys.* New York: Time-Life Books, 1973.

Frost, **Lawrence A.** *The Custer Album.* Seattle: Superior Publishing Company, 1964.

Frost, **Lawrence A.** *Custer Legends.* Bowling Green, Ohio: Bowling Green University Popular Press, 1981.

General George Crook: His Autobiography. Edited by Martin F. Schmitt. Norman: University of Oklahoma Press, 1946.

Gilbert, **Bil.** *The Trailblazers.* New York: Time-Life Books, 1973.

Godfrey, **E. S.** "Custer's Last Battle." *Century Illustrated Monthly Magazine.* Vol. 43 (January 1892).

Graham, **W. A.** *Abstract of the Official Record of Proceedings of the Reno Court of Inquiry.* Harrisburg, Pa.: The Stackpole Company, 1954.

Graham, **W. A.** *The Custer Myth: A Source Book of Custeriana.* Harrisburg, Pa.: The Stackpole Company, 1953.

Gregg, **Josiah.** *Commerce of the Prairies.* Philadelphia: J. B. Lippincott Company, 1962.

Grinnell, **George Bird.** *The Fighting Cheyennes.* Norman: University of Oklahoma Press, 1983.

Guns of the Gunfighters. Edited by Garry James. Los Angeles: Peterson Publishing Company, 1975.

Haley, **J. Evetts.** *The XIT Ranch of Texas.* Norman: University of Oklahoma Press, 1953.

Halliwell, **Leslie.** *Halliwell's Film Guide.* London: Granada Publishing, 1977.

Hammer, **Kenneth M.** *The Springfield Carbine on the Western Frontier.* Bellevue, Neb.: The Old Army Press, 1970.

Hart, **Herbert M.** *Tour Guide to Old Western Forts.* Fort Collins, Co.: The Old Army Press, 1980.

Haun, Harvey. *The Movie Quote Book.* New York: Harper & Row, 1980.

Hooker, Richard J. *Food and Drink in America.* Indianapolis: The Bobbs-Merrill Company, Inc., 1981.

Horan, James D., and Paul Sann. *Pictorial History of the Wild West.* New York: Crown Publishers, 1954.

Horn, Huston. *The Pioneers.* New York: Time-Life Books, 1974.

Hunt, Frazier, and Robert Hunt. *Horses and Heroes: The Story of the Horse in America for 450 Years.* New York: Charles Scribner's Sons, 1940.

Hunt, Frazier and Robert Hunt. *I Fought with Custer.* New York: Charles Scribner's Sons, 1947.

Hyams, Jay. *The Life and Times of the Western Movie.* New York: Gallery Books, 1983.

Hyde, George. *Red Cloud's Folk: A History of the Oglala Sioux Indians.* Norman: University of Oklahoma Press, 1957.

Irving, Washington. *Captain Bonneville.* New York: John B. Alden, 1887.

Johnson, William Webber. *The Forty-Niners.* New York: Time-Life Books, 1974.

The Journals of Lewis and Clark. Edited by John Blakeless. New York: The New American Library, 1964.

Kain, Robert G. *In the Valley of the Little Big Horn.* Newfane: Vermont Printing Company, 1969.

Katz, Ephraim. *The Film Encyclopedia.* New York: Thomas Y. Crowell, 1979.

Keating, Bern. *An Illustrated History of the Texas Rangers.* New York: Promontory Press, 1980.

King, Charles. "Custer's Last Battle." *Harper's Magazine* (August 1890).

Koller, Lawrence R. *The Fireside Book of Guns.* New York: Simon and Schuster, 1959.

Koury, Michael J. *Diaries of the Little Big Horn.* Fort Collins, Co.: The Old Army Press, 1968.

Kuhlman, Charles. *Did Custer Disobey Orders at the Battle of the Little Big Horn?* Harrisburg, Pa.: The Stackpole Company, 1957.

Kuhlman, Charles. *Legend into History: The Custer Mystery.* Harrisburg, Pa.: The Stackpole Company, 1951.

Lake, Stuart N. *Wyatt Earp: Frontier Marshal.* New York: Houghton Mifflin Company, 1931.

Laubin, Reginald, and Gladys Laubin. *The Indian Tipi.* Norman: University of Oklahoma Press, 1977.

Lavender, David. *The American Heritage History of the Great West.* New York: American Heritage Publishing Company, 1965.

Lord, Walter. *A Time to Stand: The Epic of the Alamo.* New York: Harper & Row, 1961.

Los Angeles Times.

McConnell, Ronald C. "Isaiah Dorman and the Custer Expedition," *Journal of Negro History* (July 1948).

McLoughlin, Denis. *Wild and Woolly: An Encyclopedia of the Old West.* Garden City: Doubleday & Company, Inc., 1975.

Mails, Thomas E. *Dog Soldiers, Bear Men and Buffalo Women: A Study of the Societies and Cults of the Plains Indians.* Englewood Cliffs, N.J.: Prentice-Hall, Inc., 1973.

Manchel, Frank. *Cameras West.* Englewood Cliffs, N.J.: Prentice-Hall, Inc., 1971.

Marquis, Thomas B. *Keep the Last Bullet for Yourself.* New York: Two Continents Publishing Group, 1976.

Marquis, Thomas B. *Wooden Leg: A Warrior Who Fought Custer.* Lincoln: University of Nebraska Press, 1962.

Martin, Horace T. *Castorologia: The History and Traditions of the Canadian Beaver.* London: Edward Stanford, 1892.

Mayhall, Mildred P. *The Kiowas.* Norman: University of Oklahoma Press, 1962.

The Medal of Honor of the United States Army. Edited by Thomas W. Huntington. Washington, D.C.: U.S. Government Printing Office, 1948.

Mercer, A. S. *The Banditti of the Plains.* Norman: University of Oklahoma Press, 1954.

Nadeau, Remi. *Fort Laramie and the Sioux.* Lincoln: University of Nebraska Press, 1982.

Nelson, Bruce. *Land of the Dacotahs.* Lincoln: University of Nebraska Press, 1973.

Nevin, David. *The Expressmen.* New York: Time-Life Books, 1974.

Nevin, David. *The Soldiers.* New York: Time-Life Books, 1973.

The New York Times.

Oregon *Daily Journal.*

Osgood, Ernest S. *The Day of the Cattleman.* Chicago: The University of Chicago Press, 1968.

Parsons, John E. *The Peacemaker and Its Rivals.* New York: William Morrow and Company, 1950.

Parsons, John E., and John S. duMont. *Firearms Used in the Custer Battle.* Harrisburg, Pa.: The Stackpole Company, 1953.

Pointer, Larry. *In Search of Butch Cassidy.* Norman: University of Oklahoma Press, 1977.

The Reader's Encyclopedia of the American West. Edited by Howard R. Lamar. New York: Thomas Y. Crowell Company, 1977.

Reiter, Joan Swallow. *The Women.* New York: Time-Life Books, 1978.

Report of the Secretary of War: House of Representatives, 44th Congress. Volume I. Washington, D.C.: U.S. Government Printing Office, 1876.

Rickey, Don. *Forty Miles a Day on Beans and Hay.* Norman: University of Oklahoma Press, 1963.

Roe, Charles Francis. *Custer's Last Battle.* New York: National Highways Association, 1927.

Rosa, Joseph G. *The Gunfighter: Man or Myth.* Norman: University of Oklahoma Press, 1969.

Russell, Carl P. *Guns on the Early Frontiers.* Berkeley: University of California Press, 1957.

Salisbury, Albert, and Jane Salisbury. *Here Rolled the Covered Wagons.* Seattle: Superior Publishing Company, 1948.

Sandoz, Mari. *The Beaver Men.* New York: Hastings House, Publishers, 1964.

Sandoz, Mari. *Crazy Horse, The Strange Man of the Oglalas.* Lincoln: University of Nebraska Press, 1961.

Schoenberger, Dale T. *The Gunfighters.* Caldwell, Idaho: The Caxton Printers, 1971.

Settle, William, Jr. *Jesse James Was His Name.* Columbia: University of Missouri Press, 1966.

Soldier and Brave. National Park Service. Washington, D.C.: U.S. Government Printing Office, 1971.

Steckmesser, Kent L. *The Western Hero in History and Legend.* Norman: University of Oklahoma Press, 1965.

Stewart, Edgar I. *Custer's Luck.* Norman: University of Oklahoma Press, 1955.

Stone, Eric. *Medicine Among the American Indians.* New York: Hafner Publishing Company, 1962.

Story of the Great American West. Edited by Edward S. Banard. Pleasantville, New York: The Reader's Digest Association, 1977.

Stoutenburgh, John L. *Dictionary of the American Indian.* New York: Philosophical Library, 1960.

Stratton, Joanna L. *Pioneer Women: Voices from the Kansas Frontier.* New York: Simon and Schuster, 1981.

Tanner, Ogden. *The Ranchers.* New York: Time-Life Books, 1977.

Trachtman, Paul. *The Gunfighters.* New York: Time-Life Books, 1974.

Trappers of the Far West. Edited by Leroy R. Hafen. Lincoln: University of Nebraska Press, 1983.

Tuska, Jon. *The Filming of the West.* Garden City, N.Y.: Doubleday and Company, Inc., 1976.

Unruh, John D., Jr. *The Plains Across: The Overland Emigrants and the Trans-Mississippi West, 1840–60.* Urbana: University of Illinois Press, 1979.

Utley, Robert M. *Custer and the Great Controversy.* Los Angeles: Westernlore Press, 1962.

Utley, Robert M. *Frontier Regulars: The United States Army and the Indian, 1866–1891.* New York: Macmillan Publishing Company, 1973.

Utley, Robert M. *The Indian Frontier of the American West 1846–1890.* Albuquerque: University of New Mexico Press, 1984.

Utley, Robert M., and Wilcomb E. Washburn. *The American Heritage History of the Indian Wars.* New York: American Heritage Publishing Company, 1977.

Van de Water, Frederick. *Glory-Hunter: A Life of General Custer.* Indianapolis: The Bobbs-Merrill Company, 1934.

Vestal, Stanley. *Jim Bridger: Mountain Man.* Lincoln: University of Nebraska Press, 1946.

Vestal, Stanley. *Sitting Bull: Champion of the Sioux.* Norman: University of Oklahoma Press, 1957.

Vestal, Stanley. *Warpath.* Lincoln: University of Nebraska Press, 1984.

Victor, Frances F. *Eleven Years in the Rocky Mountains and Life on the Frontier.* Hartford: R. W. Bliss and Company, 1881.

Viele, Teresa Griffin. *Following the Drum.* Lincoln: University of Nebraska Press, 1984.

Warner, Ezra J. *Generals in Blue.* Baton Rouge: Louisiana State University Press, 1964.

Waters, Frank. *The Earp Brothers of Tombstone.* New York: Clarkson N. Potter, 1960.

Wellman, Paul I. *The Indian Wars of the West.* Garden City: Doubleday and Company, 1954.

Wheeler, Keith. *The Scouts.* New York: Time-Life Books, 1978.

Wilson, R. L. *Colt: An American Legend.* New York: Abbeville Press, 1985.

Winther, Oscar O. *Via Western Express and Stagecoach.* Lincoln: University of Nebraska Press, 1945.

The World of the American Indian. Edited by Jules B. Billard. Washington, D.C.: National Geographic Society, 1974.

Index

Page numbers in *italics* refer to illustrations.

abandoned trapper, 39
Abilene, Kansas, 9, 95, 125, 128, 131, 138, 144
Absarokas, 57
Academy Awards, 187, 189, 190, 191, 194, 200
ace in the hole, 14
Acme Saloon, El Paso, 7
Adams, James Capen, 106
Adobe Walls battle, 51
adulterous Indian women, punishment of, 49
Agar, John, 194
age:
  of Army recruits, 73
  of cowboys, 117
airin' the lungs, 119
The Alamo, 28, 33
  battle of, 32, 34, 140
albino beavers, 48
Alexis, Grand Duke, 28
Allison, Clay, 1, 7, 8
  death of, 23
American Falls, Idaho, 93, 107
American Fur Company, 35, 38, 39, 42, 44
American Horse, Sioux chief, 69, 83
American River, 96
ammunition, 89, 176
among the willows, 21
Anderson, Gilbert M., 194
Angry-Men-Stand-in-Line-for-Him, 55
antelope, pronghorn, 57
Anti-Fever Pills, 112
Antrim, Henry, 3
Apache Indians, 49, 51, 52, 53, 55, 64, 68, 72, 88, 155
Apache Pass, Arizona, 77, 88
Apache Wars, 79
Appaloosa horses, 56, 139
Arapaho Indians, 52, 54
Arbuckle's, 117
Arikara Indians, 34, 48, 57, 64, 85, 170
Arizona, gold strike, 43
Arkansas River, 106
"The Arkansas Traveler," 113
Armstrong, John, 13
Army. *See* U.S. Army
The Army and Navy Journal, 84
Arnold, Philip, 103
Aronson, Max, 194
arrowhead, removal of, 82

arrow poison, 64
arrows, number of, 38
Arthur, Chester A., 58
Arthur, Jean, 196
Ash Hollow battle, 76
Ashley, William H., 28, 32, 34, 35, 48, 140
Assiniboine Indians, 64
Astor, John Jacob, 35, 42
Astoria, Washington, 42
Atchison, Topeka and Santa Fe Railway, 112
Audubon, John J., 26
Austin, Texas, 130
automobile wreck, Indian leader killed, 72
Autry, Gene, 192, 198

Baca, Elfego, 16
backhand slip, 122
Bacon, Elizabeth, 177
  See also Custer, Elizabeth
Bad Hand, 41
Bad-Light-Hair, 165
bad medicine, 6
Bain wagon, 98
The Bandit King, 191
bank robberies, 8, 19
  by Jesse James, 12, 18
Bannack, Montana, 10, 98
barbed wire, 110, 137, 150
Barnes, George, 198
Barnum, P. T., 106
barrel jacket, 78
Barry, Donald "Red," 194
Bartleson, John, 106
Bascom, George N., 79
basic training, 74, 81
Bass, Sam, 18, 159
baths, for soldiers, 73
battles:
  Adobe Walls, 51
  Ash Hollow, 76
  Bear Paw Mountain, 78
  Beecher's Island, 65, 76, 90
  Big Hole, 78, 84
  Camas Creek, 78
  Canyon Creek, 78
  Clearwater, 78
  Cow Island, 78
  Little Big Horn, 77, 150, 152, 159, 161–82, 187, 193
  Milk Creek, 65

battles (cont.)
  Palo Duro Canyon, 82
  Pierre's Hole, 41, 155
  of the Rosebud, 75
  San Jacinto, 37
  Skull Cave, 79
  Slim Buttes, 69, 83
  Soldier Spring, 84
  Solomon River, 92
  Summit Springs, 61, 80
  Tres Castillos, 69
  of the Washita, 56, 75, 87, 157
  White Bird Canyon, 78
  Wolf Mountain, 86
Baxter Springs, Kan., 122
bayonets, 75
Beadle, Erastus, 102
Bean, Roy, 3, 6, 151
  film portrayal of, 191, 197
bean-master, 121
Bear Lake, 26, 42
Bear Paw Mountain, 78
"Beautiful Dreamer," 80
beaver, 24, 43, 46, 48
  trapping of, 27, 29
Beaver, Utah, 9
Becknell, William, 102
Beckwith, Jennings, 25
Beckwourth, James Pierson, 25, 25, 29, 48,
    157
bedbugs, 100
Beecher, Frederick, 76
Beecher's Island battle, 65, 76, 90
Belknap, William W., 86
Belle Fourche, S.D., 4
belly-cheater, 121
belts, for ammunition, 89
Ben Hur, California, 95
Ben Hur, Wallace, 14
Bent, Charles, 29, 46
Bent, William, 29, 47
Benteen, Catherine, 164
Benteen, Frederick W., 152, 164, 175, 180
Benton, Jessie, 29
Benton, Thomas Hart, 29
Bent's Fort, Colorado, 29
Bent's Old Fort, 47
Bible, Indian request, 51
Bidwell, John, 106
Big Chief Who Swears, 76
Big Heart White Man, 130
Big Hole battle, 78, 84
Bighorn River Valley, 33

The Big Trail, 186, 200
Big Vermilion, 93
Billy the Kid (William Bonney), 1, 3, 7, 11,
    12, 13, 14, 20, 23, 143, 154, 186
birthplace:
  Billy the Kid, 1
  Jim Bridger, 24
  Butch Cassidy, 9
  Gary Cooper, 188
  General Custer, 161
  William S. Hart, 195
  Howard Hawks, 193
  Bat Masterson, 4
  the Sundance Kid, 9
  Ben Thompson, 10
Bisbee, Arizona, 101
biscuit shooter, 121
Bismarck, N.D. 96
  Tribune, 172, 175
the bit (earmark), 131
bits (for horses), 133
Black Bart (Charles E. Boles), 4, 16
Blackfoot Indians, 37, 39, 56, 64, 68, 70, 108
Black Hawk War, 32
Black Hills, S.D., 69
Black Jack Point, 106
Black Kettle, Cheyenne chief, 56, 87, 155,
    157
Blacks, 25, 29, 76, 82
  at Little Big Horn, 164
blanket courting, 72
blizzards, 130, 144
Bloody Knife, 174, 174
blowflies, 124
Blue Creek, Nebraska, 55
blue denims, 128
blue paint, Indian, 70
body paint, 49, 56
Bogart, Humphrey, 193
Boggs, Francis, 191
bone pickers, 107
Bonner, T. D., 48, 157
Bonneville, Benjamin, 43
Bonneville, Louis Eulalie de, 41
Bonney, William. See Billy the Kid
Boone, A. G., 157
Boone, Daniel, 30, 157
boots, cowboy, 120
bordellos, 157
border draw, 4
bounty, Indian slaves killed for, 70
bourgeois, 41
Bouyer, Minton ("Mitch"), 170

Bow Strings, 53
Boyd, William, 189, 194
Bozeman, John M., 108
Bozeman Times, 175
Bozeman Trail, 45, 89, 113, 140
Brahma Bull Saloon, 114
Brahman cattle, 133
brand artists, 118
branding of cattle, 121
Brandon, Benjamin, 170
Brennan, Walter, 183, 190, 191, 197
brides, imported, 111
    mail-order, 103
Bridger, Jim, 24, 28, 32, 33, 35, 38, 39, 44,
        45, 146, 155
Bridger Pass, 45
Broken Arrow, 185, 186, 196
Broken Hand, 41
Bronson, Charles, 197
brothers:
    fur traders, 39
    outlaws, 8, 10, 11
Brown, Johnny Mack, 186, 194
Brown, Margaret Tobin, 104
Brule Sioux Indians, 62, 76
Bryan, John N., 112
Brynner, Yul, 197
bucking and gagging, 87
buffalo, 28, 31, 149
    dried meat, 33, 54
    hunters, 29, 37, 41, 58, 66, 68
    marrow, 26
    preservation of, 120
Buffalo Bill. *See* Cody, William F.
    Buffalo Bill's Wild West Show, 3, 22, 65
buffalo bones, 107
buffalo chips, 70, 95
buffalo grass, 118
Buffalo Jim, 104
buffalo robes, 32
bugle calls, 81
Bugles in the Afternoon, 193
bullboats, 42
bulldogging, 133
bullets, for Colt .45, 7
bunkhouses, 129, *129*, 135
bunky, 91
Buntline, Ned, 30
Buntline Special (Colt .45), 6
burial, in wagon box, 112
burial place:
    Frederick Benteen, 180
    Calamity Jane, 18

Crazy Horse, 57
General Custer, 175, 176, 177, 178, 181
Wyatt Earp, 16
Thomas Fitzpatrick, 44
Geronimo, 55
Wild Bill Hickok, 18
Myles Keogh, 170
Sitting Bull, 67
Burkman, John, 181
Burnett, S. Burk, 118
Butch Cassidy and the Sundance Kid, 185, 187,
        188, 192, *192*, 200
"the Butcher," 76
butcher knife wagon, 104
Butler, Frank, 22
Butte, Montana, 100
butter, churning of, 93
B Westerns, 187, 194

cabins, 96, 107, 145, *145*
    wall covering, 111
Cache Valley, 42
Caddle, M. C., 178
Cahill, Frank P., 13
Calamity Jane (Martha Jane Canary), 18, 97,
        142, 196
calf wagon, 122
Calhoun, James, 168, 175
California, 96
    overland route, 29, 106, 111, 113
California Gold Rush, 52, 84, 95, 96, 102,
        111, 128, 138, 151
Camas Creek battle, 78
camels, 78
Camp Grant Massacre, 55, 68
campaign hats, 83
Campbell, Robert, 41, 44, 84
Canary, Martha Jane. *See* Calamity Jane
Canby, Edward R. S., 76, 90
Candlish, James, 112
cannibalism, 38, 113
cannon, Continental Divide crossing, 35
Canton, Frank M., 3
canvas, surplus, 128
Canyon Creek battle, 78
Canyon de Chelly, Arizona, 56, 80
Capitol Saloon, 110
Captain Jack, Modoc leader, 52, 66
Carnahan, John M., 181
Carolina Hotel, 22
Carr, Eugene A., 80
Carradine, John, 191

Carson, Christopher ("Kit"), 27, 32, 36, 44, 80, 143, 152
cartridge belts, 89
cartridge box, 82
Casement, Jack, 138
Cassidy, Butch, 1, 4, 6, 9, 9, 16, 19, 20, 21, 156
  film portrayal of, 188, 192, *192*, 200
Cassidy, Hopalong, 185, 189
catamounts, 106
Cat Ballou, 190
Catlin, George, 56, 154
catlinite, 56
cattle, 122, 128, *131*
  brands, 118, 121, 126
  in railroad cars, 125
  stampedes, 120, 123
  unmarked, 123
cattle drives, 118, 120, 126, 129, 132, 133, 135, 148
  cooks, 116, 135
  night hawk, 131
Cattle Drive to the Yukon, 202
Cattle king of Colorado, 119
cattle market, first in Kansas, 125
cattle rustlers, 118
Cavalry, 81, 86, 90
  See also U.S. Army
"Cavalry Trilogy," 184
cave, siege of, 79
Cayuse Indians, 108
Central Pacific Railroad, 98, 102
Chaffee, Adna R., 136
Champion, Nate, 127
Chandler, Jeff, 185
Chaney, Lon, Jr., 191
chaps, 132
Charbonneau, Jean Baptiste, 42
Charette, Missouri, 47
Charles Sitting Man, 177
charqui, 33
Chato, Apache leader, 72
Cherokee Indians, 63
Cheyenne, Wyo., 125, 133
Cheyenne Indians, 53, 56, 58, 60, 61, 63, 65, 72, 75, 76, 80, 82, 86
child, captured by Indians, 101
Chimney Rock, 93
Chinese laborers, 98, 99
  massacre of, 103
Chisholm, Jesse, 124, 151
Chisholm Trail, 124, 132
Chivington, J. M., 155

cholera, 108
Chouteau, Francois, 102
Chouteau Island, 106
Christian convert, 70
Christmas Day battle, 84
chuck wagons, *121*, 125, 127, 128, 135
churning of butter, 93
cigarettes, 128
Cimarron, 191
Civil War, 63, 80, 82
Civil War widows, 111
civilian, commanding U.S. troops, 83
Clanton, Ike, 136
Clark, William, 150
Clearwater, battle of, 78
Clift, Montgomery, 193, 197, 200
clothing, 131
  of cowboys, 116, 120
    hats, 118, 127, 136
    chaps, 132
    kerchief, 119
  of Custer, 172
  of soldiers, 147, 163
    hats, 73, 170
    Stetson hats, 125
Cloud Man, 165
clowns, Indian, 55
clubhouse, for cattlemen, 133
Clum, John, 55
Clyman, James, 32, 47
Coburn, James, 197
Cochise, 79, 185, 196
Cody, William F. ("Buffalo Bill"), 26, 28, 30, 65, 82, 198
coffee, 116, 142, 149
  cowboy, 122
Coffeyville, Kansas, 5
coffin, under bed, 30
cold, treatment of, 94
cold weather, 79, 134
Collins, Caspar W., 80
Collins, William O., 80
Colma, California, 16
Coloma, California, 96
Colorado River, 33, 40
Colt .44 #55093, 23
Colt .45, 7
  Peacemaker, 3, 8
  Buntline Special, 6
Colter, John, 33, 37, 47
Columbia River, 30, 93
Columbus Barracks, O., 74
Colvin, Al, 83

Comanche (horse), 167, 181
Comanche Indians, 43, 49, 51, 60, 66, 68, 75, 82, 84, 138, 158
Comanche Moon, 49
Concord stagecoaches, 99, 99, 112
Conestoga wagons, 98, 114
Confederate army, Indian regiment, 63
Congressional Medal of Honor, 26, 74, 75, 88, 92, 173, 179
Connor, Patrick E., 80
Conquering Bear, 91
Continental Divide, 104
    first crossings, 35, 46
Cooke, W. W., 152, 164
cooks, cowboy, 121
the coonie, 125
Cooper, Gary, 186, 187, 188, 192, 194, 196, 197
copper production, 100
cordelle, 41
cork helmets, 73
corn whiskey, 156
costs:
    beaver pelts, 24
    beaver traps, 29
    buffalo bones, 107
    firearms, 3, 161
    Lewis and Clark Expedition, 44
    mules, 105
    oxen, 105
    Pony Express, 115
    powder horns, 42
    stagecoaches, 99
    stagecoach fare, 112
    wagon, 108
    westward emigration, 108
cottonwood bark, 122
cougars, 106
Council Grove, 106
counting coup, 51
Court House Rock, 93
Court of Inquiry, Little Big Horn, 176
court-martial:
    of Benteen, 175
    of Custer, 172
courting customs, 72
cow chips, for fuel, 125
Cow Island battle, 78
cow towns, 118
cowboys, 116, 117, 117, 119, 132, 134, 134, 144, 158, 158
The Cowboys, 191
Coyote Droppings, 51

coyotes, 150
Crabb, Jack, 187, 193
Crater Lake, Oregon, 37
Crazy Dogs, 53
Crazy Horse, 49, 53, 56, 57, 60, 66, 86, 151, 156, 159, 168, 191
Creede, Colorado, 17
Crocker, Charles, 102
Crockett, Davy, 32
Cromwell, Oklahoma, 12
Crook, George, 69, 75, 77, 78, 79, 83, 139, 146, 152, 156
    death of, 86, 90
Crooked Lances, 53
the crop, 131
Crow Indians, 38, 57, 64
    scouts for Custer, 170
Crow's Nest, 165
the curb (bit), 133
Curly (Indian), 53, 175
Curly Dan, 104
curly wolf, 6
cursing, 119
Custer, Boston, 168
Custer, Elizabeth Bacon, 139, 166, 177, 181
Custer, George Armstrong, 28, 75, 87, 139, 143, 152, 154, 157, 161–82 passim, 162, 174
    film portrayal, 185, 187, 191
Custer, Lydia-Ann, 173
Custer, Thomas W., 168, 175, 177, 179, 179
Custer Avengers, 90
Custer of the West, 193
Custer's Last Stand, 193

Dakota Territory, 100
Dallas, Texas, 112
Dalton, Bob, 8
Dalton, Emmett, 8
Dalton, Grat, 8
Dalton Gang, 5, 8
dark and bloody ground in Arizona, 130
David's Island, N.Y., 74
Davis, Jefferson, 78
Davis, Jefferson C., 76, 90
Daw, Thomas, 46
dead body:
    fined by court, 6
    poker played on, 26
Dead Man's Hand, 14, 202
Deadwood, South Dakota, 14, 18, 142
death, common causes, 132
de Havilland, Olivia, 185

dehorning of cattle, 122
DeKalb, Illinois, 110
Delores, New Mexico, 105
Delta, Colorado, 4
DeMille, Cecil B., 187, 190, 198
Denig, Edwin T., 43
denim trousers, 128
dentist, 8, 129
Denver, Colorado, 111
Denver, James W., 111
Denver and Rio Grande Western Railroad, 104
Dern, Bruce, 191
desertion rate, 83, 84
De Smet, Pierre Jean, 97
Destry Rides Again, 186, 201
Devil's Gate, 93, 107
Devil's Half-Acre, 95
de Wilde, Brandon, 189
De Wolf, James M., 170
De Young's Broadway Studio, 6
diamond field hoax, 103
diapers, Indian, 70
dicehouse, 129
Dickinson, Angie, 197
die-up, 128
Digger Indians, 52
dime novels, 102
"Dinah Had a Wooden Leg," 113
Dingus, 20
dirt floors, 96
diseases, 73, 74, 98, 108
dishwater, 135
the dive, 129
Doan's Store, 126
Doc, 199
Dodge, Grenville M., 138
Dodge City, 189
Dodge City, Kansas, 15, 31, 97, 124, 124
the doghouse, 129
Dog Men, 52
dog robbers, 86
dogs, sheepherders', 142, 150
Dog Soldiers, 53
dog stew, 43
dogtrot cabin, 107
Dolin gang, 12
Donner, George, 113
Donner, Jacob, 113
Donner disaster, 154
Dorman, Isaiah, 164
dough-boxer, 121
Dover, New Jersey, 185
"The Dreary Black Hills," 80

Drovers Cottage, 128
drunkenness, 78
Duchouquette, Francois, 29
dugouts, 42
Dull Knife Battle, 60, 89
the dump, 129
du Pont de Nemours, Eleuthere Irenee, 39
Dutch John, 104
Dutch ovens, 121
Duvall, Robert, 188
dysentery, 73

Eagle Brewery, 110
ear to the ground, 151
earmarks of cattle, 131
Earp, Allie Sullivan, 19
Earp, Mattie, 19
Earp, Morgan, 5
Earp, Newton J., 13
Earp, Virgil, 5, 19
Earp, Wyatt Berry Stapp, 1, 5, 5, 6, 9, 10, 12, 13, 15, 16, 19, 21, 158, 197
    film portrayal of, 187, 199, 199
    quotes, 136, 140
Eastlick, Merton, 97
Eastwood, Clint, 188, 198
Edwards, Ethan, 201
Eel River, California, 29
eggs, packing of, 110
1875 Smith & Wesson Schofield, 20
1873 Colt Peacemaker, 3
elk antlers, pile of, 63
Elk Bear, 165
Elliott, Joel H., 75
Elliott, William, 194
El Paso, Texas, 7
emigrants, 108, 146, 148
    Chinese, 99
The Emigrant's Guide to Oregon and California,
    Hastings, 110
Encyclopedia Americana, 111
enema, Indian-made, 68
enlisted men, at Little Big Horn, 182
enlistment term, 86
entertainment, in cow towns, 118
Eskiminzin, Apache chief, 55
Evans, Andrew W., 84
Evans, Dale, 193
Exact (ship), 103
Exeter, Montana, 4, 20

Faber, Charles, 1
false teeth, 183

Far West (ship), 173
Fargo, William George, 105
Farnum, Dustin, 187, 188
Farnum, William, 196
faro, 101, *101*
fatigue duty, 91
fencing, barbed wire, 110
Fetterman, William J., 78
fever, 94, 98
fiddles, 98, 113
field command, at Little Big Horn, 170
Fighting Blood, 184
fingers, severed, 63
Fink, Mike, 34, 144, 152
firearms, 16, 18, 20, 37, 38, 39, 75,
    86, 123
  flintlock, 33, 35, 37
  Hawken rifle, 26, 38
  of Seventh Cavalry, 161, 165, 182
  Winchester Model 1866, 12, 15
fires, lighting of, 97
A *Fistful of Dollars*, 188
Fitzpatrick, Thomas, 41, 44
Fitzsimmons, Bob, 19
five beans in the wheel, 11
flag, at Little Big Horn, 163, 170
Flaming Star, 194
Flathead Indians, 60
Fletcher (steamboat), 176
flintlocks, 33, 35, 37
floors, 96, 136
Florence, Arizona, 183
flour sacks, 123
Floyd, Charles, 26
Floyd, John, 143
Flying-By, 165
Flynn, Errol, 185, 189, 191
Folsom, New Mexico, 4, 16
Fonda, Henry, 190, 194, 199, *199*
Fontenelle, Lucien, 44
food:
  beaver tail, 43
  buffalo meat, 28
  dog stew, 43
  jerky, 33
  pemmican, 54
  of Plains Indians, 57
  of soldiers, 74, 175
For a Few Dollars More, 188
Ford, Bob, 7, 17, *17*
Ford, John, 184, 186, 190, 191, 193, 194, 196,
    200
forefooting, 122

foreign-born soldiers, 90
  at Little Big Horn, 165
Forsyth, George A., 76, 90
Forsyth, James, 80
Forsyth, John, 181
Fort Abraham Lincoln, 96, 173, 178
Fort Apache, 88
Fort Apache, 184, 190, 194, 199
Fort Bayard, N.M., 81
Fort Benton, 35
Fort Berthold reservation, 57
Fort Bonneville, 35, 41
Fort Bowie, Arizona, 69, 77, 88
Fort Bridger, 33, 35, 45, 93
Fort C. F. Smith, 83, 89
Fort Caspar, Wyoming, 80
Fort Collins, Col., 80
Fort Concho, 83
Fort Davis, 83
Fort Davy Crockett, 35
Fort Dodge, Kansas, 52
Fort Douglas, Utah, 80
Fort Grant, Arizona, 13
Fort Griffin, 83
Fort Hall, 35
Fort Keogh, Montana, 85
Fort Klamath, Oregon, 66
Fort Laramie, Wyoming, 84, 91
Fort Laramie Treaty, 52
Fort Leavenworth, Kan., 84
Fort Lisa, 35
Fort Lyon, Colorado, 36
Fort Mandan, 35
Fort Marion, Fla., 55, 60
Fort McKeen, 178
Fort Nonsense, 41
Fort Phil Kearny, 78, 89
Fort Reno, 89
Fort Richardson, 83
Fort Robinson, Neb., 156
Fort Ross, Cal., 107
forts, defense of, 87
Fort Sill, Okla., 55, 77
Fort Smith, Ark., 18, 104
Fort Stanton, N.M., *71*
Fort Stockton, 83
Fort Sumner, N.M., 20
Fort Union, 43, 64
Fort Vancouver, 93
Fort Wallace, Kansas, 99
Fort Walla Walla, 35
Fort Washakie, 143
Fort Yates, N.D., 67

free trappers, 28
Fremont, John C., 29, 43, 92
Frisco, New Mexico, 16
Fritz (horse), 185, 195
From Here to Eternity, 189
Frontier Marshal, 187, 199
frontier whiskey, 28, 156
funerals:
    of Custer, 181, 182
    of Wyatt Earp, 197
fur trade, 28, 30, 31, 32, 34, 35, 46, 48

Gaither, John, 46
Galaxy, 84
Gall, Sioux chief, 59, 168
gambling, 95, 101
games, 101
    favorite of Custer, 173
Garrett, Pat, 14, 20, 23
"Garry Owen," 87, 167, 171
Gate of Death, 107
general, killed by Indians, 76
Gentles, William, 49
Geronimo, 50, 51, 53, 55, 69, 70, 72, 75, 77,
        139, 146
Ghost Dance Movement, 63, 65
ghost towns, 95
Gibson, Edward Richard ("Hoot"), 197
Girard, F. F., 150
The Girl from Montana, 191
"The Girl I Left Behind Me," 167
"Give the Fiddler a Dram," 113
Glass, Hugh, 39, 48
Glidden, Joseph Farwell, 110
Goes Ahead, 175
Gold Rush. *See* California Gold Rush
gold strikes:
    Arizona, 43
    California, 111
    Montana, 98
    New Mexico, 105
Goldfish, Samuel, 194
Goldwyn, Samuel, 194, 198
The Good, the Bad and the Ugly, 188
Goodnight, Charles, 117, 121, 127
Goodnight-Loving Trail, 121
Goodnight Ranch, 117
goose grease, 94
Goshen, Indiana, 193
Goyakla, 51
grama grass, 118
Grand Canyon, 40
Grand River, S.D., 72

Grant Teton Mountains, 33, 46, 145
Grant, Richard, 132
Grant's Fort, 35
grass, wild, 118
Grasshopper Creek, Montana, 98
Grattan, John L., 91
Gray, Robert, 30
Gray Goat, 171
greasy belly, 121
The Greasy Grass, 161
Great Diamond Hoax, 103
The Greatest Show on Earth, 187
Great Plains, 27
Great Register, 106
Great Salt Lake, 32, 45
The Great Train Robbery, 185, 190, 198
Greeley, Horace, 151
Green River, Wyo., 40, 42
Green River knife, 24
Gregg, Josiah, 29
Grey, Zane, movies, 184
Grey Beard, Cheyenne chief, 60
Grierson, Benjamin H., 82
Griffith, D. W., 184
grizzly bears, 44, 47, 60
    injury by, 42, 47, 106
Gros Ventre Indians, 64
The Grotto, 110
grub-line riding, 132
guidebooks, 113
gun fanners, 6
Gunfight at the O.K. Corral, 199
gun flints, 33
gunmen, hired, 9
gunpowder, 39
gun tippers, 6
Gurley, C. L., 166
gut robber, 121

Hairy Moccasin, 175
half-breed (bit), 133
Hancock, Winfield S., 52, 61
handprints, on horses, 57
Hanging Judge, 10
hangings, 104
    of Judge Roy Bean, 3
Hardin, John Wesley, 7, 13, 19
Harney, William S., 76
Harper's Magazine, 12
Harper's Weekly, 84
Harrington, Henry M., 166
Harris, Richard, 196
Harris, William, 15

Harrison, Arkansas, 20
Hart, William S., 185, 195, 197
Hastings, Lansford W., 110, 113
Hastings Cutoff, 110
hats, 38, 125, 170, 127
   of cowboys, 118, 136
   U.S. Army, 73, 83
Hawaii, miners from, 102
Hawk Man, 165
Hawken rifle, 26, 38
Hawks, Howard, 190, 193, 194, 197, 200
Hayden, Ferdinand B., 95
Hayes, Rutherford B., 176
Hayfield Fight, 83
Hazen, Nevada, *137*
head, pickled, 11
Headquarters for Hospitality, 130
heart and hand women, 103
heeling, 122
Helena, Montana, 188
Helena Herald, 175
heliograph stations, 89
helmets, white cork, 73
Henry, Andrew, 35, 46
Henry, B. Tyler, 123
Henry rifles, 15, 123
Henry's Fork, 42, 46
Henryville, Quebec, 4
heyokas, 55
Hickok, James Butler ("Wild Bill"), 4, 8, 9,
   12, 14, 16, 159
   film portrayal of, 196
Hidatsa Indians, 57
High Noon, 186, 187, 188, 193, 194, 196, 197,
   200
Hillman, John Wesley, 37
hired gunmen, 9, 19
His First Ride, 191
hoax, diamond field, 103
Hoffman, Dustin, 187, 193
hog ranches, 79
Hole in the Wall, 20
Holliday, Doc, 5, 21, 158, 199, *199*
Holt, Tim, 194
Holy Dog, 61
Homestead Act, 95
Hook, George, 98
the hoolihan, 122
hoosegow, 125
Hopalong Cassidy films, 185, 189
Hopi Indians, 64
Hopkins, Mark, 102
Horn, Tom, 159

Horner, Joseph, 3
"the Hornet," 76
horse bits, 133
horse feed, 122
Horsely, David, 190
Horsemeat March, 77, *77*
horses, 57, 144, 198, 200
   Indian, 56, 61, 68
   at Little Big Horn, 163, 168, 171, 181
horse thieves, 1, 4
hotels, 102, 127, 128
Hour of the Gun, 199
Houston, Sam, 37
Howard, J. D., 4
Howard, Oliver Otis, 78, 82, 90
Howard University, 90
Hoyt, George, 15
Hudson's Bay Company, 30, 35, 37
Hudspeth Cut-Off, 111
Hughes, Robert, 170
human sacrifice, 53
Hunkpapa Sioux Indians, 59, 61, 72
hunting trips, 28, 35
Huntington, Collis P., 102

ice cutting, *91*
Iliff, John Wesley, 119, 160
Independence, Mo., 37, 96
Independence Rock, 93, 106
Indian language, first film use, 186
Indian raids, 49, 51, 95
   See also Massacres
Indian reservations, 58
Indians, 43, 49–72, 101
   at Little Big Horn, 165, 172, 177
The Indians Are Coming, 186
Indian uprisings, 51, 57
Indian villages:
   burned, 61
   oldest, 64
Indian wars, end to, 71
insanity of General, 86
"In the Sweet By and By," 119
"Irish Washer Woman," 113
Iron Hail, 177
The Iron Horse, 193
Italian Westerns, 188

Jack, Ute chief, 65
Jackson, David E., 34
Jackson County, Ind., 10
Jackson County, Mo., 37
Jackson Hole, Wyo., 34, 200

Jackson Lake, Wyo. 34
jail, name for, 125
James, Edwin, 36
James, Frank, 4, 8, 11, 13, 14
James, Jesse, 3, 4, 7, 8, 11, 13, 17, 18, 20
  film portrayal of, 191
James, Jesse, Jr., 18
James, Robert, 3
James, Zerelda Cole, 3
James Gang, 12
jaw cracker, 123
Jayne, William, 100
Jefferson, Thomas, 44
Jefferson Barracks, Missouri, 74
Jefferson River, Montana, 39
the jehu, 113
Jenny Lind, 85
Jeremiah Johnson, 185
jerky, 33
Jesse James, 191
"Jesus, Lover of My Soul," 119
jinglebob, 130
John B., 118
Johnson, John, 38, 185
Johnson County War, 3, 9, 19, 127
Jones, Buck, 194
Jones, Shirley, 197
Joseph, Nez Perce chief, 53, 64, 66, 70,
  147
Judas steer, 118
Judson, Edward Z. C., 30
Julesburg, Colorado, 11
Julius Caesar's New York Coffee House, 110
Justins, 120

Kane, Will, 186, 188, 196
Kansas City Fairgrounds robbery, 10
Karotofsky, Jacob, 131
Kaycee, Wyoming, 20
keelboats, 27, 41
Kelawatset Indians, 46, 48
Kellogg, Mark, 172
Kelly, Grace, 197
Kelly, "Yellowstone," 82
Keogh, Myles W., 167, 170, 175, 181
kerchief, uses for, 119
Kill, Miss, 25
King, Nelson, 15
King, Richard, 129
King of Kings, 189
King of the Thimbleriggers, 103
King Ranch, 117, 129
Kintpuash, 52

Kiowa Indians, 51, 52, 55, 58, 66, 70, 72, 75,
  82, 84, 159
Kit Foxes, 53
Knottingly, England, 10
Krag-Jorgensen rifle, 86
Kramer, Stanley, 196
Kristofferson, Kris, 186
Kuskov, I. A., 107

Ladd, Alan, 183, 189
Lake, Stuart, 187
Lamar, Missouri, 13
Lame White Man, Cheyenne chief, 168, 172
Langford, N. P., 46
Lapoint, Joseph, 46
lariats, 118
LaRue, Lash, 194
Las Animas, Colorado, 1
Lasky, Jesse, 198
The Last Roundup, 184
laundry, on Army post, 76
Law and Order, 199
law enforcement officers, 8, 16, 18, 37
  Wyatt Earp, 13, 15
lawlessness, 147
Lazarus, Emanuel, 46
Lead, South Dakota, 182
Leadville, Colorado, 98
leather slappers, 6
Lee's Summit, Missouri, 4
The Left-Handed Gun, 7
Lewis, Meriwether, 47, 139
Lewis and Clark expedition, 26, 42, 43, 44,
  47, 150
Liberty, Missouri, 8
The Life and Adventures of James P. Beckwourth,
  48
Life of Buffalo Bill, 198
Lincoln, Abraham, 32, 100
  inaugural speech, 110
Lincoln County jail, 12
Lincoln County War, 11
"Little Annie Roonie," 80
Little Big Horn, 193
Little Big Horn, battle, 77, 150, 152, 159,
  161–82
  film versions, 187, 193
  officers at, 171
  relatives of Custer at, 168
  survivors, 175, 176, 177, 182
Little Big Man, 187, 193
Little Crow, Sioux chief, 51, 57
Little Mary, 122

Little Sure Shot, 21
Little Thunder, Sioux chief, 76
Little Wolf, Cheyenne leader, 60
locations, 185
    Red River, 200
    Shane, 200
    The Searchers, 196
lodge pole pines, 52
log stockades, 87
Lonesome Charley, 171
Long, Stephen H., 27, 36
Longabaugh, Harry, 1, 4, 6
    See also Sundance Kid
Long and Norton Bank, 18
Long Branch Saloon, 15
Long Dog, 165
longhorn cattle, 119, 120, 135
Longley, Bill, 144
"Long Walk," 56
Lookout Mountain, South Dakota, 140
Lordsburg, N.M., 200
Lounsberry, Clement A., 172
Love, Harry, 11
Loving, Oliver, 121
Lowe, Albert, 10
luggage, of cowboy, 129
Lytle, John T., 122

McCall, Jack, 14
McCarty, Henry, 3
McCaskey, William S., 166
McCord, Whip, 193
McCoy, Martin, 46
McCrea, Gordon, 197
McCrea, Joel, 187, 198
McKeever, Samuel, 82
Mackenzie, Ranald S., 82, 86, 89
Mackinaw Gun, 35
mackinaws, 42
McLintock!, 188, 197
McQueen, Steve, 197
The Magnificent Seven, 197
mail, cross-country, 94
mail-order brides, 103
mail-order cowboy, 125
makin's, 128
malaria, 73, 98, 112
A Man Called Horse, 196
Man Chief, 53
The Man from Laramie, 186
The Man Who Shot Liberty Valance, 186, 202
Mandan Indians, 57, 63, 64
Mangas Coloradas, 52

Many Lice, 165
marching songs, 87
Marsh, Grant, 173
Marshall, James Wilson, 96, 111, 138
Martin, Dean, 190
Martinez, California, 28
Martini, Giovanni, 167, 172
Marvin, Lee, 186, 190
Massacre Rocks, 107
massacres, 46, 48, 78
    of Chinese workers, 103
    of Indians, 56, 63, 68, 80, 155
    of missionaries, 108
    of trappers, 46, 48
Massey, Raymond, 185
Masterson, William Barclay ("Bat"), 4, 6, 18, 21
matches, substitute, 97
Matchless Mine, 115
Mature, Victor, 199, 199
Maverick, Samuel A., 123
Maxwell, Pete, 20
Maynard, Ken, 194, 200
meals, call to, 148
measles epidemic, 108
Medicine Dog, 61
Medicine Tail Coulee, 163
Meek, Joe, 26
Meeker, Nathan C., 65
Mercer, Asa, 111
Mexican Mountains, 30
Middleton, J. V. D., 166
Miles, Nelson A., 69, 75, 78, 79, 83, 86, 147
    death of, 92
Milk Creek battle, 65
milk sick, 111
Mills, Anson, 89
Milner, "California Joe," 82
Mimms, Zerelda, 13
mining camps, 95
Minnesota Uprising, 51, 57, 64, 145, 155
Miss Kill, 25
missionaries, 51, 97, 108, 145, 156
Missouri Fur Company, 46
Missouri Mountains, 30
Missouri River, 68
Mitchum, Robert, 185
Mix, Tom, 183, 197, 198
Modoc Indians, 76
Modoc War, 52, 66, 90
Mojave Indians, 48, 64
Montana Gold Rush, 98
Montana Pinch, 127

Montana Territory, 12, 98
Monte Walsh, 196
Montpelier, Idaho, 4
Monument Valley, 186, 196
Moonie, George A., 170
Morning Star, Cheyenne chief, 60
Morrison, Marion, 183
"Mother, Kiss Me in My Dreams," 80
mountain lions, 106
Mount Moriah Cemetery, 18
Mozee, Phoebe Anne, 3
mule teams, 78, 105
Murieta, Joaquin, 11
music, 113, 119
   for battle, 87, 167
musical instruments, 98
My Darling Clementine, 187, 191, 199, *199*
Myrick, Andrew J., 145

The Naked Spur, 186
Nation, Carry A., 114
Nation, David, 114
Navaho Indians, 56, 80
"Nearer My God to Thee," 119
Nelson, Ricky, 190
Newburgh, New York, 195
Newhouse, Sewall, 27
Newman, Paul, 185, 186, 188, 192, *192,* 200
New Mexico Territory, 14, 46, *145*
New Rumley, Ohio, 161
newspaper reports of Little Big Horn, 171, 172, 175
newspapers, wall covering, 111
Newton, Kansas, 21
New York *Herald,* 84
New York *Morning Telegraph,* 21
New York–Someday, 103
Nez Perce Indians, 51, 56, 60, 64, 66, 139
   Retreat (1877), 66
   War, 64, 78, 84, 147
nice kitty, 126
Nichols, Charles H., 7
Nichols, George Ward, 12
nicknames, 86, 113
   Jim Bridger, 28
   Custer, 164
   Jesse James, 20
night hawk, 131
Nolichuky River, 32
Nome, Alaska, 6, 10
noncommissioned officers' quarters, 76
norther, 130

Northwest Gun, 35
Nuttall, Thomas, 137

O'Feeney, Sean, 186
O.K. Corral gunfight, 5, 18, 23, 137, 138
   film version, 191
Oakley, Annie, 3, 6, 14, 21, 22, *22*
Oatman, Olive, 101
Ogden, Peter Skene, 37, 41
Ogden, Utah, 37
Oglala Sioux Indians, 52, 53
Oklahoma!, 197
The Oklahoma Kid, 193
"Old Dan Tucker," 119
Old Gabe. *See* Bridger, Jim
Old Gray Head, 78
Old Oraibi, 64
Old Shalcross, 104
Old Spanish Trail, 100
"The Old Time Religion," 119
Olikut, Nez Perce leader, 64
Olivares, Antonio de San Buenaventura, 24
Olympic Dance Hall, 1
Omaha Thunder Society, 57
One-Arm Howard, 82
one-armed explorer, 40
One-eyed Charlie, 104
One-Who-Yawns, 51
Oregon Territory, 108
Oregon Trail, 33, 35, 45, 84, 93, 98, 106, 107, 111, 113, 143
   burial on, 112
   cattle drives, 133
   objects discarded, 103
Oriental Saloon, 110
Ortiz, Jose, 105
Osage Trace, 116
Oscars. *See* Academy Awards
Oumessourits Indians, 68
over-under swivel-barrel rifle, 38
Overland Mail Company, 94, 112, 113
oversharp bit, 131
overslope bit, 131
Owl Prophet, Kiowa chief, 70
Owns-Red-Horse, 165
oxen, 105, *105,* 152

painters, 106
Paiute Indians, 63
Palance, Jack, 196
Palmer, Joel, 148
Palmer, Joseph, 46
Palo Duro Canyon battle, 82

panthers, 106
Papago Indians, 68
Paraguay, U.S. minister, 134
Paris, Tennessee, 34
Parker, Cynthia Ann, 69
Parker, Isaac C., 10, 11, 18
Parker, Quannah, 51, 58, 69, 154
Parker, Robert LeRoy. See Cassidy, Butch
Parker, Samuel, 145
Parkhurst, Charlie, 96
the Pathfinder, 29
Patkanim, Snohomish chief, 71
Pawnee Indians, 53
Pawnee Rock, 106
pay rates:
    in Army, 85, 91, 154
    of Pony Express, 108
    of Texas Rangers, 11
    for trail drives, 134
Payson, Arizona, 126
Peacemaker (Colt .45), 3
Peckinpah, Sam, 198
Pecos, Texas, 23, 126
pemmican, 54
Pensacola, Florida, 13
Pepper, Ned, 188
periodicals, popular, 84
Pershing, John J., 89
Peta Nacona, Comanche chief, 69
Philadelphia Inquirer, 171
Philip, James, 120
Phillips, William T., 21
Phoenixville, Penn., 9
Pickett, Bill, 133
Pierce, Abel Head ("Shanghai"), 127, 133
Pierre's Hole, Idaho, 38, 42
    battle of, 41, 155
Pike, Zebulon M., 30, 36
    death of, 47
Pike's Peak, 30, 36, 36
piket, 126
Pinal, Arizona, 19
Pine Ridge, S.D., 62, 80
Pinehurst, N.C., 22
pipe bowls, stone for, 56
pistol, hidden, 14
the pitch, 122
Place, Etta, 6
Place of the Rye Grass, 108
Plains Indians, 51, 55, 57, 60, 62, 62, 72
    polygamy of, 155
    See also name of tribe
The Plainsman, 196

Platte River, 142
Pleasant Valley War, 128
plumbing, bunkhouse, 135
Plummer, Henry, 10
Plymouth Cordage Company, 122
Poinsett, Joel R., 29
Point-au-Sable, Jean Baptiste, 29
poison, for arrows, 64
Poison Spider Creek, 93
Poke Flat, 95
poker hands, 14, 202
pole cat, 126
Police Gazette, 84
polygamy, 58, 155
ponies, Indian, 61
Pony Express, 96, 108, 109, 110, 115, 160
Popo Agie River, 26, 42
popular music, 80, 113
Porter, Edwin S., 190
Porter, James E., 166
possum belly, 125
powder horns, 42
Powder River, 187
Powell, James W., 87
Powell, John Wesley, 40, 40
Power, Tyrone, 191
prairie coal, 95
prairie fires, 39, 127
Prairie Hen River, 42
Praying General, 82
pregnant women, delivery induced, 70
Prescott, Arizona, 126
President of U.S., visit to Indians, 58
Presley, Elvis, 194
price. See cost
prizefight, Wyatt Earp as referee, 19
professions, civilian, of soldiers, 88
prohibition, 115
promotion, in post–Civil War Army, 76
pronghorn antelope, 57
Provo, Utah, 38
Provost, Etienne, 38
public hangings, 104
Pueblo, Colorado, 112
Puff, 171
pumas, 106
punishment, methods, 87

quinine, 112
Quinn, Anthony, 191

race-car driver, 193
Raft River Turnoff, 111

railhead cattle markets, 125
railroad, 98
The Rainbow Trail, 184
rainfall, to increase, 95
ram pasture, 129
ranch, largest, 117, 135
Rapid City, S.D., 97
Rapid Creek, S.D., 53
"Rawhide," 188
Reagan, Ronald, 185
"The Real McCoys," 191
Red Cloud, Sioux chief, 52, 55, 66, 140, 156
Red Cloud Agency, 49, 66
Red Face, 165
Redford, Robert, 185, 187, 188, 192, 192
red-light district, 97
    Abilene, Kansas, 138
Red River, 183, 193, 194, 197, 200, 201
Red River War, 60, 82, 136
Red Shields, 53
Red Sleeves, Apache, 52
Red Tomahawk, 65
Reed, Harry Armstrong ("Autie"), 168
regimental command, Seventh Cavalry, 87,
    167
"The Regular Army, O," 80
remedies, 94
Rendezvous, 42, 44, 144
    Bear Lake, 26
    Pierre's Hole, 38, 41
    Popo Agie River, 26
Reni, Jules, 11
Reno, John, 10
Reno, Marcus A., 150, 161, 168, 169, 176,
    178, 182
Reno, Simeon, 10
Reno Hill, 169, 172
respiratory illnesses, 73
Returns-Again, 72
Revenge of the Creature, 198
rewards offered:
    for James brothers, 13
    for Vasquez, 14
Reynolds, Charles A., 82, 171
Richards, Charles B., 8
richest city, 125
Richmond, Kentucky, 32
Richmond, Texas, 114
Richmond, Virginia, 24
Riders of Destiny, 191
Riders of the Purple Sage, 184
Ride the High Country, 198
the ring (bit), 133

Ringo, John, 12
Ringo Kid, 190
Rio Bravo, 190, 197
Rio Gallinas, 106
Rio Grande, 184
Rische, August, 98
Ritter, Tex, 200
road-agent's spin, 19
Roan County, Tenn., 28
Rock Springs, Wyo., 103
Rocky Mountain Fur Company, 28, 32, 34, 38
Rocky Mountains, 29, 30
    South Pass, 98
rodeos, 126
Rogers, Roy, 193, 196, 198, 202
Roman Nose, Cheyenne leader, 65
Roosevelt, Theodore, 18, 70, 126
rope, manufacture of, 122
rope throws, 122
Rose, Edward, 29
Rose, Henry M., 110
Rosebud, battle of, 75
Rough Riders, 88
Round Grove, 106
Round Mound, 106
Round Rock, Tex., 18, 159
Russell, Charles, 126
Russell, John, 24
Russell, Majors and Waddell, 96, 115
Russellville, Ky., 18
Russian emigrants, 107
rustlers, 118
Ryan, John, 173

sabers, 75, 92
Sacagawea, 42, 150
saddle horn, 127
Saint Joseph, Mo., 4, 115
Saint Louis, Mo., 31
Saint Peters (boat), 64
Saint Vrain, Ceran, 29
salary. See pay rates
Salish Indians, 60
Sallie, 121
saloons, 95, 114, 137, 137
Salt Lake Tribune, 84, 175
San Antonio, Texas, 18
Sand Creek Massacre, 56, 155
San Francisco, Ca., 108
    Palace Hotel, 102
San Jacinto, battle, 37
San Miguel, 106
San Miguel Valley Bank, 19

San Pedro River, 200
San Rogue River, 30
Santa Fe, New Mexico, 126
Santa Fe Trail, 29, 96, 102, 106
The Santa Fe Trail, 185
Santee Sioux Indians, 51, 97, 145
Santschi, Tom, 196
Sappington, John, 112
Satanta, Kiowa chief, 52, 58
scalping, 58, 93, 155
scar, on Custer's forehead, 173
Scarborough, George, 19
The Scarlet West, 193
Schaefer, Jack, 196
Schofield, John M., 181
Schuler, John, 38
Schutler wagon, 98
Scott, Randolph, 191, 198
Scott's Bluff, 93
scouts, 78, 82, 174, 175, 178
screw worms, 124
Scyrene, Texas, 8
The Searchers, 196, 201, *201*
Seattle, Wash., 104, 111
Seeds-Kee-Dee, 42
Selman, John Henry, 7, 19
Seven Samurai, 197
Seventh Cavalry, 73, 161–82 *passim*
The Seventh Cavalry, 193
73 Ranch, 120
the shack, 129
Shane, 183, 185, 189, 196, 200
Sharkey, Tom, 19
Shawnee Trail, 116, 122
She Wore a Yellow Ribbon, 184, *184*, 198, 201
sheep, 119
sheepdogs, 142, 150
sheep shearers, 104
sheep wagons, 112
shell game, 103
Sheridan, Michael V., 176
Sheridan, Philip, 152
Sherman, William T., 70, 77, 86, 147, 171
Shining Mountains, 30
Shirley, Myra Belle, 8
The Shootist, 200
Shoshone Indians, 38, 58
shotguns, 132
Sibley, Henry H., 155
Sieber, Albert, 78
Sierra Nevada Mountains, 113
silver, discovery of, 98
"singing cowboy," 192

Sioux Campaign, 1876, 177
Sioux Indians, 56, 58, 62, *62*, 63, 66, 69, 75, 76, 86, 91, 97, 143, 148, 160
  heyokas, 55
  Hunkpapa, 59, 61, 72
  massacre of, 63, 80, 83
  Oglala, 52, 53
Sitting Bull, 21, 61, 65, 67, 72, 144, 148, 157, 168
six-shot revolvers, 11
Skagway, Alaska, 103
Skull Cave battle, 79
skunk, 126
Slack, John, 103
Slaughter, C. C., 135
Slim Buttes battle, 69, 83
Slow, 72
Slye, Leonard, 202
smallpox epidemic, 57, 64, 139
Smith, Algernon E., 175
Smith, Horace, 18
Smith, Jackson and Sublette, 34
Smith, Jedediah S., 29, 34, 43, 46, 47, 48
Smith, Jefferson R., 103
Smith, Theobald, 120
Smith, Tom, 9
Smith & Wesson handguns, 16, 18, 20
Smithsonian Institution, 43
Snake River, 33
snakes in sod houses, 100
Snohomish Indians, 71
snowstorm, in June, 173
Snowy Mountains, 30
Snyder, Dudley H., 154
Society of the Ten Bravest, 72
Soda Springs, 93
sod houses, 96, 100, 136
sod schoolhouse, *114*
solar eclipse, 63
"sold his saddle," 135
soldiers, 73, 74, 84, 86, 88, 89, 90, 91
  basic training, 81, *81*
  black, 82
  pay rates, 85, 91, 154
Soldier Spring battle, 84
Solomon River battle, 92
songs, 80, 119
  of Seventh Cavalry, 171
sourdough bread, 100
South Pass, 93, 98
souvenirs of battle, 89
the spade, 133
Spalding, Eliza, 97, 156

Spirit Dog, 61
the split (earmark), 131
The Spoilers, 196
Spotted Tail, Sioux chief, 58
Spotted Wolf, 72
spring, Indian signs, 68
Springfield rifles, 75, 86, 161, 165
spurs, new, 130
The Squaw Man, 188, 190, 198
squirrel can, 128
Stagecoach, 186, 190, 200, 201
stagecoaches, 94, 99, 112
    drivers, 96, 104, 107, 113
    length of trip, 113
    robberies, 4, 16
stampedes, 120, 123
Standing Rock reservation, 59
Stand Watie, 63
Stanford, Leland, 102
Stanwyck, Barbara, 187
Starr, Belle, 8, 11, 156
    death of, 13
Starr, Henry, 20, 158
Steele, Bob, 194, 197
steel traps, 27, 29
steeple fork earmark, 131
Sternberg, Sigismund, 83
Stetson, John B., 118, 125
Stevens, George, 186, 200
Stevenson, James, 46
Stewart, James, 185, 186, 201
Stewart, William Drummond, 44
stockades, 87
Stony Mountains, 30
Story, Nelson, 132
Strauss, Levi, 128
street howitzer, 21
Stuart, Granville, 134
Studebaker wagon, 98
Stumbling Bear, Kiowa chief, 77
Sturgis, James G., 166
Sturgis, Samuel D., 167
Sublette, Andrew, 39, 42
Sublette, Milton, 34, 39
Sublette, Pinckney, 39
Sublette, Solomon, 39
Sublette, William L., 34, 39, 41, 84
suds row, 76
Sullivan, Amelia, 19
Summit Springs battle, 61, 80
Sumner, Edwin V., 92
Sun Dance, 55, 63
Sundance, Wyoming, 4

Sundance Kid, 1, 4, 6, 9, 9, 21
    film portrayal, 187, 188, 192, *192*
Sunday school, 144
Sutter, John A., 111
swallow fork earmark, 131
Swan, Alexander H., 119
Swift, Charles, 46
Swift Cloud, 165
Switzer's Creek, 106

Tabor, Elizabeth ("Baby Doe"), 115
Tabor, Horace, 115
Taft, William Howard, 18
tailing a steer, 127
Tall Bull, Cheyenne chief, 61
The Taming of the Shrew, 188
Taos Indians, 46
Tarzan (horse), 200
tattoos, of Tom Custer, 177
Taylor, Babcock and Company, 130
Taylor, Robert, 186
telegraph, account of Little Big Horn battle,
    181
Telluride, Colorado, 19
temperance movement, 114
Temple, Shirley, 194
tepee poles, 52
Terrazas, Joaquin, 69
Terry, Alfred H., 165, 168, 171
Tewksbury, John, 130
Texas, 53, 130, 135
Texas fever, 120, 135
Texas longhorn cattle, 119, 120
"The Texas Lullaby," 119
Texas Panhandle, battle in, 82
Texas Rangers, 11, 146
Texas Road, 116
They Died with Their Boots On, 191, 193
Thoen, Louis, 140
Thompson, Ben, 10, 18
Thompson, William, 93
Thornburgh, Thomas T., 65
Three Forks, Montana, 37
Thunderbolt of the Rocky Mountains, 34
Thunder-Rolling-Down-from-the-Mountains,
    53
Thunder Society, 57
tick fever, 120, 133
Tilghman, William M., 12
Tipton, Wyoming, 4
Tombstone, Arizona, 5, 12, 23, 110
Tonka, 193
Tonto Basin Campaign, 79

Tony (horse), 198
tooth, wrongly drilled, 8
To the Last Man, 184
trading posts, 35
trail drivers, 122
train, wrecked by Indians, 72
train robbery, 10
  Butch Cassidy, 16, 20
  James gang, 12
transcontinental railroad, 98
trappers, 39, 41, 140
  Rendezvous, 42, 44, 144
trapper's butter, 26
Travis, William B., 140
tremetol, 111
Tres Castillos battle, 69
Trinity River, 112
trophies from dead enemies, 69
Troy Grove, Illinois, 4
True Grit, 188, 194, 201
Tucson Committee of Public Safety, 68
Tumbling Tumbleweeds, 192
tunes, popular, 113
Tunstall, John, 11
"Turkey in the Straw," 113
turpentine, as cold remedy, 94

umbilical cord, worn by child, 56
unbranded cattle, 123
Uncle Billy, 12
Uncle Jim Miller, 104
undersharp earmark, 131
underslope earmark, 131
Uniforms, Army, 83, 163
Union Pacific, 187
Union Pacific Railroad, 98, 138
United States Army, 73, 79, 81, 83, 87,
      175
  cavalry enlistments, 86
  desertion rate, 83, 84
  Eighth Cavalry, *74*
  Fifth Infantry, 86
  First Cavalry, *74*
  First New Mexico Volunteers, 80
  Fourth Cavalry, 87
  heliograph stations, 89
  Ninth Cavalry, 76
  officer ranks, 87, 147
  pay rates, 85, 91
  Seventh Cavalry, 73, 77, *77,* 80, 87, 89,
      142, 143, 161–82 *passim*
  Sixth Cavalry, 81
  Tenth Cavalry, 76, 82

Third Cavalry, 84
Twenty-fifth Infantry, 76
Twenty-fourth Infantry, 76, 79
Twenty-second Infantry, 85, 86
Twenty-seventh Infantry, 87
Unsinkable Molly Brown, 104
Uruguay, U.S. minister, 134
Ute Indians, 63, 65

Van Buren, Arkansas, 1
Vanderburg, William Henry, 39
The Vanishing American, 184
Varnum, Charles, 170
Vasquez, Louis, 33
Vasquez, Tiburcio, 14, 147
venereal disease, 73
vests, of cowboys, 116
Victorio, Apache chief, 69
vigilantes in Montana, 12
Virgin, Thomas, 46
Virginia City, Mont., 98
The Virginian, 187, 188, 192, 194
Voight, Henry C., 170
Voigt, Andrew, 130
The Volga Boatman, 189

Wagon Box Fight, 87
wagons, 98, 108
wagon trains, 94, *94,* 146
Waiilatpu mission, 108
Wakpala, South Dakota, 59
Walkara, Ute chief, 63
Walker, Joseph R., 28, 37, 43, 155
Walker Lake, Nev., 43
Walker Pass, Calif., 43
Walker River, Nev., 43
Wallace, Lew, 14
Wallach, Eli, 197
wall covering, 111
Wallis, Hal B., 194
Walsh, Raoul, 183, 200
war bag, 129
War of 1812, 47
war paint, 56
Washakie, Shoshone chief, 58, 143
Washita battle, 56, 75, 87, 157
"The Wasp," 76
Watkins, R. O., 126
Wayne, John, 183–202 *passim, 184, 201*
Wayne, Michael, 201
weapons. *See* firearms
weather, cold, 79, 134
Webner, Frank, *109*

Weir, Thomas B., 172, 177
Wells, Fargo and Company, 105
Wesson, Daniel, 18
Western Trail, 126
The Westerner, 191, 197
West Point:
  Custer at, 172, 178
    burial, 176, 181
  most demerits, 161
Westport, Mo., 45, 102
Wharton, Okla., 5
the whip, 113
whiskey, 43
  frontier, 28, 156
White Bear, Kiowa chief, 159
White Bird Canyon battle, 78
White-Hunter-Who-Never-Goes-Out-for-
    Nothing, 171
White Man Runs Him, 175
Whitman, Marcus, 97, 108, 155
Whitman, Narcissa Prentiss, 97, 108
Wichita, 199
Wild Bill (horse), 171
Wild Bunch, 4, 6
Wilson, Jack, 63
Winchester, Oliver F., 123
Winchester Model 1866, 12, 15, 123
Winchester Model 1873, 123
Winchester '73, 186
Windolph, Charles, 182
window panes, 107
Wind River reservation, 58, 143
Winnemucca, Nevada, 4
winter, 43, 79, 134
  work for cowboys, 132
Wister, Owen, *The Virginian*, 187
Withered Hand, 41
wolf meat, 157
Wolf Mountain battle, 86

Wolf Necklace, Sioux leader, 138
wolves, 106
women, 96, 97, 111, 148
  Annie Oakley, 3, 6, 14, 21
  Belle Starr, 8, 11
  Calamity Jane, 97
  Indian, 49, 143
  mail-order brides, 103
  missionaries, 156
  pregnant, inducement of labor, 70
  views of, 150, 151
  in Western movies, 193
Wood, Leonard, 88
wood pussy, 126
woollies, 132
wounded, from Little Big Horn, 173
Wounded Knee Massacre, 63, 71, 80,
    148
Wovoka, 63
wreck pan, 128
Wyatt Earp: Frontier Marshall, Lake, 187
Wyoming Stock Growers Association, 19

XIT Ranch, 117, 130

Yankee Jims, 95
Yates, George W., 175
Yates, Rowdy, 188
Yavapai Indians, 79
Yellowstone Lake, 33
You Bet, 95
Young, Brigham, 19, 80
Younger, Bob, 10, 142
Younger, Cole, 4, 8, 10
Younger, John, 7
Young Skunk, 165
Yuma, Arizona, 13

Zinneman, Fred, 193